Working in East Germany

Also by Jeannette Z. Madarász

CONFLICT AND COMPROMISE IN EAST GERMANY, 1971–89: A Precarious Stability

Working in East Germany
Normality in a Socialist Dictatorship, 1961–79

Jeannette Z. Madarász

palgrave
macmillan

First published 2006 by
PALGRAVE MACMILLAN
Houndmills, Basingstoke, Hampshire RG21 6XS and
175 Fifth Avenue, New York, N.Y. 10010
Companies and representatives throughout the world

PALGRAVE MACMILLAN is the global academic imprint of the Palgrave Macmillan division of St. Martin's Press, LLC and of Palgrave Macmillan Ltd. Macmillan® is a registered trademark in the United States, United Kingdom and other countries. Palgrave is a registered trademark in the European Union and other countries.

ISBN 13: 978–0–230–00160–2
ISBN 10: 0–230–00160–2

This book is printed on paper suitable for recycling and made from fully managed and sustained forest sources.

A catalogue record for this book is available from the British Library.

Library of Congress Cataloging-in-Publication Data
Madarász, Jeannette Z., 1973–
    Working in East Germany : normality in a socialist dictatorship,
1961–1979 / Jeannette Z. Madarász.
       p. cm.
    Includes bibliographical references and index.
    ISBN 0–230–00160–2 (cloth)
    1. Working class–Germany (East)–Political activity–History. 2. Socialism–Germany (East)–History. 3. Germany (East)–Economic conditions. I. Title.
    HD8460.5.M33 2007
    305.5′620943109046–dc22   2006046068

10   9   8   7   6   5   4   3   2   1
15 14 13 12 11 10 09 08 07 06

Printed and bound in Great Britain by
Antony Rowe Ltd, Chippenham and Eastbourne

For my loved ones, whether they are sadly missed,
happily alive or yet unborn

Contents

Preface ix

Acknowledgements x

List of Abbreviations xi

Introduction: Life in a Socialist Dictatorship 1

'We' and 'I' as reflections of socio-political change 4
Historiography 8
An appreciation of the 'little man' (or woman) 16
Methodology 17
Structure 18

1 Economic Politics and Company Culture 21

The economic system 22
Work in the GDR 26
Differentiation 30
Dynamics of power: interaction and stabilization 34
Routinization and internalization 36
Conclusion 41

2 Transformatorenwerk Berlin: Success and Failure 43

Characteristics 43
The economic reforms 44
Blessing or curse? Central authorities getting involved 48
Summary 61
Voices 62

3 Berliner Glühlampenwerk: Working and Living 66
Conditions

Characteristics 66
The early 1960s at the BGW 67
The improvement of working and living conditions 73
Summary 80
Voices 83

4   *Erdölverarbeitungswerk Schwedt*: Privileged Within   86
    a Shortage Economy

    Characteristics   86
    Control and privilege   87
    Economic planning – a farce?   93
    Conclusion   101
    Voices   102

5   *Halbleiterwerk Frankfurt/Oder*: Falling Behind the Times 105

    Characteristics   105
    A new factory in the storms of the NES   106
    Changing circumstances: the creation of *Kombinate* and   111
        its impact on the HFO
    Conclusion   118
    Voices   120

6   *Chemiefaserwerk Premnitz*: Creating a Home for   123
    Thousands

    Characteristics   123
    Social effort in Premnitz   125
    Conclusion   136
    Voices   138

7   **Conflicts and Solutions**   141

    Eigen-Sinn   143
    General problems   144
    Work, politics and private life intertwining   151
    Conclusion   159
    Excursus: spying for the Stasi   160

    Conclusion: Normality in the GDR   166

    Arrival in the everyday   167
    Broken promises   168
    Socialist normality   171
    Conclusion   175

Notes   176

Bibliography   198

Index   204

Preface

This book analyses the economic processes, political relationships and social situations that combined to create a specific socio-political habitat in East Germany after the building of the Berlin Wall. Fundamental to East German society was the search for a collective spirit, which found some popular support in the 1960s but soon massively constrained the individual. Everyday life reflected changing reactions to this restrictive context. Eventually, the political system was challenged by those who felt disillusioned by the Communist Party's broken promises. This framework vastly contributed to the collapse of the system in 1989.

Working life delineated the everyday experiences of most adults within the East German dictatorship. In the work place, mentalities, attitudes and behaviour patterns were shaped according to the specific circumstances that confronted the individual. This book explores the working lives of the East German people and their changing perceptions of 'socialist normality' in the 1960s and 1970s.

JEANNETTE Z. MADARÁSZ

Acknowledgements

I am particularly grateful to the Arts and Humanities Research Council (AHRC) for funding the research project entitled '"Normalisation of Rule"? State and Society in the GDR, 1961–79', which is currently underway at the German Department of UCL. Without the AHRC's continuous and generous financial support, this book would not have been written.

My special thanks also go to the other participants in this project: Esther von Richthofen, George Last and, especially, Mary Fulbrook. Their unfaltering enthusiasm, insightful comments and original thoughts have helped me to clarify issues and focus research. Furthermore, I would like to thank Corey Ross. His insightful comments have benefited the manuscript immensely.

I wish to thank staff at the *Bundesarchiv Berlin*, the *Landesarchiv Berlin* and the *Brandenburgisches Landeshauptarchiv*; the archivists Frau Müller and Frau Forcke have been especially helpful. Special thanks are due to Dagmar Semmelmann for allowing me to use her unpublished notes and to Herr Degner for his unwavering support. I have also received much help from former employees of the five state-owned factories analysed in this study.

I would like to acknowledge the immense debt I owe to Mary, Esther and Merrilyn, not only for their critical appraisal of the manuscript but also for their friendship, which has helped me through the ups and downs of academic life. I would also like to thank Fränzi and Nicole, who have been excellent friends for a long time now. Perry shall be mentioned here with much gratitude as the soul mate he has always been. Last but not least, I want to thank Heiko and Anna for adding an entirely new dimension to my life.

JEANNETTE Z. MADARÁSZ

List of Abbreviations

APO	SED organization of a department
BGW	*Berliner Glühlampenwerk*
BKV	Contract between workforce and management of a factory
BPO	SED organization of a factory
CFW	*Chemiefaserwerk Premnitz*
DFD	East German women's organization
EVW	*Erdölverarbeitungswerk Schwedt*
FDGB	East German central trade union
FDJ	East German youth organization
FRG	Federal Republic of Germany
GDR	German Democratic Republic
HFO	*Halbleiterwerk Frankfurt/Oder*
IM	Unofficial collaborator of the Stasi
NES	New Economic System of Planning and Management
SAPMO	*Stiftung für das Archiv der Parteien and Massenorganisationen der DDR*
SED	East Germany's Communist Party
SED BL	District organization of the SED
SPK	State planning commission
Stasi	East German security police
TRO	*Transformatorenwerk Berlin*
VVB	Union of state-owned factories
VWR	People's economic council
WOA	Scientific organization of labour

Introduction: Life in a Socialist Dictatorship

For a variety of reasons, life in socialist dictatorships changed over time. In the German Democratic Republic (GDR), outside influences in the course of the Cold War and those resulting from shifts on the world market repeatedly left the East German political elite desperately searching for new means to stabilize its planned state system. Power struggles and domestic crises initiated policy changes which more often than not had a noticeable impact on the East German population's experiences of everyday life. The building of the Berlin Wall in 1961 may be the most extreme example but it had massive implications for both the position of the communist Socialist Unity Party (SED) and the attitudes of the population. This dramatic event prepared the ground for far-reaching policy changes with a direct influence on the public and the private sphere. The economic reforms in the 1960s, shifts in cultural priorities, social relations and even ideological adjustments followed it. Official doctrine began to contemplate the role of material interest within socialist planning. It also became more open to the masses' social and cultural needs which differed, and this the political elite accepted only slowly, from the highbrow expectations of the 1950s.

Another bout of far-reaching political shifts was caused when the Prague Spring in 1968 overlapped with a massive economic crisis in the GDR, resulting in a leadership change that eventually led to important alterations in relation to economic, social and cultural policy in the 1970s. In a similar way to the reforms of the 1960s, these efforts were intended to stabilize East Germany and raise economic performance, as well as confirming the GDR's international status as an independent state. In the later 1970s, however, economic and political difficulties grew. The political elite withdrew or proved unable to deliver on some

1

of its earlier policies. After this, no major political change of course took place until the late 1980s, when the Politburo was confronted with mass demonstrations and emigration that led to the collapse of the GDR and, in 1990, to unification with West Germany.

The role of the people becomes relevant in this context of change over time. The question that has to be asked is to what extent economic, political and cultural shifts were caused by individuals or groups of people, and who those people were. The power of people, both ordinary citizens and high-level functionaries, in a socialist dictatorship is a difficult subject for various reasons, but it is also crucial to the understanding of socio-political processes in the GDR. It would be crude, even inaccurate, to describe individuals as powerless, without any influence over their own lives. If the SED's claim for total control was accepted as given, then there would be no need for more research on the GDR. However, historians would know nothing of the reasons for this dictatorship's 40-year survival. The nostalgia for the GDR that continues among many East Germans, even to this day, would be inexplicable.

The SED's hold on the East German population was never total and most aware of this fact was the Politburo itself. It understood this, at the latest, with the popular uprising on 17 June 1953. This knowledge never left the political elite and had a major bearing on central policy up to the revolutionary autumn of 1989. East Germans nonetheless became increasingly involved with the socio-political structures implemented by the SED. Specifically after access to West Berlin as an obvious and tempting alternative had been barred by the building of the Berlin Wall, the population was forced to focus on its primary task, namely survival. Survival in a wider sense includes not only physical needs but a stable context in which it is possible to work, bring up children and generally live one's life. This, at least, state and party institutions promised to provide. After 1961, East German society had to adjust to this self-built cage, which housed all citizens of the GDR including the political elite, economic, trade union, cultural and political functionaries, workers, intellectuals, young people, old people, women and men. They were all forced to adjust to each other and to accommodate a variety of expectations. Both the Politburo's concern for keeping the domestic peace and the population's interest in a functioning socio-political environment ensured a mutual search for socialist normality.

This book will argue that the expansion of social policy during the 1960s and 1970s was a reflection of the interaction between all levels of the East German state. It was not solely a strategy employed by the central decision makers to subdue the East German people. Rather, the working population in particular had an impact on central policy. Furthermore, up to the late 1970s, there was at least a partial concurrence between the interests voiced by the population and the ruling elite's intentions.

This constellation led to changes in the mentalities of East Germans, which reflected the specific socio-political situation to which they were exposed over many years. Psychological learning curves are not unusual in the context of long-term sociological processes. They were also encouraged by official ideology: the creation of a so-called 'socialist personality' was a major aim of the SED. This ideal personality type was to espouse the Marxist idea of collective life by giving up its individual concerns in favour of the betterment of socialist society. Subordination to the patriarchal state was one aspect of this personality but so also was reliance on 'father state' for the fulfilment of basic needs such as work, food, accommodation, education and social security. In response to constant propaganda and the real circumstances of life in the East German dictatorship, both aspects slowly ingrained themselves into East Germans' expectations, attitudes and behaviour, establishing new social norms in the process. In the 1970s, however, a paradigm shift occurred whereby individualization processes moved to the foreground in response to an economic and political stagnation that was irreconcilable with official propaganda. Arguably, this process prepared the way for the collapse of the regime in 1989. Nevertheless, for most East Germans, adjustment to the realities of a Western market economy proved difficult after the initial euphoria over the unification process. The expectations and methods for dealing with the difficulties of everyday life had to be changed almost entirely to comply with the requirements of a fundamentally different system.

Life in the socialist dictatorship was, at least to some extent, shaped by the population, which accommodated the Communist Party's expectations but also forced modifications of central policy. Over time, changes in normative behaviour accompanied the growing integration of state and society. Eventually, however, growing resentment against an overbearing state sparked the search for individual fulfilment, and this undermined Marxist principles of collective life. The changes in the work place and the meaning of work during the 1960s and 1970s were crucial aspects of this process. In the following pages, this assertion will be laid out before the reader in more detail to provide a guide through this study's argumentation and intention.

'We' and 'I' as reflections of socio-political change

The repercussions of the Third Reich, the Second World War and post-war Germany (1945–9) proved to be of long-term relevance to the new East German state. Specifically the sociological consequences of life in Nazi Germany at war cannot be ignored. Much of the GDR's claim to legitimacy, structures and socio-political orientation was based on the rejection of Nazi Germany's activities and ideology. However, the people rebuilding the new state had been shaped by the experience of living at least through parts of the following pandemonium: two lost World Wars, the uncertainties of the Weimar Republic, a worldwide economic crisis, the horrors of the Third Reich and foreign occupation. Furthermore, most of the new East German political elite had also had to deal with Stalin's notorious reprisals during their Moscow exile and had undergone intensive political training in the Soviet Union prior to their return to Berlin in 1945. These influences built the foundations of the GDR and scarred its entire existence in terms of political, economic, social, cultural and even sociological views. In addition, Soviet plans for post-war Germany, the beginnings of the Cold War, Stalin's death and the popular uprising in 1953 defined the socio-political framework within which East German society moved during the 1960s and 1970s.

In the 1960s, the population was forced to learn to exist in a socialist dictatorship. Many were hoping for a better future without war. The ideals that were pronounced again and again by the Politburo, particularly regarding peace and social fairness, were principles that at least a part of the East German population could and did support at the time. Adjustments had been made since the foundation of the GDR in 1949 but were required even more radically after the border was closed. They were based on sheer need and a lack of alternatives. Also, for about twelve months, the SED returned to what has been called the 'professed terror' of the 1950s.[1] The human suffering caused by the Politburo's decision to close the borders, especially the tearing apart of whole communities, friends and even families must have been unimaginably immense but cannot be described here.

Nevertheless, with time many East Germans, especially those generations that grew up after the Second World War, developed an emotional bond with the GDR, which was after all their homeland.[2] This homeland defined itself as distinctly different from its Western brother, as socialist, as belonging to the Eastern Bloc. It expected its people to work for the common good. Toeing the party line was one option and playing the system another; and many people learned both from their everyday experiences and encounters with state and party functionaries. In one sense, East Germans acquired a new method, or language, with which they could communicate effectively in the given environment of a socialist dictatorship. The new modus operandi was shaped primarily by official doctrine, economic requirements and social initiatives. In the long term, it led the population to rely on the state for jobs and social security. It also conveyed to the political elite a false sense of stability.

Whilst adjustments to ideological demands had been forced on the population in the harsh 1950s, more positive attitudes were encouraged by socio-economic changes in the 1960s and consumerism in the 1970s. In the shadow of the Berlin Wall, the SED felt both able and required to apply its power more subtly. After the initial increase in persecutions, the head of state, Walter Ulbricht, soon opted for milder law enforcement. Introducing economic reforms in 1963, he attempted to deal with the socio-economic crisis by providing both an economic perspective and, eventually, some social improvements for the working population. Material interest became a legitimate concern as doctrine, temporarily, had to yield its place to economic considerations.

In the late 1960s, when a change in leadership began to become evident, power politics moved to the foreground again. Ultimately, Ulbricht's successor, Erich Honecker, replaced the economic reforms with debt-funded consumerism, an extensive social programme and renewed politicization. Indoctrination became all-important again, party functionaries reclaimed the economic sector from the technocrats, and the East German security police, the Stasi, grew in sheer size, if not in influence. Nevertheless, the intention of encouraging acceptance and building up the Communist Party's legitimacy continued to dominate central policy.

In the 1960s, the political leadership had made greater efforts to involve the population, thereby overcoming the state–society divide at least to some extent. The slogan 'Vom Ich zum Wir' ('From me to us') succinctly expressed central political intentions. It offered the population the feeling of being a part of the socialist project in return for its endorsement. Supporting this general trend towards collective responsibility, the efforts to improve working and living conditions had an effect not only on people's places of work but also on their families, how spare time was spent, and on political and cultural activities. The importance of state-owned factories[3] for their employees highlights, more than all other aspects of life in the East German dictatorship, the point that the definition of private and public spheres needs revising for the GDR, at least from the late 1960s onwards.

Socio-political efforts in the 1960s had led to a level of involvement that created high expectations regarding social provisions and economic success. These were put forward forcefully by the population but were not seen to be fulfilled in spite of undeniable efforts at the central level of political decision-making. Debt was rising whilst the SED was struggling to uphold assurances it had made with regard to accommodation needs, the support of mothers and young families, childcare, the improvement of service industries and the supply of goods. In the early 1970s, the drive for an increase in the standard of living raised people's hopes but set the GDR on the path of economic decline, political inflexibility and stagnation from the late 1970s onwards. Its economic and moral failure became ever more apparent, although much had been expected of Honecker when he first came to power. Instead, from the late 1960s onwards, growing standardization and institutionalization had created more rigid structures in and around people's lives.[4] Young people and women, who saw their lives mapped out in detail and restrained by the needs of the state, were particularly affected.[5] During this period both social groups were disadvantaged in their search for self-realization; this was in contrast to the 1950s and 1960s when social advancement had flourished and women had been encouraged into full-time employment and further education. In the 1970s most had to submit to standardized biographies with impeded career opportunities. At least some of these women and young people expressed their concerns in literature or political groups, often by joining subcultures, moving into alternative lifestyles or subversive activities. These initiatives faced repression. However, a strong concern for Western financial credits prevented a return to the open terror of the 1950s.

In the late 1980s, a massive economic crisis, political upheaval and international developments combined to destabilize East Germany. All three aspects had their roots in the socio-political strategies of the late 1960s and 1970s. When Honecker began to replace Ulbricht's economic reforms with debt-funded growth and consumerism, he did not take an entirely wrong path. However, when his investment strategies went wrong, he refused to adjust his policies according to contemporary needs. Equally important, the East German population had been given high hopes, which they insisted upon in millions of petitions to government and party institutions. Their economic expectations were not being fulfilled any more in the late 1980s. They could not be fulfilled in the face of international trends, both economical and political. In the end, unification with West Germany proved the best option for a run-down country with a disappointed population. Nevertheless, even the East Germans' behaviour at demonstrations was marked by the collective lesson that had been learned over the preceding 40 years: avoiding open confrontation but expressing one's demands in language central institutions would have to accept. Specific methods were used to subdue potential terror, such as isolating the provocative Stasi agent, carrying candles calling for non-violence and giving flowers to border guards. Slogans such as 'We are the people' expressed what East Germans had been taught for many years in the Workers' and Peasants' State. Disappointed with realities that did not match promises, the people on the streets were claiming back their lives but they were doing it in the language they had employed in their daily haggling for privileges, goods and supplies or personal security. The behaviour patterns linked to the East German experience continued beyond the collapse of the state. Even young people, who could be expected to be more flexible than older generations, suffered a loss of orientation in the transformation process. In the 1990s, many former citizens of the GDR, most of whom had not taken to the streets in the autumn of 1989, felt themselves to be second- and even third-class citizens in the united Germany.[6] The habitat, to which the majority of East Germans had successfully adapted in spite of the limitations and struggles of life in a socialist dictatorship, had been lost.

In summary, adjustment to the socialist dictatorship was encouraged in the 1960s and 1970s by an attempt to increase the integration of state and society. This primary aim defined both Ulbricht's and Honecker's times in power, although they used different methods to achieve it. In the 1960s, greater efforts were made to involve the population, which raised expectations that the SED was unable to fulfil in the long run. Instead, under Honecker institutionalization and standardization replaced the perspectives of the 1960s. The 1970s also introduced a growing rigidity to the socio-political system, which provoked upheaval. Albeit mostly on an individual basis, these protests against socialist reality marked a shift towards subjectivity. Socialist normality started to break apart as both international and domestic developments began to question its intrinsic validity.

In analysing these changes, this study will pay special attention to the impact of the Politburo's socio-political and economic concepts on everyday life, specifically people's experiences in state-owned factories. At the same time, however, grassroots' influence on the development and implementation of central policy will be considered. Here, middle-level functionaries, such as works directors, played an important role in the transmission of expectations and demands from the grassroots to central authorities.

Taken in the context of international events and combined with sub-jective experiences of former East Germans, as reflected in petitions from the period in question and memory reports written some time afterwards, the focus on work and company culture will create a lively illustration of the normalization that both powered and marked East German society in the 1960s and 1970s.

Historiography

Current debates call for an in-depth discussion of concepts that are crucial to this book's main argument. The usage of terms such as nor-mality and normalization has been controversial in socio-political interpretations and historical analyses of the GDR. In most cases, these terms spark off discussions based on fundamental political convictions and historical method, especially when speaking of an emerging 'socialist normality' in the GDR of the 1960s and 1970s. Nevertheless, the process of normalization lies at the centre of this thesis. Describing its causes, structure and intrinsic motivation will constitute the back-bone of the book's argument. The notion of a socialist normality and the related topic of social norms will be discussed with reference to two concepts that are critical to an understanding of socio-political processes within East German society, namely the social contract (Rousseau) and individualization. Before moving on to these issues, other historical interpretations will be reviewed to locate the study within current research on the GDR.

Current debates

Deliberations on the GDR's social, political and economic history have progressed very far from the often one-sided and tendentious appraisals that were common in the early 1990s. By now, detailed micro-studies[7] and wider attempts to describe the circumstances and structures of life in the workers' and peasants' state[8] have provided important insights, analyses and interpretations, on the basis of which an understanding of socio-political relations, motivation and interac-tion can be developed. The cultural sector has received much attention with regard to the literary production of individual writers, specific events, the alternative cultural scene and the involvement of the Stasi.[9] The activities of the Stasi have attracted particular interest, leading to many excellent studies.[10] The planned economy has been thoroughly examined with a view to its structure, policy changes and to particular industrial sectors such as microelectronics and the chemical industry.

Tendencies have been highlighted that show systemic shortcomings as well as the dependency on international developments.[11] Also, the socio-economic situation in socialist industry and the behaviour of its employees has been analysed in detail. In this context, studies on gender relations should be mentioned as well as research that has focused on the everyday experiences and attitudes of workers.[12]

As a result of these crucial studies, concepts were introduced with the intention of naming or categorizing either specific aspects of society, such as *Eigen-Sinn* (Alf Lüdtke, Thomas Lindenberger), or even the entire system, such as niche society (Günter Gauss), *Fürsorgediktatur* (Konrad Jarausch), *entdifferenzierte Gesellschaft* (Sigrid Meuschel) or *durchherrschte Gesellschaft* (Alf Lüdtke). These concepts present interesting approaches that offer particular insights and suggest a general answer to all the basic 'whys' and 'hows' of GDR history. However, these terms have often been unable to delineate the complexities and differentiations, the multitude of individual experiences and the changes in politics, culture and social relations that marked East German society during the 40 years of its existence. Furthermore, totalitarianism has been applied to the GDR although with little success in describing, not to speak of explaining, the realities of life in this socialist dictatorship.[13] Today, it seems more appropriate to stop looking for labels that are supposed to depict an entire society over 40 years. Rather, historians should co-operate with sociologists, economists and Germanists, possibly even psychologists, across national borders and consider long-term processes, behaviour and attitudes that may be comparable to other societies and periods. The history of everyday life (*Alltagsgeschichte*) has already done much in this area of research, but regarding GDR history it seems high time to increase efforts to use material that was a direct witness of what has since been written about extensively but often from an outsider's point of view. Specifically, the memories of the historical witness (*Zeitzeuge*), diaries, sound records and similar sources need to be secured while they still exist. Their take on life in the GDR needs to be considered when trying to write German history for future generations.[14]

Furthermore, current debates suggest a more intense focus on *Herrschaft als soziale Praxis*, which can be roughly translated as power politics practised in society. This approach is interested in questions relating to the translation and realization of power in societal practice. Interactive elements within an asymmetrical relationship are explored whereby the artificial division between state and society, perpetrator and victim, are minimized. This seems the right way forward.

Nevertheless, many studies still employ dichotomies that are unable to either reflect or do justice to the realities of East German society. For example, the use of the term 'social contract' for the relationship between state and society in the 1970s and much of the 1980s has been widely accepted, as a result of which the concept is often utilized implicitly rather than explicitly.[15] However, this terminology is misleading. It is taken to show that the masses have agreed, in exchange for social benefits, to comply with political repression without further concern for collective and individual interests. It implies passivity and stagnation on the part of the East German population. Such an approach ignores processes before and after the early 1970s, which were marked by societal interactivity that both engaged and shaped the East German population. For some time it stabilized the GDR.

In the following section, the term 'social contract' will be discussed in relation to concepts that seem more suited to describing the developments in East German society. 'Normalization' and 'individualization' allow more space for the people's individual responsibility for their own lives and experiences, even for their active involvement in the East German dictatorship.[16]

Social contract

Speaking of a 'social contract', in the Rousseau sense, does not mean that the masses agree to be passive in a politically repressive environment.[17] In the context of GDR history, the term 'social contract' has been used primarily to describe the early 1970s, when various Eastern Bloc regimes started to offer social benefits and higher standards of living to their populations in exchange for political acquiescence. In the GDR, Honecker's rise to power was quickly followed by an intense building programme, a rise in the standard of living and an immense social programme. However, to describe social and consumerist policy solely as part of a 'social contract' that was meant to quieten political tension or to buy off discontent is problematic, as Mary Fulbrook has pointed out. She suggests that 'soft strategies' may be seen as the result of the rulers' genuine intentions.[18] In addition, the SED's focus on economic considerations should be taken into account. Economic success was tantamount to political victory in the Cold War. This truth stood unshaken from the beginning of the GDR's existence, reaching back to Soviet experiences, and forward to its very end, when it collapsed in the face of a disgruntled population, unable to serve growing borrowing costs.

To employ the concept of a 'social contract' as an explanatory tool means that only the Communist Party's bribes in the form of social benefits and the more subtle use of repressive practices are discussed. The population's impact on, and long-term reactions to, changes in central policy are left out of the analysis; the description and categorization of the complex situation on the ground are missing. To capture the wider picture of life in a socialist dictatorship, socio-political relations need to be investigated to pinpoint values and norms which fashioned the general conception of normality in East German society. For this, it is important to describe the interaction between central authorities, party and economic functionaries and the working population. Furthermore, the often very subtle changes over time, their causes and results, need to be traced meticulously.

Normalization

East German society was differentiated, not withering away and not at all in a state of constant civil war. The GDR underwent phases of increased stability and more precarious periods. More importantly, the SED sought to achieve stability by fostering the normalization of everyday life.

Normalization is a concept which is built on various processes that contextualized societal evolution not just in a socialist dictatorship such as the GDR but also in almost any socio-political system. Stabilization after political or social upheaval will be followed by routinization that, if given enough time, will lead to a mostly unconscious internalization of at least some of the repeatedly propagated and experienced norms. These norms will define the popular perception of normality, especially when no comparison with other socio-political systems is possible. It is particularly relevant to the intention of the normalization concept that it is based on various processes, which means that no final state of achievement is declared. It is intended to trace the steps that lead towards a perceived normality which always also includes a variety of difficulties and crises. Furthermore, the normalization concept does not assume the totality of these processes. Within any society, there will always be niches, subcultures and behaviour patterns that run counter to the main stream. No state or party will ever be able to control a country and its population totally. Rather, some latitude may go a long way towards achieving acquiescence. Even this, however, will depend on issues such as social and cultural opportunities and, an imperative, economic success.

The assessment of economic success depends, obviously, on perspective and expectations. Whilst some Third World countries must be called successful when they prevent starvation, industrialized countries have different goals. Also, under Communist rule, the Polish economy, for example, was described as a shortage economy. The East German economy, in the same period, was in notably better condition than Poland but has been called by the same name. What are the criteria here? Success and normality is a matter of perception, influenced by both chronology and context. In this context, the analysis of the economic sector, and specifically of the experience of state-owned factories, can provide us with some crucial insights into the vertical relationship between central policy and actions at the grassroots. Normalization focuses on the negotiation, establishment and stabilization of power structures and the effects thereof, such as behaviour patterns in dealing with authority or expectations directed at the state. The concept emphasizes the involvement of large parts of the population in stabilization processes based on socio-economic policy.[19] It signifies processes of stabilization, routinization and internalization in the 1960s and 1970s that had some lasting impact on the attitudes and behaviour of the East German population. A backlash to normalization occurred in the late 1970s, when tendencies towards individualization were growing.

Individualization

Individualization is a process of socialization (Habermas) based on the liberation of individuals from traditional social structures. This process marks a categorical change in the relationship between the individual and society. Some doubt the possibility of self-determination in centrally organized states; biographies from childhood to choice of profession standardized by governmental institutions. However, individualization does not mean autonomy, emancipation, or limitless self-realization; rather it means on the one side self-responsibility and on the other side dependency on existing conditions. Individualization, institutionalization and standardization are aspects of the same socialization process.[20] According to T. W. Adorno (1956), individuals are never just objects of societal accommodation. They are actively engaged in shaping societal reality and do not just experience socialization passively.

Individualization in the GDR

From the beginning, the idea of collectiveness was fundamental to the socialist dictatorship. It was taken on slowly by the East German population. In the 1960s, the slogan 'From me to us' and the search for the idealized 'socialist personality' expressed the intended type of society perhaps most clearly. However, both the slogan and the ideal reflected the ambivalence of processes in the 1960s, when Ulbricht proclaimed the ideal of collective life but established the foundations on which individualization would prosper. The search for the 'socialist personality' was announced in the middle of the 1960s. It was intended to describe large units of people, even an entire population, displaying unitary characteristics. The concept spoke of persons who would subordinate themselves to the interests of socialist society. Nevertheless, it still required individuals rather than a faceless mass to develop specific convictions. Such ambiguous policies could also be found in the economy, where the economic reforms tried to introduce the uncertainties of a market economy into a planned society with socialist ideals. The message was, to say the least, mixed.

Individualization – what does it mean in a socialist dictatorship? The concept depicts a new focus on the individual and not the group any more; on an individual's wishes, aims, tastes and hopes rather than their subordination to a higher category of social organization. In fact this concept works against the collective ideas put forward by socialist regimes; although possibly they were in line with Marx's original thoughts on the position of an individual in a socialist (or even communist) society. In his autobiographical novel *Abendlicht* (1979), Stephan Hermlin described the problem:

> Among the sentences [from the Communist Manifest], which had become natural to me a long time ago, there was one that went as follows: 'Replacing the old bourgeois society with its classes and class differences, there will be an association, within which the free development of all will be the precondition for the free development of every single person.' I do not know when I had begun to read this sentence as it stands here. I read this sentence in this way; this sentence existed for me in this way, because this sentence matched my understanding of the world in this way. How great was my surprise, my dismay even, when I found out, after many years, that this sentence, in reality, meant the opposite: 'within which the free development of every single person is the precondition for the free development of all'.[21]

Hermlin does not say when exactly he noted the difference in the two sentences, the one in his mind and the original. He published the novel in 1979 and, perhaps, he recognized the difference in the sentences' meaning in the 1970s; recognition brought about because, as he indicated in the quoted text, the sentence in question was a reflection of his understanding of the world and not just a misread line of words. Keeping in mind the 'no taboos' promise to the arts and its harsh withdrawal in the late 1970s, conceivably the Honecker era made such differentiation between illusion and original meaning not just possible but necessary. What changed under Honecker?

There are various changes that took place under Honecker, both in foreign and domestic policy, that may have contributed to the socio-political shifts in the 1970s. An increased orientation towards the West, which had been started under Ulbricht but was continued and even expanded under Honecker, may provide one aspect of the expla-nation. Possibly, this was a backlash to the ideal of collective life pushed forward in the 1960s. Furthermore, individualization has been described as an aspect of modernity and, for some time now, it has been debated whether the GDR was a modern state or presented perhaps an alternative modernity. Accordingly, some sociologists may interpret the proliferation of individualism as an argument suggesting that the GDR foundered on modernity. Also, one needs to consider the possibility that individualization emerged from international develop-ments such as globalization. Under Honecker the GDR took part in the Helsinki process and, as a result of economic problems, was opening up to the world market.

However, domestic developments in the 1960s may also have con-tributed to the changes. The concern for working and living condi-tions, for example, meant that individuals and their wishes and demands were considered by the regime to a greater extent than previ-ously. The rehabilitation of material interest[22] and the increase in the individual responsibility of works directors – these were results of the economic reforms under Ulbricht which had been introduced in response to the economic crisis. In fact, the reforms moved the country away from the total plan and total control. Nevertheless, economic success always remained top priority; it was crucial to the GDR's domestic and international legitimacy.

Changes were manifold and particularly sociological studies at the time document a shift in popular perceptions and priorities.[23] A ten-dency towards individualization was detectable by the 1970s at the latest and became more pronounced in the 1980s.[24] It is important to point out that such tendencies varied in strength according to the social milieu and a person's standard of education, perhaps even profession. Those engaged in artistic activities, working at universities or within the Christian community may have been more inclined towards individualization, although these tendencies were not limited to them. Both artists and academics are often, by virtue of their professions, forced to develop their individuality, and the Christian community in East Germany also focused on encouraging their members to stand up to socialist society as individuals. On the shop-floor, in contrast, working at least eight hours a day within a team, and with pressure to comply with group behaviour, one would perhaps expect less space for developing one's own personality and interests as an individual person. However, there are examples of workers who loathed this type of group pressure in the work place and may have reacted against it quite forcefully. In the late 1970s, clear tendencies towards individualization can be traced among the working population, independent of age, gender or qualification.

Various indicators suggest that the backdrop to these developments was a backlash against the growing institutionalization and standardization of biographies, which became recognizable in the 1970s. Individualization was further encouraged by the general dissatisfaction with the discrepancy between the proclaimed ideal and real-life experiences; resentment against an apparently unsuccessful state certainly contributed to the tendency to focus on one's individual concerns rather than on the collective good. Common norms and basic values were so far established by the 1970s that the insufficiencies of reality were perceived not only as a threat to the future of socialist society but also of the individual's expectations. In 1976, for example, a dramatic increase in the number of petitions indicated growing dissatisfaction among the population, which occurred in spite of Honecker's expansive social programme. Furthermore, a shift in the interpretation of petitions took place in the 1970s. They were not used any more for pinpointing problems and finding solutions. Rather, those complaining were described as selfish and egotistic. In this way the state was ignoring information, even withdrawing from the promise that had been made implicitly when the petitions system was expanded in the 1960s, namely that the state would look for solutions and concepts to solve problems at the grassroots level. By ignoring and rejecting petitions out of hand, the regime negated a societal discourse which obliged everybody to help in the elimination of difficulties. It can be argued that this encouraged individuals to take care of their own concerns.

An appreciation of the 'little man' (or woman)

The line of argument developed here in response to current debates on GDR history has led us from Rousseau's 'social contract' to normalization processes and tendencies towards individualization in an attempt to depict the complex structures and processes of life in a socialist dictatorship, and also to give some indication of some possible long-term causes for its eventual collapse in 1989. The underlying purpose was to focus attention on the situation encountered on the ground after the Berlin Wall had been built. Rather than describing solely what the political elite expected to achieve from major policy changes, researchers need to be examining in more detail the long-term reactions to the changing circumstances and continued difficulties of living in a socialist dictatorship. Only then will historians be able to explain adequately the GDR's 40 years of existence.

What has been called a 'social contract' by some historians was not really a pact between the regime and the population at all. The implied differentiation between two apparently clearly definable groups opposing each other within the ominous construct of a socialist state is itself unsuited to the manifold, nuanced and complex relationships that slowly developed within and without the structures of governmental and party institutions. Furthermore, the relationship was defined primarily by a set of values and promises introduced by the Politburo, which became the basis for a whole value system and encouraged the development of social norms and behaviour patterns suited to the circumstances of life in a socialist dictatorship. Arguably, most East Germans adopted this value system, even propped it up by behaviour appropriate to its requirements. In addition, people were not reluctant to demand that both governmental and party institutions, even the political elite, should conform to this system and fulfil promises that had been made within this value system.

Nevertheless, the institutionalization and standardization of this value system also created a rigidity which was rejected by some sections of society, particularly young people and women of a certain milieu, mainly artistically inclined and well educated. Individual choice and self-fulfilment were moved to the fore of the value system. Increasingly, in the late 1970s and the 1980s, individualization spread and was further encouraged by an obviously failing economy, Gorbachev's reform politics, the peace movement and the growing citizens' movement, this latter becoming more visible in the late 1980s. In the end, people went on to the streets for various reasons, both international and domestic, with personal and more general concerns. However, it is also important to remember that only a minority of the 16 million East Germans demonstrated and left the country in 1989. The majority, even now, over 15 years after the fall of the Berlin Wall, remember fondly good things about living in a socialist dictatorship.

Methodology

Normalization processes will be explored with reference to changes in social relations and economic, political and cultural developments in various sections of East German society. Attention will mainly be given, however, to ordinary citizens of the GDR: the workforce of five selected state-owned factories. Change over time is seen to be crucial to the description and analysis of everyday life in a wider political and economic context. A combination of archival material and other sources such as diaries, retrospective memory reports and oral history interviews will be used to highlight nuances that can often only be suspected on the basis of documents available in central archives such as the *Bundesarchiv* and *SAPMO*. These archival materials are, of course, crucial to research on the GDR and have been used extensively for this project, specifically the files of the Politburo, the *Staatliche Plankommission* (SPK), the *Volkswirtschaftsrat* (VWR), relevant ministries or *Vereinigung Volkseigener Betriebe* (VVBs), the trade union, specific sections of the SED's Central Committee (ZK SED), the SED's district organizations (SED BL), and the offices of Walter Ulbricht, Erich Honecker and Günter Mittag.

A major problem has been that specific archives and certain types of evidence are still underused, although they provide insights that may be essential to the understanding of the workings of the regime. Archives that are very small or localized, concerned with only specific parts of East German society, unconcerned with the actual making of central policy, or based on the research of GDR academics are often ignored by historians and sociologists, who have access to plenty of material in the central archives.

Archives of former state-owned factories, for example, need to be used more to explore aspects of central policy. Archives were set up for every factory in East Germany to keep documentation relating to almost everything going on: from the activities of small workers' groups, so-called brigades, to management meetings and obligatory reports to central institutions. Not only the planning process but even the menus at the canteen were recorded. Crucially, this material illuminates both the differentiations in the implementation of central policy at the local level and the impact of grassroots' concerns on central policy makers. Particularly important to the argument of this book were archival materials stored in the *Landesarchiv Berlin* and the *Brandenburgisches Landeshauptarchiv* in Potsdam. A selection of five state-owned factories has been made according to specific criteria, these being, for example, location, gender ratios and the factory's history, in order to achieve a variety in the samples that allows for some differentiation in work culture.

The brigade diaries available for the five state-owned factories have been analysed.[25] Petitions and material from the conflict commissions, which were founded in response to the upheaval of 1953, were researched. Works directors' meetings and discussions within the trade union organization and the individual factories' SED organizations, the BPOs, were looked at in the local archives. I have also researched the archival material of the various SED BLs and of the East German youth organization, the FDJ. The archivist's warning that the FDJ did not tend to keep documents as it should have done and little useful material would have survived was well founded.

In addition, people who worked in the five state-owned factories in various capacities have been questioned with regard to their experiences in their specific work environment and to wider questions relating to life in the GDR generally. This type of material is often influenced by subjective opinions, changed memories and a one-sided presentation of events, even propaganda. Nevertheless, it is immensely valuable to any attempt to describe life in the socialist dictatorship as it was experienced by the majority of East Germans most of the time. Finally, some material from the archive of the Stasi will be used in the shape of a case study to describe the aims and methods that were employed to infiltrate and influence state-owned factories.[26]

Structure

The book is structured thematically, with the focus remaining on the 1960s and 1970s as the period in which a socio-political normalization can be traced most clearly. As will become apparent, an effort has been made to balance documentary evidence with the voices of former citizens of the GDR.

The first chapter sets out the main arguments of this book, preparing the reader for an analysis of the GDR's economic and socio-political motivations during the 1960s and 1970s. First of all, developments within the East German economy and working conditions in the GDR will be highlighted to provide the reader with the necessary background information. Secondly, the mainstay of this study will be laid out: the description of the experiences and problems of state-owned factories during the 1960s and 1970s. Common issues will be discussed but with reference also to the various individual circumstances that had an impact on the individual history of selected factories.

In the following chapters, case studies of five state-owned factories will outline the specific impact of various themes on the company culture of individual factories. The drive for the improvement of working and living conditions, which became crucial to company politics in the 1960s, will be discussed, highlighting communication between the workforce, company management and central institutions regarding not only social policy but also norms, salaries and productivity. Furthermore, the impact of central policy changes, particularly the economic reforms under Ulbricht and Honecker's guiding policy, the Unity of Social and Economic Policy, will be described. High politics, such as the increase in Honecker's influence from 1967 onwards, will be a part of these case studies, but mostly in order to highlight the repercussions of such developments within the selected state-owned factories. The case studies are intended to stress the differentiation between East German state-owned factories and, thereby, emphasize the variations in the experiences of the workforces during the 1960s and 1970s. Every case study will be backed up by memory reports from former employees to illustrate socio-cultural developments.

Using these case studies as a background, in Chapter 7 attention will shift to conflicts and solutions that shaped the working day. Specifically the motivations and actions of the workforce when dealing with everyday problems or being entangled in conflicts will be described. Conflicts affecting the workforce were manifold throughout the 1960s and 1970s. However, with time, ways of dealing with conflicts or problems changed noticeably, which may have been linked to the fact that public life and private concerns started to overlap in a way that became specific to the GDR. It will become apparent that, in response to changes in social relations and economic and political circumstances, open conflicts were avoided and solutions were sought in compromises suitable to all sides concerned. The Conclusion will highlight once more the relationship between long-term processes and individual experiences. Here, the working population's changing perceptions of 'socialist normality' in the GDR will feature dominantly.

In summary, this book explores the working lives of East Germans 'who may be neither kings nor politicians nor seen as *important* in conventional terms, but who constitute precisely the vast majority of the population and who therefore have greater historical significance than the merely *important*'.[27]

1
Economic Politics and Company Culture

This study will apply the normalization concept to company politics and company culture, specifically within East German state-owned factories during the 1960s and 1970s. It will be argued that stabilization during the 1960s relied to a large extent on the finding of common interests and the establishment of a limited dialogue or, at least, inter-action between central decision makers and the factories. When talking of state-owned factories as proactive units, it is to be understood that a variety of persons and groups with different interests and intentions influenced and prepared actions that issued from any specific factory. To explain this further: the works director was the person directly responsible to superior institutions such as an appropriate ministry or VVB. VVBs were institutions that were responsible for a number of fac-tories categorized into specific sections of the economy. In the 1960s VVBs occupied a liaising role between the individual factories and the relevant ministries. From the late 1960s onwards, the VVBs lost their influence and large factories were subordinated directly to their relevant ministry. Within every factory, the party secretary of the SED also had an impact on decisions and in many cases this was not restricted to political issues. Also, the works director was in a position in which one of his main tasks was to negotiate between his employees and central institutions. Administrative staff, economic functionaries, trade union functionaries and functionaries representing other mass organizations such as the FDJ – all these people and groups contributed to this exchange and shaped the dialogue with central institutions. Production workers and technical staff also had their own individual agendas, which they tried to defend within the context of ongoing interaction, often relying on seemingly suitable functionaries for the representation of their interests. This complex constellation of interests furthered the mutual exchange of demands and offers, which led to fine adjustments and shifts within original interest patterns at all levels. There was inter-action between different interest groups and individual personalities in state-owned factories and also with central institutions. These vertical relationships within the East German economic system lie at the heart of this analysis. Horizontal relationships, for example co-operation with other companies or with the local community, enriched this complex pattern of interaction. However, interaction is defined by the context in which the exchange takes place, particularly in dictatorial societies.[1]

Therefore, the following three themes will be discussed: differenti-ations between factories, changes over time, and interaction between the working population and central authorities. Here, the influence of central policy on individual factories and, crucially, that of state-owned factories (or related groups or persons) on central policy will be traced with a specific focus on the improvement of working and living conditions. Interaction, rather than the strict adherence to ideological and political tenets, marked the East German state after the building of the Berlin Wall. In this context, routinization will receive particular attention in order to highlight its impact on attitudes and behaviour patterns at all levels of East German society, furthering the internaliza-tion of values but also leading to a backlash against standardized lives and the ever more apparent discrepancy between official propaganda and real conditions in the later 1970s. Routine as a concept seems espe-cially suitable to describe a process of learning and playing the rules of the societal game as it was negotiated in the 1960s and 1970s.[2] Arguably, individual interests shifted to some extent to suit the condi-tions of life in a dictatorship and shortage economy, but they were not given up entirely.

The economic system

The East German economy was based on a planned system which repeatedly encountered crises. It stood in constant competition with the West German economy and was dependent on supplies of raw materials, especially oil, from the Soviet Union. Also, the East German economic system was hampered by its political context.[3] The right to work, for example, was embodied in the constitution and proved a for-midable hindrance to effective work organization in state-owned facto-ries. Employees could neither be easily shifted according to economic needs nor could they be threatened with unemployment when lacking work discipline.[4]

Furthermore, in the workers' and peasants' state, political self-definition and legitimacy relied to a great extent on heroic images of work and working people. In the GDR, workers were the most sought-after social group but also, after the upheaval in June 1953, the most feared potential opponents of both state and party. Not only would open proletarian opposition to the leadership claims of the SED have undermined the ideological base of the GDR; a nationwide strike would also have shaken an already unstable economy to its foundations. Because work was a highly political issue in the GDR, much was done to avoid open confrontation. This was a major problem in terms of economic effectiveness.

Central policies

Economic success was an issue of legitimacy to the SED.[5] It was vital to the political stability of the socialist dictatorship, partly also because the GDR had been pitted against the economic achievement of the Federal Republic of Germany (FRG) by both Stalin and Ulbricht from the very beginning of its existence.[6] Failure and success were felt most acutely and were measured by the working population on the basis of its deteriorating or improving working and living conditions.

The central decision makers had already recognized the uses of social policy by the 1950s. Especially after 1953, in an attempt to calm tensions, efforts were made to improve social and cultural provisions. State-owned factories were ordered to offer sport facilities, expand childcare capacities, build up services such as laundries, and finance holiday accommodation for the workforce.[7] At a time when labour was starting to be in short supply, these offerings were intended to increase the attraction of state-owned factories over those of private firms, and to increase the employment of women.[8] However, to a large extent, these plans never came to fruition in the 1950s.[9] The provision of workers with hot meals and industrial safety and health regulations remained as priorities but even these were mostly not realized to a satisfactory standard.[10] Economic difficulties and the centralized structure of the East German economy prevented a more expansive use of factories' resources for the improvement of working and living conditions.

The very difficult economic and political circumstances of the late 1950s and early 1960s clearly reflected upon the grassroots of society. Workers and functionaries reacted in various subtle but effectual ways, both to express their dissatisfaction and to alleviate some of the pressure forced on them by difficult working conditions: there was poor labour discipline and high levels of sickness and turnover. These in turn led to low productivity and failing plans. Moreover, at the beginning of the 1960s, Soviet subsidies were reduced dramatically and the newly built Berlin Wall was causing disquiet. It became of the utmost importance to implement policies that would enhance economic performance whilst easing some of the political tension that was undermining the stability of everyday life. In 1961, with the introduction of the new work law, social benefits provided within the factories had already been somewhat expanded.[11] However, more fundamental changes were brought about by Ulbricht's economic reforms.

In 1963, Ulbricht introduced the so-called New Economic System of Planning and Management (NES), which was intended to decentralize the East German economic system slightly. It introduced some limited competition between the economic units and also put new emphasis on both the material interests of the workforce and rewards for economic success at this level. The NES relocated some powers of decision to the VVBs[12] and, to some extent, also to the management teams (*Betriebsleitung*) and particularly to the works directors.[13] In many cases, the economic restructuring upset the precarious balance most economic units had only just maintained. Although structural changes were undoubtedly necessary, more realistic book-keeping and the adjustment of industrial prices had direct consequences for the state-owned factories' ability (here more correctly, inability) to fulfil the plans that had been drawn up for them at the central level.[14] More than ever, management came under pressure from both its workforces and central institutions to find ways to increase productivity.

Part of the effort to increase productivity was the attempt to expand the state-owned factories' social provisions in order to stabilize the workforce in the face of high turnover and sickness rates. The economic restructuring forced works directors to take the initiative. They were also directly exposed to expectations and demands, especially of those production workers who were working under difficult conditions caused by the deficiencies of the state planned economy. A lack of production capacities combined with a politically influenced allocation of scarce resources and a deeply flawed system of planning hindered any possibility that the economic reforms may have presented to improve fundamentally the situation in state-owned factories.[15]

Nevertheless, the relocation of responsibility resulting from the NES had a stabilizing effect. It diverted potential blame for failure away from political institutions as it stressed the new focus on managerial self-reliance. Furthermore, efforts to improve working and living conditions were crucial aspects of normalization. This initiative was centralized under Erich Honecker's Unity of Economic and Social Policy, which ensured him some (short-lived) popularity. In the vain hope of stimulating productivity, Honecker relocated investment and incurred debts to fund his promises. In the long term, however, this policy spun out of control. Although popular needs had been recognized correctly, the inflexible handling of the issue by decision makers at the top of the political hierarchy in the late 1970s and the 1980s proved disastrous.

The following analysis will investigate the evolution of social policy in the 1960s and 1970s. Continuity and discontinuity of central policies and their connection to the interests of the workforce will be central topics in this discussion. This focus will provide some much-needed insights into the relationship between central authorities and the workforce, which was more complex than has so far been allowed for by political and economic historians. Specifically the role of individuals, such as works directors or party secretaries within a state-owned factory, requires greater attention, if the varying experiences of the East German workforce are to be honoured rather than trying to submerge differences in one general account claiming to encompass 'the' East German working life.

Social policy in the 1960s and 1970s

The economic reforms featured a more pronounced use of social policy specifically to accommodate the demands of the workforce. Philip Heldmann's excellent study of consumer policy in the 1960s, which he linked to the development of social policy, has shown interest at the central level in these issues.[16] In addition, however, archival material indicates that the East German workforce was in a position to put forward its interests sufficiently strongly to influence central economic and political institutions. During the 1960s, the economic reforms included policies that responded to the long-standing demands of the workforce. Structural changes enabled works directors to use social benefits to alleviate pressures on workers, on the economic sector and on the political system. The rehabilitation of material (or personal) interest allowed not only for the increase of rewards for economic success but also for the use of social provisions for the workforce in an attempt to increase productivity. In particular, the involvement of state-owned factories in the drive to improve working and living conditions made this possible to a much larger extent than it had been in the 1950s. Related initiatives in state-owned factories touched on issues that would be central policy throughout the 1970s and 1980s.

Besides excellent studies on the central level of the East German economic and political system, some of which have been indicated already, there have also been superb analyses of various aspects of company politics.[17] Special attention has been paid to factories primarily employing women and to specific issues such as the role of functionaries.[18] Comparative approaches have yielded some fascinating results regarding the appraisal of the differentiation between individual factories and the influence of individuals, especially the works directors, on company politics and culture. However, a desideratum of historical research on the East German economic system would include an analysis of vertical relations between the central decision-making powers, the middle level and the grassroots.

Work in the GDR

East Germans' working life was marked by difficult working conditions throughout the GDR's existence. There was never enough money to pay for airy and well-lit factory halls with machines that would lighten the sheer physical demands on production workers, although exceptions existed and were hailed as great successes. Frequently, places of work were either very cold or extremely hot, depending on the season. Air-conditioning systems were insufficient, if they functioned or existed at all; cleanliness and order were regularly less than desirable in spite of efforts to combat these problems. In the *Berliner Glühlampenwerk* (BGW), for example, the mostly female production workers had to endure temperatures of up to 60°C in summer and freezing cold in winter. Production lines provided only insufficient lighting and the noise level was very high; even so, the main problem here was the monotony of work.[19] Some operations presented health hazards, mostly caused by either touching or inhaling toxic materials. As late as 1976, about 65 per cent of employees in the chemical industry were working in difficult conditions which were deemed a health hazard, and almost half were exposed to toxic chemicals on a regular basis.[20] If working conditions were recognized as a health risk by central authorities, a small bonus would be paid per hour (not more then a few *Pfennig*) and those affected would get milk free of charge; not an adequate compensation for long-term health problems and possibly death.

These very difficult working conditions were not ignored by central authorities and management teams. Laws and guidelines were meant to reduce health risks, especially for young people and pregnant women. However, the financial backing needed to improve working conditions to an acceptable standard was never forthcoming, at least not sufficiently to solve fundamental problems. In 1975, the BGW reported that 2 million marks[21] had been invested in the improvement of working conditions in 1974. However, the situation could not be improved noticeably because of a lack of production capacities. At that time over 1600 employees (more than a third of the workforce) were still working in unhealthy surroundings, of which 1000 had to deal with noise above regulation levels and difficult climatic conditions. For 1975 and 1976, it was planned to eliminate difficult conditions for 12 colleagues (from 1600!) but no real solution was expected up to 1980.[22] The hoped-for fundamental turn for the better never happened.

It is quite possible that the number of work accidents and illnesses caused by bad working conditions was hidden by official statistics, which were often unreliable.[23] However, work accidents were always thoroughly investigated. In many cases, the Stasi was involved because of the constant fear of sabotage.[24] Reports were available for those responsible, even at the highest level, so that they could know about the problems. The real issue was not ignorance or indifference but lack of money, which became more critical in the late 1970s and 1980s because investment in industry had been reduced to a dangerously low level since the early 1970s. Under Honecker, the GDR was living off its reserves. By the 1980s, in the *VEB Chemiekombinat Bitterfeld*, for example, 54 factory buildings were known to have major building damage and four of those 54 had to be evacuated during high winds because of the acute danger of collapse. Generally, in the 1980s, the main feature of the chemical industry was outdated plants with a high risk of accidents.[25]

This specific situation was worsened by old machines that kept breaking down and unreliable deliveries of raw materials and prefabricated parts, which was typical of all industrial sectors. Both problems kept interrupting production and undermined plans. Again, the main cause was a lack of investment and hard currency, with the embargo applied by Western countries on some materials, products and machines (the so-called 'Cocom' list) making it still more difficult for the GDR to ensure supplies. Annually, these difficulties led to an end of year rush with much overtime, weekend work and production lines that ran at a higher speed to catch up with the yearly production plan. It was an exhausting way of working. Throughout the year, nobody could be sure of a continuous work rhythm. Particularly towards the end of the year, the workforce was confronted with many stoppages and overtime to compensate for inefficient work organization.

Naturally, production workers were dealing with different problems than technologists, staff working in administration or management. Nevertheless, the latter also had to contend with a less than suitable environment and a lack of materials.[26] Many offices were cramped, sanitary facilities were deficient, air-conditioning was insufficient, chairs and other crucial office equipment were hard to obtain. On top of that, there was a lack of staff because of low wages, especially in administration.[27] There was a need to recycle paper and envelopes, save postage expenses and to have offices cleaned by administrative staff rather than cleaning personnel.[28] This was part of a general trend, which eventually led to school children cleaning their own classrooms and collecting old newspapers for recycling, just as employees were made responsible for cleanliness at their places of work. Without trying to condone clearly very difficult working conditions mostly born out of a lack of production capacities, arguably this trend also had roots in the nature of the socialist system and its desire for social equality. Additionally, massive savings measures were introduced in the late 1960s and early 1970s; they had not been present for most of the 1960s but became routine in the 1970s and 1980s.[29]

In the 1960s it had been intended that the NES would improve the economic system structurally. In response to the economic crisis of the late 1960s and Honecker's rise to power, however, 'rationalization' became the catchword of the period. In the 1970s it stood, mainly, for saving material, hard currency and working time. Neither money nor production capacities nor the will to change routine in the face of a rigid plan existed in sufficient measure to allow for the introduction of better machines and new technologies, which would have been part of the original intention of the rationalization concept. Any changes to work processes and new technologies were always connected to additional cost and lost time, at least in the first instance, which was not planned for in the already overstretched production plans. Therefore, management became ever more reluctant to support the transfer of new technologies into production processes.[30]

This was just one source of animosity between the various layers of the workforce. Technologists were unhappy and became cynical regarding their own work because it was seldom applied to production processes. Production workers mostly blamed economic functionaries for inadequate work organization and the higher levels of management for their inability to provide the materials required or better working conditions. Administrative staff were in a particularly difficult situation, positioned between the complaining workers and management, but themselves mostly unable to action possible solutions. However, it would be insufficient to describe a complex situation as simply divided into blue- and white-collar workers. Specifically within the socialist system, social relations shifted over time, blurring the traditional Marxist division of classes in the process.[31]

In retrospect at least, former employees regularly stress their good relations with both subordinates and superiors, although the latter were often faced with criticism concerning working conditions and work organization.[32] There was certainly a recognition of and insistence on distance between various social layers. In spite of the SED's repeated attempts to level social differences, these gaps never entirely disappeared; sometimes they widened or narrowed depending on central policy or local conditions at the time. Also, these gaps were closely linked to difficult working conditions.[33] Blaming the 'other' for inefficient production was common but at least partly based on a lack of information, which was typical of the East German economic and political system.[34] In male-dominated factories such as the *Transformatorenwerk Berlin* (TRO), gender relations were also tense. Animosity, however, more often occurred within or between the brigades; it affected the nearest social environment and only seldom those above or below.[35]

Within brigades, the smallest organizational work groups in the 1960s and 1970s, the working day was shaped by a curious mix of communal spirit, group support and disciplinary power over brigade members. Brigades incorporated an educational and controlling role which could lead to tensions. When members came to work late or not at all without excuse, when they were off sick, worked carelessly or slowly, the brigade was the smallest group within which individuals were reproached for their failure, lack of interest or discipline. In fact, brigades had a responsibility to ensure proper behaviour among their members, both at work and in the private sphere. If somebody committed a crime such as theft or caused a car accident outside work, the brigade would be informed, and also when somebody's children did well or badly at school or when people's family life turned problematic. The brigade was always involved and was expected to find solutions for problems or praise success. This may have been helpful in some situations, and most former members of brigades seem to maintain primarily positive memories of their brigades. However, some people also felt pressurized, under surveillance and imprisoned as part of these small but watchful groups of colleagues.[36] Acrimony and mobbing were possible at every level and some people felt forced to change their place of work to escape difficult situations.

However, as has been pointed out above, the general trend was divided into many different instances, events and processes that were influenced by both central policy and developments at the grassroots level. Neither ever progressed in a straight line or was applicable to every social group or section of society across the board. Within the economic sector, for example, central policy favoured specific industries. These priorities, however, changed over time. Company culture differed widely according to the history of the factory, location, size, the gender ratio of its workforce and its status. Accordingly, within different state-owned factories different problems occurred, were prioritized or ignored. Furthermore, central policy could take years to reach a specific factory and the workforce. As a result, the situation within one factory could differ greatly from the experience of another in the same area, of similar size or part of the same industrial sector. It follows that both the differences between state-owned factories and change over time must be considered meticulously when trying to describe company culture in the wider context of normalization.

Differentiation

The differences between state-owned factories is an issue worth studying in detail, particularly in response to totalitarian approaches to GDR history that assume central intentions to have been applied successfully to the everyday life of most people. Even some of those historians who recognize the limits of control with which central authorities were continuously confronted in East Germany, tend to neglect specific experience in favour of general trends. This approach, however, carries the danger of writing local history whilst claiming to describe a country's experience, discussing policy-making at the highest level whilst ignoring influences from below. Even in a centrally planned economic system, individual factories had different experiences and reacted differently to central policy. Problems differed and a variety of methods were applied to deal with difficulties. Of course, all state-owned factories were confronted more or less with the same basic problems. Working conditions and social relations have been described already. Also, André Steiner has pointed out that the economy depended on political decisions, which undermined efficiency throughout the GDR's existence. Almost every factory had to deal with unreliable supplies of materials and prefabricated parts, a lack of qualified workers and insufficient investment and production capacities. However, even with regard to these very basic issues, reality could vary dramatically. A comparative approach seems necessary to paint a fairly nuanced picture of life and work in the GDR that allows for both the general trend that may, at a second glance, turn out to be the exception in its ideal form, and an apparently discreet experience that may have been widely relevant in practice.

Sources are a problem in this context, as it seems that, at least tendentiously, archives for large, state-owned and centrally administered factories that were part of the capital goods industry are accessible most easily. However, the least a historian can do is, firstly, to select factories that existed prior to the Second World War to compare their position to those that were founded during GDR times; and, secondly, to choose units in diverse locations and with workforces of varying gender ratios and, crucially, of dissimilar status within the economic system and pay attention to the impact of personalities.[37]

Many excellent works have already given an indication of the relevance of some of these themes. Sandrine Kott's insightful study on factory workers in East Germany traced general structures and tendencies in five Berlin factories.[38] Petra Clemens has written on a traditional company employing primarily women (*Frauenbetrieb*) and Leonore Ansorg on a *Frauenbetrieb* built from scratch in a previously agricultural area, the *Obertrikotagenbetrieb Wittstock*.[39] Francesca Weil compared two factories in Leipzig and came to the conclusion that both size and composition were central to company culture. Weil also noted the importance of the works directors' networks.[40] Finally, the position of a state-owned factory within the economic system, that is to say its status, needs to be considered, as has been pointed out by Ingrid Deich, specifically with regard to a company's social efforts.[41] However, in spite of many excellent analyses, a comparative approach is still missing which stresses the individuality of companies with reference to a variety of themes in the context of the centrally planned economic system. To summarize: a state-owned factory with a long tradition of employing mostly women faced a different situation to an established factory employing mostly men, and both were in an entirely different position to an economic unit newly built in the countryside.

Significantly, these differences need to be considered as essential characteristics rather than picking and choosing from the various examples to put together a general picture, again discerning major trends rather than what in my opinion is the most defining aspect of state-owned factories in the GDR: their distinctiveness. To highlight this point, five carefully selected factories will be considered: the BGW, the TRO, the *Erdölverarbeitungswerk* in Schwedt (EVW), the *Halbleiterwerk* in Frankfurt/ Oder (HFO), and the *Chemiefaserwerk* in Premnitz (CFW).[42]

Five factories – five experiences

Both the BGW and the TRO were located in Berlin and had existed prior to the Second World War. Both were main suppliers of their products within the GDR and both exported worldwide. They employed large workforces of about four to five thousand people in the 1960s and 1970s. However, whilst the TRO employed mostly men, the majority of the BGW's employees, about 65 per cent, was female. Accordingly, they were confronted with different problems. In the 1960s, the employment of women was a growing need within the East German economy. Part of this effort was the provision of suitable places of work and childcare facilities to get mothers into employment. It is no surprise then, that the BGW was at the forefront of the new drive to improve working and living conditions. By late 1965 a suitable programme had been devised for the BGW; the TRO, employing mostly men, had to wait until 1967 for a similarly extensive package. A major contributory factor to the BGW's early success at expanding its social efforts, however, had been the activities of its works director, Rudi Rubbel.

The influence of the works director was crucial. In the GDR the principle of individual responsibility applied. It meant that works directors were held responsible for economic performance by both central authorities and the workforce.[43] It is crucial to show how this constellation worked on the ground; how it was dealt with by central authorities, the works directors themselves and the various layers of the workforce.

In many cases, a power struggle between the works director and the party secretary reflected the conflict between economic and political interests. Often enough, it was decided by personality traits or an individual's length of service and backing within a state-owned factory. In the CFW, for example, the relationship between the party secretary and the works director, who was appointed to his position in 1967, was tense from the beginning. In some cases, however, this power struggle never came to fruition. The works director of the EVW, for example, automatically became a member of the ZK SED and therefore had a direct link to the centre of the Communist Party, which no party secretary would have been able to rival.

The authority of any works director, and his success, also depended on his or her connections. Top functionaries such as Rudi Rubbel at the BGW, Helmut Wunderlich at the TRO or Werner Frohn at the EVW could rely on strong and continuous backing from central authorities. Rubbel maintained good relations with member of the Politburo Paul Verner and the executive board of the FDGB. Wunderlich, as former

Minister for General Mechanical Engineering and vice-chairman of both the SPK and the VWR, was well connected to central state authorities. Frohn was a member of the ZK SED and had close connections to the Minister for the Chemical Industry, Günther Wyschofsky. Although there were limits to their powers these people, more so than less elevated functionaries, could make things move. Their arrival almost guaranteed success.

Factories outside Berlin or any of the other larger cities were in an entirely different situation to both the BGW and the TRO. The CFW also had a long company tradition but was not only removed from the capital of the GDR but had less status within the East German industry than, for example, the EVW, which was also located in the countryside. Chemical fibres and textiles were less important to the East German economy than transformers and the products of crude oil that could be sold on the world market for hard currency. Nevertheless, the CFW was of immense consequence to the surrounding territory for which it was the main employer. People came from Premnitz and other villages and small towns such as Rathenow to work at the CFW. To enable sufficient provision of childcare facilities, schools, accommodation and other services necessary for everyday life, the CFW supported local authorities by offering financial assistance, technical expertise and labour.

This type of co-operation was vital to the establishment of a reliable workforce, especially in small towns or in agricultural areas; still more so for new state-owned factories such as the EVW in Schwedt and the HFO in Frankfurt/Oder. Both were founded in the early 1960s and had to put much effort into recruiting their workforces. Here it was important to work with local authorities to build up a suitable environment, where young families could see a future for themselves and their children. When trying to encourage people to move into an area or seek employment in a factory that was removed from the usual amenities offered by larger towns, management and local authorities had to work together to improve the surroundings. In this context, co-operation was based on mutual interest and benefited both sides.

The workforce, from production workers to technologists, administrative staff to economic functionaries, was very much interested in working at a successful plant. Employment at a state-owned factory which fulfilled its plans had a high status within the East German economic system, and access to social and cultural facilities would ensure high wages, bonuses and good working and living conditions.[44] Naturally, many fundamental problems which were based on the deficiency of the centrally planned economic system could not be solved, but they were dealt with to ensure, at least outwardly, more efficient work organization and a smoother production process. Success could bring an improvement in social relations. To a greater extent at least than in unsuccessful economic units, the production workers were given the possibility of being productive, technologists received the opportunity to be innovative, administrative staff and economic functionaries avoided some of the confrontations with both exasperated subordinates and superiors. Social peace was kept more easily in high-status factories than in failing ones and this was in the interests of almost everybody: central authorities, management and, increasingly in the 1960s and 1970s, also the workforce.

These are just a few examples, which will be discussed in greater detail in the following chapters, to highlight differences between state-owned factories. These differences had an impact on their progress and their position within an economic system that worked on the basis of selection. One other major issue was the influence of the SED, which mostly depended on the personalities of both the works director and the party secretary but also on changes in central policy. Furthermore, the interest of central authorities in a state-owned factory could vary widely and have diverse consequences, both negative and positive. Various aspects contributed to a factory's position within the economic system and those deemed deserving of promotion met with a different situation from those of lesser status. Status, however, depended on various aspects and could change with time; changes in central economic policy, a new works director or technological advancements could either hinder or help a particular factory in the constant struggle for a privileged position.

Dynamics of power: interaction and stabilization

Even slight shifts and fine differences had an impact on company politics, specifically within the centrally planned economic system. In spite of excellent studies on economic policy, on the evolution of the consumer and, linked to it, social policy at the central level and on developments in the factories, the interaction or mutual permeation between central policy and the grassroots in the context of the individuality of state-owned factories has not yet been analysed. In this section, the impact of changes in central policy at the grassroots level will highlight their consequences for individual factories.

Change over time

Changes at the central level had an impact on company culture. For example, the status of a state-owned factory could change dramatically in the context of changing central policy, which then affected, for example, working and living conditions, recruitment, the supply of materials and, thereby, economic performance. The reasons for such internal changes could be manifold, even beyond large-scale developments.

Any state-owned factory depended on decisions that were made at the central level. For example, the assignment of functionaries, particularly of a new works director, could have significant consequences, as has already been indicated. Also, integration into a *Kombinat*, a large conglomerate of factories, could have differing effects.[45] The HFO, for example, became the primary factory within a new *Kombinat* in 1978. The HFO suffered from this elevated position, however, as from then on investment for innovation and technological research went to Dresden and Erfurt, leaving a financial gap in Frankfurt/Oder.[46] In contrast to this negative example, when in 1957 the Energy Programme was introduced, the TRO benefited from additional investment and the Chemical Programme in 1958 led to the building of the EVW.

The implementation of central policy, however, did not take place seamlessly. Orders from the centre often needed some time to filter through to every factory. Their implementation could be delayed for various reasons: for example, a lack of trust, competence, will or means. Also, the chain of command provided many loopholes. On a broad middle level, between central decision makers and the workforce, many institutions and functionaries existed. They all had their own agenda and, in order to keep the system functioning, were often intent on finding a balance between the aims of the centre and the interests of the periphery. This constellation contained the possibility and the need for dialogue, and it was through the building up of structures to accommodate such dialogue that an important part of the normalization process was created. The interaction between the various levels had huge implications for stabilization in the 1960s.

The grassroots affecting central policy

In the 1960s and 1970s, both central authorities and the workforce learned a crucial lesson, with management teams and particularly some works directors taking the role of intermediary. It became apparent, in relation to both the upheaval in 1953 and the building of the Berlin Wall, that central authorities would have to live with an exacting workforce and that the workforce would have to accept equally severe government and party institutions.[47] This recognition, arguably, was the founding base of normalization. It enabled stabilization and, eventually, routinization within state-owned factories, as workers became more pliable and central authorities more aware and tolerant of the workforce's needs.

This new search for compromise, that was part of a trend to establish, learn and internalize the mutually acceptable rules of the (socialist) game, was reflected in the improvement of working and living conditions that had been an issue since the 1950s but received much more detailed attention from 1964 onwards. Prior to 1964, the provision of workers with meals and products at their places of work had been the main priority, which was a valuable help to many during times of food rationing. Similarly, medical care was provided to some extent, and also childcare and housing. However, from the middle of the 1960s social policy contained much more than those few issues, which may have been priorities for central institutions but not so for employees and management. Specifically, childcare and housing were given a higher priority and, in addition, culture, transportation to and from work, holiday provisions, sports facilities and so on were allocated funding.[48]

The establishment of programmes for the improvement of working and living conditions as part of the annual contract between management and workforce (BKV) was remarkable because of the interaction between central decision makers and state-owned factories. Works directors used the opportunity provided by the NES to stabilize factories in the sense of reducing high turnover and sickness rates. This also meant that works directors reacted to interests, demands and discontent voiced by the workforce.[49] Flexibility in the constant battle against the deficits of the planned economy was crucial in this context, although a factory's means always depended on its status and the personality and networks of its works director.[50]

The developments of the 1960s and 1970s had an impact on the attitudes of the East German population: the obligations on the employer or the state regarding social policy should be mentioned here as a prime example. Routinization and internalization are two of the main issues attached to such long-term developments.

Routinization and internalization

The concept of routine, as employed in this project, differs noticeably from ritualization,[51] a term that also has been used to describe people's behaviour in dictatorships. A ritual is stereotyped behaviour in a specific situation; ritualization takes place when behaviour turns into such a ritual. It implies outward adherence to both political expectation and the prescribed procedure for political ceremonies. It also carries connotations of conscious behaviour intended to pretend approval in spite of both inner retreat and a pronounced lack of interest.[52] In contrast, particularly to this suggestion of outward approval in spite of inward rejection, routinization is intended to emphasize long-term socio-political processes within East German society that resulted in internalization not only of the rules of the game but of values and attitudes.

Routine includes both negative and positive aspects. It has been argued that the rules of the game were both established and learned in the 1960s. From this predictability ensued, in many cases closely entwined with a progressive loss of real meaning, as for example can be seen in developments within official language with the result that functionaries often did not know the significance of the slogans they were using routinely.[53]

Besides these negative aspects, routine helped to stabilize both political and economic structures. Central authorities, functionaries and the general population were able to work with established structures that were functioning smoothly even if they were not effective. Routine set in not just in everyday life but also in crisis situations. One had learned what to expect and how to achieve a specific goal. By the 1970s, probably reinforced by the experience of the Czech people during the Prague Spring in 1968, the limits of open criticism were known and mostly kept, out of fear of Stasi involvement. Also, central authorities had acquired a customary way of dealing with crises, namely the avoidance of public awareness and the individualization of conflict.[54]

Keeping the social peace was an absolute priority after Honecker's rise to power. Under Ulbricht this had been much less the case. Not for nothing Honecker, at the beginning of his reign, insisted that 'One can never govern against the workers.'[55] Therefore, he tried to distance himself from Ulbricht's attitude, which had been hugely unpopular as he had prioritized investment in the economy before financing a higher standard of living for the population. In the 1960s, especially just after August 1961 and again with the eleventh plenary session of the ZK SED in 1965, socio-political appeasement of the population was deemed desirable but not at all costs. Ulbricht was not reluctant to introduce aggressive policies regarding salaries and the criminalization of critical voices just after the building of the Berlin Wall. Similarly, both cultural and youth policy in the 1960s, underwent radical periods and not just phases of liberation although, arguably, in these areas the initiator may have been Honecker's faction in the Politburo rather than Ulbricht.[56]

Nevertheless, by the 1970s routine had set in, ensuring a comparatively smooth functioning of socio-political relations in most sections of East German society. Dialogue was increasingly institutionalized within the petition system and pressed into an official language that accommodated political expectations. Routine led to internalization, not only for young people who knew no other socio-political environment but, to some extent, for everybody prepared to build a home under the very difficult political circumstances of life in a socialist dictatorship.

Routinization in factories

Within the economic sector, routinization became apparent in various ways from the late 1960s onwards. Central authorities became less likely to interfere in the running of state-owned factories directly, as long as the plan was fulfilled. In the 1960s interference had been a regular occurrence leading, for example, to a high turnover level for works directors. Also in the 1960s, the involvement of central authorities could be a blessing or a curse. Especially in the early years, at least some works directors still insisted on attention from central authorities, as it was hoped to solve problems by involving those who were felt to have the power to improve a difficult situation. This mostly happened when economic plans were still fulfilled albeit under difficulties. Support from superior institutions could include lower production plans, credits or simply a better supply of materials. However, when this was not the case any more, works directors were more reluctant to call on the SED BL, the VVB or the relevant ministry. The reason was that these bodies tended to implement ad-hoc measures because there were no real solutions, beyond short-lived rescue missions, within the given circumstances. Around 1967 the situation became calmer, at least outwardly. Between the late 1960s and late 1970s, works directors tended to stay in their positions. Only the new drive to create *Kombinate* resurrected the replacement of works directors in the late 1970s. Accordingly, the TRO had five different works directors in the 1960s but only one in the 1970s and the BGW had to accommodate three works directors during the 1960s but only one during the 1970s and a large part of the 1980s.

During the 1970s, a reluctance to attract attention from central authorities defined the attitude of most works directors. Possibly, it had become clear that no improvements were to be expected from their involvement. Most works directors and their management teams were glad to officially fulfil the plan. Whichever method seemed necessary was employed, including semi-legal initiatives such as unofficial networks, additional bonuses and higher wages for the workforce, or false book-keeping.[57] Any detailed attention could have been disastrous in this extremely precarious situation, in spite of officially fulfilled plans. There were two sides to routinization: outward calm and inner chaos. Neither one on its own, but the combination of both aspects, undermined morale in the long term.

On one side, most people adjusted to given circumstances and, on the other side, many exploited the system. Routinization had brought with it structures that tended to be ineffective with regard to what they were actually meant to achieve. These structures had acquired some stability and ensured the relatively smooth running of everyday processes, which was a crucial part of the sense of 'normality' that had been growing since the 1960s. Nevertheless, with time the recognition grew that these structures would not be able to help. By the late 1970s at the latest, the suspicion arose that they presented a primary part of the political system's basic deficiencies. In the 1970s most structures had become established and were regulated by laws that underwent only minor changes under Honecker. Systems became predictable and, for this reason, could be exploited – exploited in the sense of using given opportunities such as social benefits and educational possibilities to their maximum. Pursuing personal interests without useless confrontation helped many to keep a sense of self-determination in an extremely controlling environment. It allowed the majority of East Germans to create a life for themselves and their families that they felt was worth living.

State-owned factories were part of these structures and most had been able to stabilize their production processes sufficiently by the 1970s to ensure relatively smooth functioning. In spite of continuing problems such as unreliable deliveries of material, a lack of investment, and difficult working conditions, plans were fulfilled officially although the methods used were not always legal and relied on short-term solutions. By 1971, the intense focus on the improvement of working and living conditions had helped to stabilize the workforce: turnover and sickness rates had declined notably from the high levels of the mid 1960s.

However, stabilization was closely interlinked with routine. The workforce reacted ambivalently and very sensitively to routinization, which had a notable impact on company culture, as will be shown in the next chapters. People got used to political and economic circumstances that seemed unalterable and to the fact that fundamental problems would not be solved. No initiative, criticism or opposition would make the economic system efficient; at the most, they would enable the factory to fulfil the plan without necessarily working profitably, but thereby ensuring wages and bonuses.

Long-term processes also created a different attitude among workers. The extension of the programme for the improvement of working and living conditions had been a new development in the 1960s. Eventually, it was made a significant and obligatory part of the annual contract between workforce and management, laying down mutual pledges and promises. The expansion of the BKV in the 1960s was not, at least in this instance, a sign of increasing routine in all aspects of trade union work, but of a decisive achievement for the workforce. The latter's expectations and rights were embodied in these contracts, which made it possible to voice demands and criticism. By the 1970s, directors were making vague promises and blamed technical and financial difficulties for substandard working conditions.[58] This was progress: it is crucial to remember here the changes that had taken place in the 1960s. In the early 1960s it would have been neither acceptable to complain openly about working conditions nor would an economic functionary have stammered an excuse; mostly public complaints were either not made or ignored. The establishment of the programmes for the improvement of working and living conditions enabled the workforce to complain and be heard, and this it did massively during the 1970s, when investment shifts under Honecker really did cause additional technical and financial difficulties. Increasingly these benefits were taken for granted and expected although, as has been pointed out already, the level of provision depended on the status of the factory.

Furthermore, in the 1970s it became apparent that patterns of behaviour were changing. To take a specific example: initially workers who suggested technological improvements and innovations, so called *Neuerer*, were encountering hostility from some of their colleagues.[59] Management also became afraid of introducing technological improvement very quickly as it disturbed the precarious production process.[60] With time, however, potential *Neuerer* seem to have become reluctant to suggest innovative changes to the production process because they either did not want to upset their colleagues by suggesting innovations that may increase norms, or they co-operated with each other to exploit the system.[61] By the 1970s at the latest, it had become more important (or practical) to uphold cordial relations with colleagues and avoid confrontations than to work effectively. With routine, the conviction that nothing would ever change for the better arrived in the factories, causing lethargy, frustration and a growing concern for one's personal interests rather than those of society at large.[62]

The strong focus on personal interests affected East German society most severely. It undermined the desired sense of collectiveness by concentrating concern on the individual, not the group any more. Individualization, however, does not entail autonomy, emancipation, or limitless self-realization but a combination of self-determination and dependency on existing conditions. A strong tendency towards individualization became noticeable in the late 1970s, especially among young people and women, but it certainly affected almost all sections of society.[63]

Conclusion

Routinization combined stability and outward calm, even social peace, with resignation that was turning into lethargy and, eventually, individualization. Routine was based on the internalization of the rules of the game, of norms and expectations, and played a significant part in normalization. It allowed many to accept 'socialist normality', as it had developed in the 1960s and 1970s, as a given and thereby enjoy its advantages, grumble about its disadvantages and avoid its hazards and pitfalls. This 'socialist normality' included social benefits as much as it contained the presence of the Stasi. In addition, propaganda created inflated expectations whilst life in the GDR, as experienced by most people, was based on shortages, which increased the need for personal networks, and also on a surplus of expectations, which the state had unwittingly encouraged in its attempt to uphold social peace but proved unable to satisfy in the long term. It was also built on structures and language specific to the East German dictatorship, as well as on personal relationships and values that mirrored those in other modern European societies. The perception of normality was shaped by experience, expectation, hopes and fears. However, perceptions changed: the early 1960s offered a different normality to the late 1970s. Arguably, the tendency towards individualization can be described as a backlash against some aspects of routinization, especially standardized biographies, inefficient institutions and rigid structures, but also against the gap between official propaganda and everyday life, between promise and reality.

Normalization in the 1960s and 1970s had led to relative stability although fundamental problems were not solved. With time, the majority of the population began not only to adjust to but shape 'socialist normality'. On basic issues at least, common norms and mutual expectations were established. Therefore, it is insufficient to describe the 1970s by pointing to the reliance on mutual arrangements, whereby functionaries were reluctant to insist on a rigid application of central policy and the population adhered only to the required minimum. Such an approach would not explain the remnants of enthusiasm that still existed in the middle of the 1960s, or the optimism of the early 1970s, or the ensuing decline. Routine upheld outward appearances whilst underneath both ideological tenets and their practical implications, such as the centrally planned economy or the brigade movement, were breaking down. In the late 1970s, however, the tendency towards individualization, evident not just in the private sphere but also at places of work, contributed strongly to symptoms of disintegration. The long-term consequences of this process did not become apparent until the end of the 1980s.

The following five chapters will focus on the issues described above in more detail by considering in turn the experiences of five selected state-owned factories. In this way, differences between their individual positions and circumstances in the East German economy as a whole will be highlighted. Much attention will be given to changes over time and the impact of personalities on socio-economic processes.

2
Transformatorenwerk Berlin: Success and Failure

In this chapter the uneven path of a state-owned factory and its work-force through the economic reforms of the 1960s, the change of leader-ship and Honecker's first decade in power will be charted to highlight both changes and continuities in East German company culture. *Transformatorenwerk Berlin* (TRO) was located in Berlin and it was crucial to the East German economic system in terms of its production for domestic use and for export. Therefore, its experiences can stand as an example of the more privileged factories in the GDR. In compar-ison, companies located outside Berlin and in industrial sectors with lower priority will be considered in the following chapters. It is one of the insights of my research that every enterprise in the GDR had its very own identity, particular problems, specific solutions and a very individual atmosphere. Size, history, location and industrial sector are some of the most important differentiating factors. The case of the TRO will help to pinpoint some of the aspects indicated by the concept of normalization.

Characteristics

Up to 1945, the *Transformatorenwerk* had belonged to AEG, a major German company with a long tradition. After the war, the TRO was turned into a state-owned factory. It was the only company in the GDR which produced high-tension switchgear and large transformers up to 400KV and for this reason was crucial to the East German economy. It was one of the three largest such companies in Europe and set the world standard on some aggregates up to the early 1960s. From 1958 to 1967, in hierarchical terms, the TRO was subordinated to the *VVB Hochspannungsgeräte und Kabel*.

In 1960 the TRO achieved a surplus of 18 million DM after massive financial support from the state had helped to offset initial losses in the 1950s and the central Energy Programme of 1957 had yielded much-needed technological developments. By 1961, production had risen by 120 per cent[1] and in December 1962 production for the first time went above 100 million DM, a fair success at that time. At the end of 1964 just over 4000 people worked at the TRO.[2] In spite of these outward successes, in the early 1960s the TRO was already facing massive production problems caused by a lack of suitably qualified employees, difficulties in the punctual and sufficient provision of crucial materials or prefabricated parts, a lack of decisiveness among central decision makers, an underdevelopment of practical problem-solving leading to technological problems, and a lack of funding for theoretical research. These difficulties were typical of the East German economic system.[3]

The economic reforms

In 1963 Ulbricht introduced economic reforms, the NES. He took this step in response to economic difficulties in the very early 1960s, when the Soviet Union had refused to bail out the East German economic system. Ulbricht was forced to find a domestic solution to the crisis. The Berlin Wall had been one aspect of this solution, the economic reforms were the second. Kurt Hager, a long-term member of the Politburo, described the intention of the new economic system as follows:

> The main goal of the NES was to increase the independence and self-reliance of the state-owned factories and to focus their activities on to the market. They were meant to work according to the principle: as much planning as was needed, as much market (competition, profit) as was possible.[4]

The piecemeal implementation of the new guidelines began quickly, with the most important element being the attempt to connect central state institutions to an indirect steering of the state-owned factories by the use of monetary means, which were called economic levers.[5]

At the TRO a plan for necessary structural changes, according to the requirements of the NES, was prepared in April 1964. It proposed to bundle 'all economic functions under one homogenous management', the rational ordering of all departments and some other equally vague measures, which seemed neither particularly linked to the economic reforms' major aims nor geared towards the specific problems of the factory.[6] Part of the problem was that economic functionaries at the TRO and other state-owned factories were overtaxed by the NES. Annette Wilczek has argued convincingly that the rule book of the NES was too complex for most economic functionaries to apply to the specific circumstances of their factories.[7] Also, they were immersed in the practical problems of day-to-day survival and had little time, in many cases also insufficient information, for the implementation of the reforms. Although productivity was hampered by many structural deficiencies that needed to be dealt with urgently, nothing changed for some time. Soft norms were one prime example of such deficiencies.

Soft norms

One of the major structural problems facing the East German economy was the introduction of realistic norms, which was attempted but failed because of a lack of power and interest from economic functionaries.[8] After the building of the Berlin Wall, norms had been tightened slightly by the introduction of effective time, a practice that accommodated incentive wages. By this means, the period of time allocated for the production of specific parts, for example, was reduced and wages became linked to a worker's productivity. Nevertheless, norms were still easily reached. In some work places, norms had been negotiated with workers rather than established on the basis of technical findings and those responsible for timing workers were often unable to oversee the production process sufficiently to set accurate norms. The following case highlights the same assessment; throughout the existence of the GDR, functionaries were either not interested in or saw no way to change norms according to technological realities.

In summer 1964, an engineer, who was not a member of the SED, complained to the FDJ that in the *Niederschönhausen* section of the TRO, which supplied the main transformer construction with crucial parts, soft norms were applied. This meant that workers were receiving unreasonable bonuses to induce higher productivity and the plan had large buffer zones. In the engineer's opinion, the implementation of realistic norms did not founder on his colleagues' attitude but on that of the functionaries. Apparently, before contacting the FDJ, he had approached party and economic functionaries on this issue but without success. The responsible director, Wissfeld, recognized the problem but felt unable to improve the situation. In that functionary's opinion, phoney norms were the rule in the East German economic system. The party secretary also accepted the complaint but was not sure if it would be in the interest of the SED to rectify the problem. In a discussion of the plan, the criticism had been listened to but it was decided to prepare the plan as in previous years and not to risk change.[9]

The complaint caused a lot of trouble in *Niederschönhausen*. An investigation was conducted which found that the situation was quite disastrous. The whole section was divided into many different cost units allowing trade unionism to dominate economic decisions: 'Because these cost units form an independent entity, real trade unionism can be found. Efforts are not directed any more towards fulfilling the plan but towards fulfilling the wishes of colleagues.'[10] To speak of trade unionism was an extremely serious accusation. Accordingly, the party secretary suggested to the works director of the TRO that he replace Wissfeld and restructure the section. Although the episode was kept quiet and did not reach the company's weekly paper *Trafo*,[11] one can see from the files kept in the TRO's archive that the section's director and other economic, trade union and party functionaries were criticized and even replaced whilst the complaining engineer was promoted in early 1965.[12] From the archival perspective, at least, one could get the impression that it was possible to influence company politics from the lower levels of the hierarchy.

However, the engineer tells a different story. In his opinion, his promotion was intended to keep him quiet whilst nothing was changed regarding the main issue of his complaint: namely the soft norms, the plan with its inbuilt buffers and bad management in general remained. The engineer was repeatedly approached to join the SED, always with the offer of a leading function attached to this political courtship. When he agreed to become a member of the SED, a new position was created for him in order to fulfil the promise. However, only a short time later, he gave up his new position and changed to another department. Although apparently even the SPK had become interested in the whole affair, it came to nothing, except for the party secretary's bad feelings towards the complaining person, which were felt and had to be dealt with for several more years.[13]

Adding another element to this puzzle, the new director of this section, Dorothea Meinke, recalled other reasons for the replacements and her own assignment in *Niederschönhausen*: her predecessor, Wissfeld, had not been able to fulfil the plan for months and therefore was forced to take another position within the main factory, which he handled more successfully. Meinke agreed however that the engineer's complaint had been justified and based on real problems. The only solution offered was the replacement of leading functionaries. The real issues were not tackled nor were they ever solved. According to Meinke, and contrary to the engineer's assessment, any attempt to introduce real norms foundered on the attitude of the workers and not on the functionaries' work.[14] No final conclusions can be drawn from this particular case regarding the handling of soft norms. However, the complexities of the issue and the variety of viewpoints that can be taken on the same problem are apparent. This was typical of most major fault lines in the East German economy.

Economic reforms at the TRO

A variety of different problems, from soft norms to a lack of technological progress, to material supply problems were intended to be addressed by the NES. The reforms, however, were introduced only partially and in steps. Although the intention was to make the East German system more economical and competitive, and to give works directors more leeway in making economic decisions, procedures hardly changed.[15]

Nevertheless, more fundamental economic changes followed between 1964 and 1965. Deliveries of crucial raw materials from the Soviet Union fell drastically from 1964. Furthermore, the Soviet Union proved unreliable regarding trade contracts, which led to high financial losses for the GDR in the middle of the 1960s and hindered the attainment of the economic reforms.[16] With reforms lagging behind, partly sabotaged by high state functionaries,[17] it became impossible for central planners to put together a balanced plan for the period up to 1970. Erich Apel, the head of central planning and arguably the primary strategist of the NES, committed suicide in December 1965. Nevertheless, the second stage of the new economic system was introduced at the eleventh plenary session of the ZK SED.[18] Although planning and to some extent rights of disposal were further decentralized,[19] it can be argued that 1965 marked the end of the NES or, expressed differently, marked the very early beginnings of the Honecker era.[20]

Two years later, in 1967, the TRO was still not in line with the requirements of the NES. At that time, the criticism made by the works director, Paul Wolter, was that the TRO had practically not been managed in the first half of 1967 and that leading functionaries were not familiar with the implications of the economic reforms for individual factories.[21] Throughout the 1960s the situation, not only regarding the TRO, was difficult to say the least.

Blessing or curse? Central authorities getting involved

Successful co-operation with central state and party institutions was crucial to the success of all state-owned factories, but often these central institutions only got involved when the plan had not been fulfilled. Many works directors did everything they could to avoid such external involvement in economic management, as it often meant massive interference which, moreover, did not always lead to improvement. Nevertheless, the lack of central involvement was also criticized by works directors. As long as they saw a chance, with a little help from central institutions such as the VVB, to put things right and keep fulfilling the plan works directors asked for support. Often however, and increasingly in the 1970s, central involvement was not wished for, especially when problems had become overwhelming and seemingly insoluble. Particularly in the late 1970s, reluctance to call for help increased dramatically as the conviction grew that no real help would be forthcoming but rather interference from the centre would upset a carefully maintained balance that, at least, guaranteed continuity of production. Not only did managers react differently in different circumstances, as has been pointed out above, but they also changed their behaviour over time in response to the economic context.

The TRO experienced the ambiguity of central interference throughout the 1960s. The increase in production above 100 million DM in December 1962, for example, was only achieved because the SED BL of Berlin had interfered three months earlier to prevent a drastic decline in production. Specialists were sent in, plans for an emergency restructuring were implemented and the VVB was ordered to adjust the factory's plans for 1963. It was told to discuss the future prospects of the TRO with the SPK and the VWR. Special attention was to be directed at the improvement of relations between the workforce and management.[22] In spite of these efforts, the plan was not fulfilled in 1962. In 1961 the production plan was already showing a deficit of 9 million and 1962 ended with a 7 million DM deficit.[23] Continuous difficulties made success very hard to achieve. To make matters worse, relations between not only the workforce and management but also between the works director and the VVB became extremely tense in 1963.

Party politics versus economic decision making?

At the end of 1963 the works director at that time, Hans Zillgitt, complained to the BPO about the lack of support he had received from the

VVB. He explained to Werner Gerlatzek, the First Party Secretary at the TRO, that the VVB had not commented at all on his work in the last year. Zillgitt had the impression that the production problems did not interest the VVB as long as the plan was fulfilled. He predicted unfulfilled plans if nothing was done to improve the situation, which had not changed fundamentally because last year's difficulties had been dealt with only perfunctorily. Furthermore, he was regularly receiving unrealizable orders from the VVB. For example, without any prior information to the works director, the TRO had been given responsibility for an investment project to build a new transformer works in Berlin-Friedrichshain. Also, production plans for January 1964 had been increased, absolutely unrealistically, from 6.2 to 10 million DM. This decision was not only unworkable; it also undermined the entire bonus system down to the level of the *Meister*, who were highly qualified foremen with great responsibility for ensuring regular production. Finally, Zillgitt pointed out that the VVB had ordered adjustments to the accounts which ignored a substantial part of the production. He warned that the TRO would incur losses if nothing was done and, again, asked for help from the SED. He also pointed out that, in his opinion, he had repeatedly been made to feel that he was not well liked by the VVB's general director, and that other departmental heads had also had similar discouraging experiences.[24] From the archival files it is not apparent whether relations were improved by this plea for help. It is certain, however, that no long-term solution to any of the TRO's fundamental problems was found at that stage. Zillgitt was replaced about a year later.

The BPO

Particularly interesting was the BPO's position in the TRO. Not only had Zillgitt approached it for help; in addition, the BPO seems to have been notably influential in personnel decisions. In 1964, for example, it gave detailed orders regarding the employment, transfer and replacement of economic personnel. On 6 January 1964 it was decided to recommend to the works director to approve party member Schmolinski as head of the planning section.[25] In July 1964, as a result of an investigation into the management of a section located in Berlin-Rummelsburg that had production problems, the BPO demanded the replacement of its director Wilfling. He was described as a 'dictator' and there were concerns about his political attitudes, although his efforts ensured that production ran according to the plan.[26] Wilfling, in contrast, blamed central planning for the difficulties in Rummelsburg.[27] In September 1964, after much support from Zillgitt for Wilfling, who kept fulfilling the plan, his replacement was postponed once more.[28] By February 1965, however, Zillgitt was replaced and Wilfling lost his post. The BPO had won this particular battle but without any visible positive outcome regarding economic performance in Rummelsburg. Repeatedly, current directors were blamed for the exasperating situation but the section's production problems continued for many more years.[29] The SED's influence on decision making within state-owned factories such as the TRO could be immense, even during the NES period. It was enforced by the BPOs and the local party administration, to which detailed weekly and monthly reports had to be sent.[30] In most cases, however, politically motivated interference was of little help regarding the solution of economic problems.

The VVB

For the TRO, the years 1964 to 1967 were defined by reconstruction. Efforts were made to expand the production of large transformers. During this time, the company was repeatedly criticized for putting the NES reforms into action insufficiently; not incorrectly, as has been seen in relation to the influence of party functionaries on economic decision making. In the East German economic system, a factory's economic problems were often compounded by the threat of central involvement. Between 1966 and 1968, the TRO felt the full force of the central authorities' interest.

After some years of unsuccessfully trying to stabilize production, the VVB finally dictated a rescue programme in January 1966. Although Paul Wolter, the acting works director, ordered its immediate realization, he did not achieve any positive long-term effect. Also, he added his own priority to the catalogue of most immediate tasks at hand: he insisted on catching up with the political instruction of functionaries which, in his opinion, had been dangerously neglected because of the effort to tackle the TRO's economic problems, and also on keeping up the cultural learning of workers.[31] In May 1966 the VVB found irregularities in accounting at the TRO and demanded a replacement of staff and structural reorganization from the Ministry.[32] A few days later, Wolter introduced an obligatory presentation and discussion of political-ideological problems at every meeting, even those that should have been primarily concerned with economic problems.[33] Apparently, this works director was much more in line with the BPO's interests than Zillgitt had ever been. This may have been an indication of the changing temper of the times. However it did not bode well for economic success. In September 1966

Wolter was informed by telephone that an investigation of the TRO's economic and financial difficulties would take place.[34] Three months later, the TRO finally succumbed to long-term problems that had already been hindering production in the early 1960s but had never been solved. The plan could not be fulfilled anymore.[35]

Replacing works directors

Between 1961 and 1967 the TRO had three different works directors. They were all appointed and dismissed by the VVB, which was working in close co-operation with the SED BL of Berlin. This succession of works directors was a reflection of both the difficult situation during that period and the failure to introduce essential improvements. The tendency to replace people rather than tackling more fundamental issues such as the planning process, the delivery of material or improving technologies was typical of the 1960s but not very effective in the long term. In 1965, production plans were already showing a deficit of 27 million, which in 1966 reached 42.3 million Marks.[36]

In February 1967, in the course of central organizational changes, the TRO was subsumed into the new *VVB Hochspannungsgeräte* before, in July 1967, both the technical and the works directors were replaced. The former works director, Wolter, was praised for his engagement but criticized for his inability to deal with staff issues and for his lack of authority.[37] In July 1967 another new works director arrived at the TRO. He was to stay for some time, ensure plan fulfilment and, with much delay, implement at least some aspects of the economic reforms.

The new works director, Helmut Wunderlich, was appointed to stabilize production and ensure the fulfilment of the plan. Before Wunderlich came to the TRO he had been Minister for General Mechanical Engineering in 1953 and again from 1955 to 1958. Then, he had worked as vice-chairman of the SPK for two years and after that as vice-chairman of the VWR for three years. He also had some experience as a works director. Between 1963 and 1967, he headed another Berlin company, *VEB Elektrokohle Berlin-Lichtenberg*, which he took over when it was in a similar position to the TRO in 1967 and managed to stabilize it in a very short time. It is apparent that when he came to the TRO he had acquired not only vast experience in central planning and excellent contacts to the central decision-making bodies but was also a works director on a rescue mission. He stayed at the TRO until 1971, during which time he was also a member of the SED BL of Berlin.[38] Wunderlich had political and economic authority and important connections: he was a top economic functionary.

When Wunderlich arrived at the TRO, he described his first impressions succinctly:

> At the SED BL of Berlin, I said that I had never before seen such chaos in a socialist factory as I found in the TRO, although I know hundreds of state-owned factories. Such lack of organization, such chaos, such an attitude to the fulfilment of the plan as in the TRO, is probably present in no other factory in the whole of the GDR.[39]

First of all, he worked on structural issues, liaised with workers' collectives and brigades, brought in specialists, ensured the use of improved technologies and rationalized production processes.[40] His primary task at the TRO was the fastest possible return to the plan; a task that he achieved in just about eighteen months. However, he was not solely responsible for this success: in September 1967 a special 'Committee for the restoration of the TRO's economic viability' was put to work and, in December 1967, the Ministry for Electronics and Electrical Engineering decided on a specific course to ensure a speedy recovery.[41] The committee left in October 1968, and from December 1968 onwards the TRO was able to fulfil its plans although its products were not competitive on the world market any more.[42]

The replacement of economic functionaries from the middle of the 1960s was not just typical of the TRO.[43] This large-scale effort to employ works directors with qualifications which were appropriate for their positions had been preceded by changes within the VVBs. In 1964 many VVB functionaries were sent to work in state-owned factories where they were supposed to increase their experience and qualifications.[44] The replacement of works directors, noticeable especially between 1967 and 1970, was a trend that affected factories throughout the GDR.[45] Steiner has argued that the political elite discussed the priority of economic over political competency throughout the 1960s, with political competency being increasingly favoured towards the end of the 1960s.[46] Arguably this process reflected Honecker's rise to power. In addition, the replacement of works directors also had practical motives. It was intended to improve the qualification structure across the East German economy, partly to keep up with developments in West Germany.[47] Particularly in the 1960s, the strong belief in technological progress and its relevance to the shaping of society, put forward by supporters of cybernetics, encouraged this trend of looking to the best qualified for an answer to all the major problems of the East German economy.[48] Wilczek, in her comparison of two *Kombinate*, points out that the management team of the *VEB Elektrogerätewerk Suhl* was repeatedly replaced in the 1970s.[49] Nevertheless, she concludes that it became more difficult to get qualified staff to take on managerial positions at the highest level in the 1970s and, therefore, older managers were kept in their positions as long as possible.[50] Another possible explanation would be that under Honecker many of the economic functionaries had only been put into their positions in the late 1960s. Most were still relatively young in the 1970s and highly qualified. Also, routine set in. In contrast to the fundamental changes under Ulbricht, central decision makers now aimed for stability rather than accepting upheaval in the interests of long-term economic success.

The personality, qualification and connections of a works director were crucial to the success of a state-owned factory, particularly because the underlying structural problems of the East German economy were never solved and could not have been solved without changing the political context of the socialist dictatorship. What mattered most was that the plan needed to be fulfilled and social peace to be kept. Furthermore, the new works directors conveyed a new management style which stressed good relations between workers and management although it is unclear if this was intended by central institutions or rather a reflection of the temper of the times.[51] In any case, these changes were very well received by employees, as shown by the reaction to the new works director of the TRO, Wunderlich, when he promised to spend a great part of his time on the shop floor:

> And it caused spontaneous clapping among the SED activists present when Wunderlich announced that he would spend the greatest part of his working hours in the production workshops with the collectives and socialist brigades.[52]

The replacements were linked to central efforts to improve the standard of qualification among economic functionaries, which began in the first half of the 1960s and were directly based on the requirements of the NES.[53] Many of those works directors, who came into their positions between 1967 and 1970, stayed there for many years, thereby putting an end to the volatile staff turnover at this level in the 1960s.

From about 1967 onwards, possibly complementing the replacement of works directors, another aspect of company management changed. There was a notable increase, or return to, a politicization of economic management, which was an early sign of Honecker's growing influence.

The influence of the SED within economic units had always been high. However, in tune with the NES, technical know-how and economic management had been moved to the foreground of decision making. Nonetheless in July 1967 a discussion at the SED meeting of the *VVB Hochspannungsgeräte*, during which Wunderlich sat on the management committee, came to the following conclusion:

> It has become crucial that functionaries, whether SED members or not, get used again with all its consequences to the fact that party decisions are binding for them as they are for every party functionary and that they have to participate in party life.[54]

The influence of the SED on economic management became ever more pronounced after 1967,[55] although this also always depended on the personalities of the party secretary, works director and the VVBs' general directors. In the same year, the general director of the *VVB Hochspannungsgeräte* claimed that he would not be able, in the future, to work with leading functionaries who had not developed a clear class consciousness, that is to say supported the SED's activities.[56] In 1970, the TRO's party secretary Schellknecht was giving not recommendations but orders to the works director, defining the BPO's role as pacemaker leading the factory out of the crisis.[57]

Difficult years: the 1970s

In 1967, the TRO had been confronted with industrial price reforms, which meant that prices did not reflect the actual work and cost involved in the production of transformers. The TRO was producing too expensively compared with world market prices.[58] The resulting difficulties were immense but not unique to the TRO. In the late 1960s, the East German economy underwent a massive crisis which reflected back onto the TRO in various ways. Specifically, the provision of materials became haphazard. To take just one example: to build transformers, copper was needed. Copper, however, had to be bought with hard currency. In the 1970s, it became increasingly difficult to ensure a continuous supply of this expensive but crucial material because of rising prices for raw materials on the world market. Nevertheless, the TRO officially continued to fulfil its plans and production of goods reached an output above 150 million Marks. However, there are indications that productivity stagnated whilst accounts showed an unbroken rise.[59] The 1970s were to be difficult years for the TRO.

In 1969 and 1970 seven major breakdowns of transformers shook the plant severely. Furthermore, in 1969, the Ministry for Electronics and Electrical Engineering ordered investment cuts. The TRO was advised that the plan for the 1970s should not be limited by these cuts but the freed resources would be 'centralized', which meant that they would be lost to the factories. It was not pointed out how this was to be done although such cuts would have not been easy to make considering the already low level of investment.[60] Nevertheless, in 1971 the TRO achieved the best results within the *VVB Automatisierungs- und Elektroanlagenbau (AEA)*.

Even so, the situation within the TRO was difficult at the turn of the decade. Accordingly, between 1968 and 1970 Wunderlich repeatedly sent pleas for help to Paul Verner, First Secretary of the SED BL of Berlin and member of the Politburo. At that time Verner was probably the person in Berlin with the greatest power to allocate sparse resources and help with formal or administrative hindrances. The TRO must have been in dire straits to justify applying to Verner for help. The workforce, both management and workers, certainly felt dejected. In August 1970 many brigades were reported to doubt that management would be able to solve existing problems. It was pointed out that, so far, problems that had been occurring regularly had only been tackled to an extent which allowed the immediate bridging of production stoppages but not the finding of fundamental solutions. At that time, as was noted by the BPO, workers were already becoming increasingly concerned about their own material advantage and were much less interested in the overall performance of the company.[61] In December 1970, in a consultation with the local SED administration in Köpenick, the Berlin borough in which the TRO was located, growing tensions between central authorities and the TRO were discussed. In particular delays in decision making seem to have had a negative impact on the already complicated situation within the TRO and were undermining the workforce's trust in central authorities.[62] In spite of fulfilled plans, the inside of TRO was rotting, a process which neither a well-connected works director nor the replacement of the very unpopular Ulbricht in 1971 could contain entirely.

Late in 1971 Manfred Friedrich replaced Wunderlich, who after his successful rescue mission in the TRO had been sent to another crucial East German factory, the *VEB Carl Zeiss Jena*. In the TRO, after some initial optimism in the early 1970s when Honecker came to power, it became quickly apparent to the workforce that neither the new works director nor the new head of state would implement any fundamental changes. In 1975 discussions about the plan, which always involved the entire workforce, reflected the mood in the production halls. Criticism was directed at working conditions, especially the lack of important tools and the worn out and defective machines, unreliable delivery of materials, the ventilation of production halls and the provision of meals for workers. Also, many sections had unfilled positions, registered high levels of overtime and complained about insufficiently qualified production helpers.[63] All in all, the catalogue of grievances looked similar to those voiced over a decade earlier. Apparently, not much had changed since the early 1960s except for the fact that machines and equipment had worn out.

The late 1970s were marked by massive production problems. Apparently, however, new ways of dealing with them were used by the works director. In 1978 disciplinary proceedings were brought against Friedrich for forging statistics. The accounts for a number of months had contained unfinished and incomplete products, thereby suggesting results that were not achieved in reality.[64] These practices seem to have been used for some time to embellish the accounts and may be part of the explanation for the nationwide trend of fulfilled plans in spite of obvious economic problems in the 1970s and 1980s.[65] Nevertheless, Friedrich continued as works director and was there during the TRO's integration into the *Kombinat Elektroenergieanlagenbau* (VEB KEA) in January 1979.

Social issues, sickness rates and turnover

In spite of the many economic difficulties described above, the TRO had always been a privileged factory because of its export obligations. Therefore it had been able to build up over the years a whole complex of social, cultural and medical facilities for use by its workforce. Here, management made some special efforts even in difficult periods. In 1964, a sewing room was opened, for 1965 a sauna was planned. In 1966, a programme for the improvement of working and living conditions existed which included the building of a kindergarten and a holiday home in spite of massive financial difficulties.[66] In 1969 a new hairdresser was opened. By 1974 it boasted a polyclinic, childcare facilities for toddlers and children beneath school age, holiday camps for children, young people and water-sports enthusiasts, a folk dance group, an orchestra for mandolins and accordions, a general orchestra and a library containing about 8000 books. These facilities, part of an effort to attract and retain employees, took off in the middle of the 1960s in response to high staff turnover rates.

From the late 1950s onwards all state-owned factories were confronted with a constant shortfall in their workforces; for the TRO the recruitment of qualified staff was a particular problem. This situation was worsened by labour-intensive production processes and high sickness rates in the early 1960s. In most cases it was impossible to offer higher wages as an incentive. The alternative proved to be social benefits. The programme for the improvement of working and living conditions was a response to this need for a stable workforce.

Turnover of staff and sickness rates were crucial issues for every works director. Firstly, although a certain number of sick days were allowed for, anything above this minimal number endangered the plan. Furthermore, the recruitment of new staff was difficult and also always meant an initial period during which productivity would be low. The reasons for leaving a place of work in the 1960s varied widely and it is difficult, to some extent even speculative, to pinpoint these for any particular period and factory. Although some state-owned factories kept statistics on numbers and reasons for those who decided to leave, one cannot rely on the reasons given. People may have put forward explanations that seemed socially more acceptable than the real causes in order to avoid negative sanctions. Problems with a particular superior functionary would have been perceived to be less acceptable than claiming that one had to look after an elderly relative. Nevertheless, trends can be deduced. Generally, in the 1960s staff turnover was very high up to the middle of the decade. It declined in the second half of the 1960s, which can be linked to more pronounced efforts to tie workers in by offering social incentives such as accommodation, childcare and a variety of social, medical and cultural facilities. Furthermore, in 1967 the introduction of annual bonuses at the end of the year probably had an initial suppressing impact on levels of staff turnover although it did not last. In 1968 the SED BL of Berlin blamed high staff turnover rates on the many jobs available in the capital of the GDR,[67] which does not account for similar problems in less industrialized areas of the GDR.

The TRO never had a very acute staff turnover problem because of its comparatively high wage level. In 1968 average staff turnover reached only 7 per cent.[68] After that, however, rates started to rise to about 11 per cent by September 1970[69] and even 15 per cent in 1972, whilst 1973 saw a decline to 11.2 per cent.[70] An analysis of the causes of staff turnover prepared in 1970 concluded that other Berlin factories offered better working conditions, in some cases even better wages and social benefits.[71] This only became an issue of concern for management in the late 1970s.[72] By this time, however, attitudes had changed enough from the 1960s to make anybody seem suspect who changed his place of work more than once or twice. A study conducted by the Central Institute for Youth Research (ZIJ) came to the conclusion that a large proportion of young employees was given the impression that those people who often changed their employer would have a difficult time with the management and even within their work groups.[73] Apparently, the drive of the 1960s to strengthen the bond between factories and their workforce had been successful at least in this sense.[74] In the late 1970s the TRO was particularly successful in reducing turnover rates after the introduction of a special working group to tackle this problem. Rates had been reduced to about 5 per cent in the first half of 1978 and 4.1 per cent in the same period of 1979.[75]

The general trend for sickness rates, with which the TRO was pretty closely in line, was a notable increase in the early to middle 1960s, after they had been quite low around 1960. The rates declined in the late 1960s, arguably in reaction to changes in social policy as reflected in the programme for the improvement of working and living conditions.[76] After Honecker came to power, sickness leave started to rise again, overtaking in the late 1970s the comparatively high level of the mid 1960s.[77] The development of sickness rates in the TRO went from around 7.7 per cent in 1960 to 6.3 per cent in 1963, rising to around 6.8 per cent in 1965. A decline to 6.3 per cent in 1966 and around 6.4 cent in 1968 can be traced. From then on, the rate increased again to around 7.4 per cent in 1970. A short dip in 1972 (7 per cent) can probably be explained by the short-lived optimism following Honecker's rise to power. However, very quickly sickness rates began to rise again: to 7.6 per cent in 1973 and even 8.6 per cent in 1978, which was comparatively high.[78]

One explanation for the increase may have been the onset of drastic saving and rationalization measures, the so-called 'Scientific Organization of Labour' (WOA), which reduced buffer zones within the working day to increase productivity and extended shift work, particularly the three-shift system.[79] One report from August 1978 claimed an increase in alcohol consumption during working hours, a tendency which may both reflect the stress levels involved in working within a shift system and be the cause of higher levels of sick leave.[80]

It can also be argued that Honecker's centralization of social policy issues undermined the bond between the working population and their employers that had been carefully crafted in the 1960s. In particular the improvement of working and living conditions, social benefits for women, and the central building programme, which was to provide sufficient accommodation by 1990, became centrally administered under Honecker. This left state-owned factories with fewer material and production capacities, and less room for initiative and influence.[81]

Furthermore, in 1979 a report to the ZK SED explained high sickness rates not by a particularly bad bout of flu or the sheer exhaustion of the workforce but by egoistic attitudes: 'It is obvious that our social benefits system is being exploited egoistically by many employees.'[82] Apparently, physicians outside the factory's own polyclinic were not reluctant to accept a person's claim to be ill although he or she was obviously simulating it. Also, within work brigades, colleagues could be extremely tolerant of those colleagues who called in sick without cause.[83] Those who did not produce an excuse for missing work, however, were not supported by their work colleagues. Here, fine lines of differentiation were being drawn, which separated integrated work colleagues from those who tended towards what was called 'asocial' behaviour:

> Here, our colleagues react correctly, according to their class (*klassen-mässig*), but achieve a change in only very few cases ... In discussions, they declare ... 'Our laws are made for the future [and] one should treat these dodgers, who today still live amongst us, quite differently. They should be sent to prison and then they should be made to work their fingers to the bone.'[84]

So, whilst most colleagues' sick calls were accepted, other colleagues were ostracized. To some extent, this differentiation was encouraged by both official rhetoric and law.[85] It helped central control institutions such as the police force and the Stasi to pressurize those people who, for various reasons, were not able or willing to participate fully in the stylized work culture of the GDR. After all, the education of the masses was the major aim of the socialist dictatorship.

Changing attitudes

With time, large sections of the population supported official guidelines wherever they reflected their own expectations, for example regarding young people's attitudes to music, fashion and leisure time, behaviour in public and, as shown above, at the work place. The ideas of a 'proper' lifestyle were largely characterized by traditional petit bourgeois values, which the East German political elite also adhered to on the basis of their own upbringing and experience. The impact of the socialist propaganda drive should also not be underestimated. Highly prized, up to the middle of the 1970s at least, were values such as a general readiness to work for collective interests, a strong interest in social fairness, and engagement in the immediate social environment, be it at school, at work, with friends or family. In the late 1970s, the tendency towards individualization became more dominant and undermined the collective ideas of socialism.[86]

In 1978 a BPO report noted a change in the attitude of workers. It stated that a more or less large part of the workforce used working hours less intensively, that loss of working time through sickness and people missing from work without an excuse had increased and that additional work was not done voluntarily any more but only in exchange for more pay.[87] Similar tendencies were noted by Dagmar Semmelmann. She had studied philosophy but had been sent to work in production after she had been too forthcoming with her students following the Biermann affair, by arranging a viewing of the singer's Cologne concert, which had led to his banishment in 1976.[88] Semmelmann came to the TRO in the late 1970s, where for some time she worked in the department responsible for devising and controlling the campaign called '*Sozialistischer Wettbewerb*' (socialist contest). According to her observations, by then this campaign followed rigid guidelines and procedures that were counterproductive to its original intention and meaning:

> Rather, an illusory life takes place here, in a more or less perfect manner, sprinkled with the appropriate external highlights. It is kept going from 'above', i.e. by the state functionaries, the party functionaries and the trade union representatives, kept within certain rules, worked in a specific pattern and already got used to.[89]

Furthermore, the working climate at the TRO was marked by production stress, a constant frustration of initiative, even disillusionment and defeatism. The workforce was primarily interested in keeping norms low, earning money and dealing with sometimes very difficult working conditions. A socialist consciousness, as may have been expressed by a concern for society in general and the factory's success in particular, seemed to have stagnated at a low level and, in fact, appeared to be receding. Conflicts within the brigades and also between brigades and management were kept quiet or played down, in spite of widespread displeasure and dissatisfaction with economic organization and dysfunctional structures. On both sides, the feeling was that at least compromises kept production going and open confrontation would be unhelpful and, possibly, cause problems rather than bringing about fundamental and lasting improvement. Apparently the experience of working at the TRO for many years had ingrained the conviction in both the workforce and management that nothing would ever change for the better.[90]

Outwardly, the TRO was fulfilling its plans but inwardly, working and living conditions, the attitude of the workforce and the management's behaviour combined to produce a lethargic lack of interest in anything other than one's own concerns, primarily earning sufficient money and surviving the working day. This situation seemed to cause stress, with unreliable working conditions and uncertain prospects for a factory that was obviously struggling to keep up appearances whilst every single employee knew of its rotten core.

Summary

In the early 1960s efforts were already being made to stabilize the East German economy and, thereby, the political system in general. However, the introduction of the NES did not achieve what it was intended to do: structures did not change enough to achieve lasting stability. As has been shown for the TRO, it took a long time before the measures based on the economic reforms reached the shop floor, even longer for them to be implemented, and sometimes it never happened. Procedures and problems remained the same beyond the 1960s. Soft norms were an issue that hampered productivity up to 1989. The interference of central authorities in the management of state-owned factories continued throughout the 1960s although the NES was meant to extend the leeway of individual works directors.

In the second half of the 1960s, SED involvement in the day-to-day running of the factory increased again after there had been a slight retreat in the years prior to 1967. Works directors were most successful when they had good backing within the district organizations of the SED. Wunderlich was not a miracle worker but he was well connected. Not even this top functionary, however, could solve the TRO's problems in the long term. Nevertheless, slowly a new, socialist normality took shape – marked by both central politics and developments at the grassroots. It brought some stability to everyday life without necessarily solving basic problems; rather, routinization encouraged both the establishment of and, eventually, the internalization of the rules of the game.

In the 1960s we still find many instances of adjustment, which could be painful, and even struggles against the deficiencies of the planned system. In contrast, the 1970s were marked increasingly by frustration and exploitation of the system. These were difficult years for the TRO, in spite of the optimism in the early years of the decade. Not only was there the same catalogue of complaints, difficulties and shortcomings to deal with as in the 1960s, but the workforce was becoming unwilling to accept these problems as a necessary part of building socialism, as propaganda had put it in the 1950s and 1960s. Although much had been done since the 1960s to improve working and living conditions by providing services, social and cultural care, there were notable signs of stagnation in the 1970s. Also, sickness and staff turnover rates rose again drastically in the 1970s, reaching further even than the high levels of the mid 1960s.

By the late 1970s this situation was reflected in the changing attitudes of the workforce. Lethargy and resignation regarding the future of the TRO was coupled with a growing concern for one's own interests, be these financial or material. Nobody was rewarded for working hard to finish a job; in the end there would always be an offer of overtime and bonuses to ensure the plan was fulfilled. This is not to say that work in East German factories was undemanding. On the contrary: working conditions often were extremely arduous, and demanded flexibility and creativity to overcome both material and technical problems. The experience of working in the TRO for many years seems to have taught its workforce to take it as easy as possible because there would always be much overtime and stress and never a continuous, productive and efficient flow of production. People, especially those who had been in employment for some time, were exhausted and had little hope left by the end of the 1970s. The TRO did not stand alone: almost all state-owned factories within the East German economy struggled with similar problems, although each had its own specific constellation of issues to deal with.

In the following chapters, the experience of four other state-owned factories will be analysed to highlight both general trends and individual stumbling-blocks. This will create a context for the discussion both of conflicts that dominated people's work experience and solutions that may have been offered.

Voices

A section called 'Voices' will conclude every chapter that deals with one of the five selected state-owned factories. These sections are intended to give an insight into the specific company culture of every factory, as it is remembered by its former employees. These are memory reports that were collected by the author in 2005, many years after the collapse of the GDR. Therefore the excerpts presented here need to be read with caution: they are subjective accounts marked by an individual's character and experiences. In addition, people's memories change constantly and are influenced by current circumstances. Many of those who have the opportunity to voice their memories in this section will have lost their jobs, the basis of their livelihood, after German unification. Their memories will be marked by this experience. Nevertheless, these reports provide many interesting details which delineate the working days (and nights) of the workforce.

In the following excerpts, differences in experiences between production workers and economic functionaries at different levels are highlighted by the accounts of three people, who had all been working at the TRO for two decades or more before the upheavals of 1989.

H. K. (born 1940): female, skilled worker (finished school at 15), member of the SED from 1971:

> Within the sections, the various work groups supported each other; and it could happen that material was delivered irregularly and problems regarding the fulfilment of the plan occurred towards the end of the month. With special shifts and socialist help [by means of which workers came into a specific work group to help] we mostly managed to catch up.
>
> It is said that people grow with their responsibilities. This was also my way with the party (SED), which I joined in 1971 ... There were not many party members [in the section *Schalterbau*] but we could be counted on. With our work we encouraged even those who doubted that the plan could be fulfilled. The motto 'not possible is not an option' originated with the plant's management and was realized with much effort. In spite of everything.

D.S. (born 1943): male, junior departmental manager (finished school at 15):

> *A working day, 7am to 4pm:*
> 6.45am checking the workshop to find out whether all ordered parts had been finished. Or, in urgent cases, having machines adjusted to accommodate different parts, which annoyed colleagues. However, as I got on well with most people, things were possible. Or, from time to time, half a bottle of schnapps and everything worked out

fine (forbidden!). Then administration, between 9am and 10am travel to the main plant, scheduling and finding out personally how things were doing in the workshops. More administration and then, between 2.30pm and 3.30pm, again in the workshop.

A successful day:
When you could report to the works director: schedules kept.

A bad day:
31.12., New Years Eve, at 2.30pm I was told to go to the main plant immediately to collect a shaft. The department was already cleaning up. I was received with grumbling. Got back with the required shaft ... end of my day. It could have waited until the 2.1. of the new year. Thanks very much.

D.M. (born 1934): female, Director of Production (finished school at 16, engineer's diploma), member of the SED 1961 to 1990:

Acceptance of a woman in a managerial position within a plant that mostly employed men:
At the beginning, after higher education, work was not easy: I was not always taken seriously as an engineer, people were waiting for me to get married, have children and then interrupt my career. That was between 1958 and 1963. Furthermore, I had to fight for equal pay but was given great support in this battle by the trade union and the SED, which wanted to foster women in technical professions. With time, there was a change in the attitudes of men, mostly because of good work and noticeable ambition.

A successful day:
Positive appraisal of one's work was primarily linked to the fulfilment of tasks although, sometimes, demands could not be met. For example, the fulfilment of the production plan in spite of a desperate lack of materials or delayed deliveries happened more often than not or discussions with production workers regarding the effective use of the working day and the fulfilment of their norms.

Company culture:
What was positive regarding everyday life at the plant and company culture was that colleagues had done most of their learning at the TRO and afterwards had undertaken a qualification course as super-

visor or engineer and in 30 to 40 years of belonging to the same plant very friendly inter-personal relations had developed, which had no negative effects on the managerial hierarchy. Often, couples had met at the plant and children got their vocational training here, so that the collapse of the TRO after 1989 [the *Wende*] led to personal tragedies and even deaths.

What was negative for the TRO was ... that incompetent people from superior outside institutions such as the VVB or the ministry and party functionaries were interfering with the management of the plant.

3
Berliner Glühlampenwerk: Working and Living Conditions

Over the years, the priorities put forward by central institutions changed in more than one sense. External problems such as the world-wide oil crises, for example, reflected directly on to state-owned factories. In some industries, investment was withdrawn because of a sheer lack of finances; others had to reorientate production to deal with reduced supplies of crude oil. Some factories had to accommodate production lines which may have been environmentally unfriendly and posed health hazards for the workforce, such as the revived processing of brown coal. Also, the Energy Programme and the Chemical Programme from the late 1950s fundamentally altered the situation of existing companies, such as has been described in the case of the TRO in the previous chapter, and created new companies, such as in the case of the EVW. The appointment of a new works director may also have had an immense and long-term impact, sometimes even causing major policy adjustments. *Berliner Glühlampenwerk* (BGW) was an excellent example of this, as will be shown in this chapter.

Characteristics

Like the TRO, the BGW had been owned by a long-established German firm, OSRAM, until 1946, when it was taken over by the Soviet occupation forces. Between 1945 and 1949 crucial technical equipment and part of the production output was taken from the BGW to make reparations to the Soviet Union.[1] Like the TRO, the BGW was a Berlin factory which, in the period of the East German dictatorship, was an advantage both in terms of the allocation of investment and the availability of a large and diverse workforce. The BGW employed up to 5000 employees in the 1980s. It was the most important producer of light bulbs for the East German market and exported to both Eastern Bloc and Western countries. NARVA, a conglomerate of bulb-producing factories established in 1969 and expanded in 1978, of which the BGW was the primary factory, became one of the largest producers of bulbs (and other sources of light) worldwide.

As a factory with a long tradition, the BGW had to deal with problems similar to those faced by the TRO: in particular, old technical equipment and unsuitable building stock hampered technological progress and productivity. Also, particularly in the early years and up to the middle of the 1960s, employees who had worked for the BGW prior to the Second World War were still harking back to the 'good old times', when the factory had belonged to OSRAM.[2] Often, comparisons were drawn between the efficiency of the old days and the disorganization, approaching chaos, that dominated the working day, especially during the late 1950s and early 1960s. Naturally the BGW endured the usual problems facing East German factories such as unreliable delivery of materials and prefabricated parts, unsuitable production plans and an unsatisfactory transfer of new technologies into production. Of course the BGW also enjoyed the advantages of an established factory. Specifically the existence of a workforce, skilled and experienced in the production of bulbs, was a major asset which benefited the BGW from very early on. Shortly after the war, for example, former employees rescued and refitted old machinery ensuring that production could begin again very quickly. Emotional bonds and basic disciplinary norms were already present and ensured some commitment to the future of the company. They encouraged reliability and a concern for quality work among the workforce. The privileges available to the BGW did not compare with those enjoyed by the TRO; the former produced lightbulbs, the latter large transformers for sale expensively on the world market. Also, the BGW employed mostly women. These differences had a notable impact on the development of the BGW in the 1960s and 1970s.

The early 1960s at the BGW

The early 1960s were marked by an almost chaotic situation, with the archival files referring to the activities of the BGW's management team giving an impression of helplessness, and a lack of order, knowledge and authority. Problems recurred and were addressed again and again by the same superficial actions without ever being solved.[3] The most lively and emotional recollections of the situation in the BGW during the early 1960s can be found in brigade diaries, which during this period still gave a day-by-day account of experience on the production lines. Production workers were dealing with a variety of difficulties that impeded their work and during night shifts.

The machines kept breaking down and repairs often took some time, not to speak of delays because of missing spare parts or difficulties in getting the often very old machines started again. Sometimes critical materials or prefabricated parts were unavailable or of low quality, both of which slowed down or even stopped the production process entirely.[4] Furthermore, workers arriving late for work or calling in sick, not always with a sick note or even an acceptable explanation, repeatedly threw any prior work schedule into disarray. Sudden resignations were also not uncommon, especially among women who, at that time, still tended to be less focused on paid employment than men. Especially up to the middle of the 1960s, this was an enormous problem that was exacerbated by high sickness rates and a lack of work discipline. These difficulties were linked to low pay and dreadful working conditions. Production brigades repeatedly criticized management for bad work organization but were mostly ignored and their criticism was certainly not acted upon. This did not improve the attitude to work, affecting both quality and quantity of output, although many brigades and individual workers tried very hard to deal with the horrendous problems they encountered.[5] Nevertheless, rising sickness and staff turnover rates reduced productivity noticeably and endangered the fulfilment of the plan. In the 1960s it became ever more urgently necessary to put more effort into improving working conditions and encouraging emotional links to the factory.

Furthermore, criticism, even from economic functionaries, seems to have been less than welcome to the management team, as one incident highlighted in 1963. When the two eminent physicists Gustav Hertz and Max Steenbeck visited the BGW, one colleague used the opportunity to indicate that 'some of the management team hinder the implementation of measures intended to improve quality quickly'. This was probably not a false accusation. It was a problem almost every economic unit was struggling with up to the late 1980s, because innovations almost always entailed changes to the plan and that was not rewarded within the East German economy. Nevertheless, the works director reacted to this indiscretion by naming the colleague responsible and ordering the management team to make sure that in talks with anybody from outside the BGW only factual depictions of the factory's problems were given so that no 'personal speculations' should become public information.[6] This desperate struggle to keep internal problems secret was not untypical of a company already in dire straits. Often it hindered both fundamental improvements and intervention from the outside. In most cases, this tactic just delayed the recognition of threatening collapse at the central level. In 1963 the BGW was in dire straits and revival was not on the cards for some time yet, partly because fundamental solutions were not sought.

In the summer of 1964, for example, the works director noted that the BGW was encountering problems because of extremely unreliable, or the complete lack of, deliveries of material. At the same time, he was informed that production was taking up far more material than planned. Rather than trying to reduce the use of material, he ordered those responsible for organizing and distributing deliveries of material to ensure that there would always be material available, thereby avoiding any stoppages in production.[7] This, however, meant that these people would either have to hoard material, which was illegal and undermined the concept of the economic plan, or they would have to generate, somehow miraculously, more material than was being delivered. However, without constructive help from the works director, the department for the procurement of materials (*Materialwirtschaft*) had neither sufficient connections nor bargaining power to alleviate the problem even temporarily. Similarly, management kept complaining about a shortage of workers without, however, ever trying to restructure in order to use the available workforce more efficiently.[8] Not surprisingly, that particular works director did not achieve any improvement in the situation during his time at the BGW.

In July 1964, Paul Verner visited the BGW to assess the situation. Only a short time later, Rudi Rubbel arrived as the new works director. He was confronted with debts, inefficiency and a disgruntled workforce. He was to become something like the mythical good fairy of the BGW: the person who managed to turn chaos into long-term success that continued even after he had left.[9]

Rudi Rubbel

Rubbel was born in 1920, which meant that he was 44 years old when he arrived at the BGW. He had been a co-founder of the rationalization and innovation movement at the beginning of the 1950s. During the second half of the 1950s, he supported reform efforts designed to increase the participation of employees in the planning process and management. He contributed to discussions on the improvement of productivity in newspaper articles, in which he and Erich Apel demanded the right to independent norm regulation and certain disciplinary and personnel competences for brigades. In 1961 he graduated from the Humboldt University as an economist. Between 1960 and 1963 Rubbel was a member of the FDGB managing board, and between1963 and 1964 was secretary for economics in the SED BL of Berlin. Between 1961 and 1963 he worked first as director for work and then was put in charge of the *VEB Elektrokohle Berlin-Lichtenberg*, where he was less successful than at the BGW. In 1969 he became general director of NARVA, the newly established *Kombinat*. After his assignment at the BGW, he was sent on another rescue mission for a large Berlin factory in difficulties. Rubbel was a holder of the *Nationalpreis*, one of the highest honours of the GDR. He died in a car accident in 1971.

When Rubbel came to the BGW in August 1964, he offered both experience and good connections within the SED and the FDGB.[10] Within 18 months he stabilized production and ensured the fulfilment of the plan. He also drew up a development strategy for that entire branch of the industry.[11]

When he first arrived at the BGW, he was most concerned with improving the situation generally and structurally. At the directors' meetings an issue was made of the high costs incurred by the inefficient use of materials, stoppages, and lost working time caused partly by party, trade union or FDJ meetings and other related activities that had nothing to do with production. Also, salary structures and inadequate management were dealt with as the most immediate problems.[12] Furthermore, Rubbel was the type of manager who refused to stay aloof from his employees whilst at the same time showing strong paternalistic tendencies. He sought direct contact. Shortly after his arrival, he demanded better co-operation between management and the workforce, citing high staff turnover rates as one reason for his concern: 'Good comradely work with colleagues is the basic principle of every manager, because we cannot allow ourselves any more to have even one more colleague leaving the factory.'[13] With the arrival of Rubbel, the BGW underwent a fundamental restructuring, not only in organizational terms but also regarding social cohesion.

In order to increase motivation, production workers had to be able to recognize that changes had to take place and for this to be achieved, he asked for their opinions. As can be seen from various brigade diaries, production workers who had criticized the situation for many years were happy to point out specific problems.[14] To increase the transfer of information, in the middle of August 1964 the BGW's newspaper was

already describing various measures that Rubbel intended to implement. He insisted on better work discipline, order and cleanliness at
the work place, enhanced qualifications and regular quality controls, to
name just a few items on a long list, in order to increase the quality of
production. In addition, on 30 September 1964 Rubbel made a speech
to the entire workforce, again asking for order and cleanliness at the
work place. He promised more control over plan discipline and
announced changes to shift working times.[15] At the beginning of
October, the '*Sozialistischer Wettbewerb*' was restructured.

Further alterations, as noted in brigade diaries, adjusted the bonus
system, which was used more pointedly to motivate brigades. Also,
rewards became more personalized, arguably even more tuned to the
needs of a primarily female workforce; praise from the works director, a
doll that was handed on to the best brigade every month and even
receptions with Rubbel for good work and additional shifts.[16] His focus
on personal contact seems to have had a highly motivating effect.

One young technologist and member of the FDJ, for example,
decades later described how he was able simply to enter the works
director's office without having an appointment and ask about his
management style. Rubbel, the FDJ member remembers, took the time
to answer his questions patiently. The answers have long been forgot-
ten but not the experience of speaking to the works director, in spite of
having no appointment and no other recommendation for himself
other than showing interest.[17]

Besides these personalized motivation strategies, more direct measures were introduced. For management, the introduction of salaries
based on bonuses, in January 1965, probably injected motivation, just
as the rise in wages for the entire workforce in the middle of 1965
would have helped to bind workers to the plant and reduce their
financial need to search for more fruitful employment elsewhere.[18]

In addition, Rubbel focused on exports and technological advances
to improve the trading position of the BGW. In January 1965 he initiated an internal discussion which resulted in 320 suggestions on
possible organizational, technical and structural improvements. The
innovation movement was kick-started into new life. Rubbel's attempts
to incorporate the entire workforce into the recovery effort and
encourage internal discussion on how best to achieve it showed their
first signs of success in the middle of 1965. For example, in July 1965,
for the first time, entries in brigade diaries elaborated on the economic
role of the bulbs produced by the brigades. Succinctly, the case was put
that 65 watt bulbs were in higher demand, brought more profit and,

therefore, production should be adjusted – a deduction worthy of a market economy and reflective of the new spirit not only within the BGW but also the NES.

In contrast to these practical efforts based on sound economic judgement, central planners deliberately inflated the BGW's plan for 1965 for propaganda purposes.[19] Political reasoning was still interfering in economic decision making, thereby endangering the recovery of the BGW. The production plan, for example, operated on the basis of 4830 employees working full-time, although only 3230 production workers were available in reality. The small but important wiring section (*Drahtbereich*), for example, was short of 50 workers.[20] Nevertheless, the BGW fulfilled this plan and received a high-quality mark at the end of 1965. Only one year later it had officially redeemed all its plan debts. From then on, and particularly in the 1970s, it managed to fulfil plans at a continuously rising level.

The efforts of the new works director had focused primarily on the quality of work, trying to regain quality marks and ensuring the fulfilment of the plan, both of which would bring more money. His methods were, firstly, to increase motivation at all levels and, secondly, to introduce a strict rapport and control system.[21] In his time at the BGW, Rubbel presented himself and, significantly, is remembered by former employees as an authoritative father figure.

The importance of connections

Crucially, his former position within the SED BL of Berlin provided Rubbel with a direct line to Paul Verner. In September 1964 Rubbel and Verner had already met to discuss the recovery of the BGW and had developed some crucial ideas, which had most probably been advanced by the new works director but would not have been realizable without Verner's backing. For example, it was decided to allow the BGW to advertise for new employees; a similar application by the previous works director to the municipal authority of Berlin had been declined only two months earlier. Furthermore, Verner accepted that a new programme to improve the working and living conditions of the workforce needed to be developed in order to stem discontent. This was a crucial decision, as will be shown below. Rubbel even got permission to shift working times and implement holiday restrictions for the next year, whereby entire work brigades were to be sent on holiday at the same time.[22] These certainly would not have been popular measures, and were a potential cause of tension, but they were economically sound as the workforce recognized in good time. To summarize, Rubbel was given remarkable leeway where others before him had been severely restricted. This kind of status, backed up also by the FDGB, and continuous support from a member of the Politburo were crucial to Rubbel's, and thereby the BGW's, long-term success.

However, his influence also had limits, especially when central policy ran counter to the interests of the BGW. With the introduction of the Microelectronics Programme, for example, the BGW lost its most important supplier of special machinery and technical equipment, the *VEB Elektromat Dresden*, which had been ordered to focus on the production of equipment for the new microelectronics industry. The BGW's own capacity to build the required special equipment had been reduced in the years prior to this decision and Rubbel's efforts to rebuild it were not successful in spite of his good connections. Therefore, the potential for future innovation was drastically curtailed and the already-existing technological backlog could not be reduced.[23]

Also, upon his arrival at the BGW Rubbel, in close co-operation with trade union functionaries, tried very hard to get permission to increase the workforce's wages.[24] He had argued that this would help to reduce staff turnover rates, and encourage a more positive attitude to work which was difficult and took place under less than perfect conditions. His applications, however, were repeatedly rejected by central authorities, at least up to the middle of 1965 when the minimum wage was increased nationwide. To alleviate the negative circumstances, at least to some extent, Rubbel turned to an alternative: during the last months of 1964 he had already developed a complex programme for the improvement of working and living conditions, which probably went beyond what Verner had imagined when first introduced to the idea in September 1964.

The improvement of working and living conditions

In contrast to the TRO, where only 25 per cent of the workforce was female in 1970, the BGW employed primarily women. Most of the women worked on the production lines. They had to endure dire working conditions under great pressure to hit targets.[25] In the production halls of the very old buildings it was cold in winter and very hot in summer. It was dirty and the ventilation was insufficient. Particularly at the end of the year, these women were strongly encouraged to work additional shifts, often for weeks, to catch up with the plan. This was an extreme burden for many, especially those who had families to take care of and who were not as flexible as single women without children.

However, volunteers were always found, partly because of group pressure from other brigade members and also because of the additional money that could be earned. This situation was nevertheless a concern for the new works director, whose management philosophy was aimed at linking workers to the factory and making it possible for them to work productively.[26]

The employment of women required adequate social provisions such as childcare facilities and suitable working hours. This was a particular issue at the BGW and of much less consequence to state-owned factories employing mostly men, such as the TRO. Also, salaries were lower than at the TRO. Particular women working on the production lines tended to be less qualified than their male colleagues and, therefore, received lower wages. As Rubbel was unable to increase wages straightaway, he decided on a different strategy, whereby the working conditions in the BGW would be made more bearable, reducing discontent, staff turnover rates and high sickness rates in the process. Rubbel's efforts were possibly based on a patriarchal concern for the well-being of his workforce but, ultimately, they were certainly also aimed at increasing the quantity and quality of production.

It was the introduction of the NES which allowed Rubbel to develop his new strategy to improve working and living conditions. First of all, for some time Ulbricht had paid special attention to the employment of women, calling for the improvement of childcare to make it possible for mothers to cope with their workload. Secondly, the structural changes introduced by the economic reforms allowed individual works directors slightly more leeway in management decisions and gave them more responsibility for obtaining profits. These aspects encouraged initiatives to turn state-owned factories into cleaner, safer, more socially and culturally active places of work, suitable for the employment of mothers and women. Rubbel was not the only one to choose this path. Many works directors seem to have become concerned about rising turnover and sickness rates, low productivity and the slow erosion of and need for an experienced and committed core workforce, as will be shown below. At the central level, alarm over the consequences of poor working and living conditions was also being voiced and efforts were being initiated to counteract low productivity.

Central order or individual initiatives?

This section will concentrate on the period from the middle of the 1960s to the early 1970s. It will focus on the development of the programme for the improvement of working and living conditions, which to some extent already existed in the 1950s but which became more complex, relevant and influential from the middle of the 1960s onwards. At this time, central decision makers as well as individual factories started to advance ideas on how to expand the programme. The main aim of the management teams was to establish an experienced and reliable core workforce to counteract the high staff turnover and sickness rates reached by the middle of the 1960s. An increase in productivity was the long-term concern of most works directors, at a time when the economic reforms had given them more direct responsibility for the economic success of their factories.

This case study will highlight an overlap between central and individual initiatives, with the suggestions from works directors such as Rubbel being much more complex and comprehensive than the ideas voiced in the Politburo. Eventually, it was the more expansive approach that was accepted, generalized and implemented throughout the GDR. The close co-operation with local authorities, which became an important and far-reaching part of the project, was in the mid 1960s still individually regulated. Only towards the end of the 1960s were these efforts centralized and, thereby, standardized. This was counter-productive though, because it resulted in them being watered down and becoming less effective. When Honecker took over power in 1971, he centralized social policy and thereby undermined the social efforts of the state-owned factories. This brief outline will suffice as an introduction; in the following analysis the whole process will be laid out in detail with special attention given to the interaction between central and individual initiatives.

In the first half of the 1960s, the situation in state-owned factories was dire: productivity was low and plans were not being fulfilled.[27] Because salaries were meant to stay low, other ways needed to be found to motivate the workforce. At the central level, first steps were taken after Ulbricht announced at the fifth plenary session of the ZK SED in February 1964:

> because of this, the proposed plan up to 1970 sets out to develop the provision of meals and foodstuffs for workers (*Arbeiterversorgung*), particularly in factories of the primary industrial sectors, in such a way that the principle of material interest in high productivity is realized.[28]

Characteristically, Ulbricht was speaking only of the 'primary' industrial sectors. Not every state-owned factory would be included in this programme for the improvement of working and living conditions straight away; some would benefit from additional funds for social benefits and institutions but many would not. However, as Ulbricht's statement indicated and the programme, which was discussed at a Politburo meeting in September 1964, showed, central efforts were concentrated almost solely on warm meals for workers, childcare to encourage mothers into work and the building of accommodation blocks.

During the Politburo meeting it was noted that those factories that had improved working and living conditions had been more successful in fulfilling their plans than those that had not done anything to better provisions for the workforce. Accordingly, it was decided to send the proposed plan to the VVBs to be forwarded to selected state-owned factories with exact orders on how to implement it, including directions on the co-operation with local authorities.[29] It is crucial, when studying the GDR, to combine any analysis of the central level with a consideration of developments at the grassroots level. These had a decisive influence on central policy, at least regarding social policy in state-owned factories, as we will see when turning back to the BGW.

The reaction of individual works directors to these central orders differed: some implemented them, some ignored them to a large extent because they had more immediate problems, and some took the initiative into their own hands.[30] At the BGW Rudi Rubbel had been planning to raise standards of cleanliness, provisions for workers, and social benefits for the workforce since his arrival in August 1964. He also tried to raise wages but the attempt to have the BGW classified as a heavy machinery plant and, thereby, achieve higher wages, had been stalled by the FDGB and the VWR. The explanation given was that wage increases were not acceptable as new guidelines for an increase in minimum wages were currently being drawn up.

When the VWR, in agreement with the Industrial Commission and the Electronics Department of the FDGB, offered the BGW the opportunity to improve working and living conditions instead, specifically to combat high staff turnover rates, Rubbel drafted a complex programme that went far beyond the programme that had been accepted by the Politburo in September 1964.[31] It contained eight distinct sections concerning not just the provision of food, childcare and accommodation. The programme included a section on 'material working conditions' which incorporated accident prevention as well as the provision of meals for workers; there were also sections on social and medical care, on provisions for holidays and spare time, on sports, on culture and on public transport for workers to the factory halls. Rubbel also included another plea for an increase in wages.[32] Although this last point was refused, the main programme was approved and implemented accordingly.

Almost at the same time, other large economic units seem to have been developing similar extensive programmes, which were discussed with their entire workforce and included in their plans for the following years. In contrast to Rubbel, who had developed his programme in response to an offer from central authorities, these others had been developed internally, without support from the outside or even the responsible VVB's knowledge. The factories' trade union and party organizations had backed the process. The workforce had discussed and supported the programmes. In particular, the *Leuna – Werke* and the *VEB Reifenwerke Fürstenwalde* were singled out in an SPK report of February 1965, in which it was pointed out that these state-owned factories would need to be reorientated towards the main issues such as provisions for workers, would need to be made to co-operate with local authorities, and would have to include the VVB in the planning process. However, these were not the only cases. The FDGB had noticed similar occurrences in other companies, for example the *VEB Filmfabrik Wolfen* and the *Fischkombinat Rostock*.[33]

To summarize, some works directors had gone beyond the Politburo's instructions, just as some had ignored them, to fashion the programme for the improvement of working and living conditions according to the needs of their own workforce, possibly even taking up the demands of that workforce, in the long-term interests of the factories. It cannot be said exactly where the programme with its eight main sections originated, although Rudi Rubbel at the BGW seems to have put forward a very early version. In any case, in May 1965 the Council of Ministers published a central order on the improvement of working and living conditions incorporating the major points of Rubbel's programme.[34]

Possibly, the FDGB had encouraged this development – a reasonable supposition especially considering Rubbel's background.[35] Trade union leaders were actively demanding improvements in working and living conditions going beyond arrangements solely concerning places of work, only a little time after the ZK SED's eleventh plenary session.[36] However, an exchange of views between various works directors, based on Rubbel's status, connections and character, seems a more feasible explanation, especially as almost every management team was dealing with similar problems at that time. Some managers must have seen the possibility in the programme that central authorities had intended to address urgent problems without increasing wages. Works directors also perceived the problems to be far more extensive than was suggested by the focus on provisions for workers, childcare and accommodation put forward by the centrally produced programme of September 1964. Managements were forced to offer much more in order to stem discontent, increase motivation and, most important, reduce staff turnover rates. This initiative, however, was greeted with less than enthusiasm by the SPK, which had demanded the curtailment and control of these efforts. Eventually, however, the catalogue of eight sections as introduced by Rubbel and other works directors was accepted and turned into a central order which was applied to all companies. By about 1967, most state-owned factories seem to have been working with the extended programme.

Up to the middle of the 1960s, difficult working conditions had been recognizable but were presented as a necessary part of building socialism. Some party functionaries would have rejected any criticism as paramount to treason until Ulbricht began to change the party line. The increasingly open criticism among the workforce was most certainly linked both to statements from central authorities, particularly Ulbricht, and to examples from other, more progressive, state-owned factories. By 1967, however, a campaign to standardize and recentralize not just programmes for the improvement of working and living conditions but the political, economic and social system of the GDR in general was well under way. It reflected the rising influence and future policies of Honecker.

Honecker's impact

In the late 1960s, various developments in state-owned factories suggested major changes at the central level. Party functionaries again became more influential in factories and local administrations. The influence of local SED organizations on state-owned factories grew, especially with regard to working and living conditions. Based on state orders, regional administrations and factories had been working together since the early 1960s to ensure sufficient recruitment of workers and, specifically, to draw in more women and expand childcare facilities. In the middle of the 1960s, however, co-operation was extended to include the improvement of working and living conditions in general. These contracts benefited the entire region as building capacities were shared and, in many cases, the factories provided the necessary finances for such projects. Many such projects developed predominantly in response to difficult economic circumstances that were undermining the social stability of the state-owned factories and their surrounding region.[37]

In September 1967 the Council of State decided to develop the towns and rural communes, thereby supporting co-operation between the VVBs and local administrations. From 1968 onwards, contracts between state-owned factories and local administrations became a requirement. Central decision makers intended to contain and use the factories' social initiatives. In the face of the Prague Spring and the economic crisis at the end of the 1960s, according responsibility to the state-owned factories for the towns and wider territory surrounding them was crucial to the stability of the regime.[38] The Council of Ministers supported this new orientation in July 1968, when it decreed the planning of contractual relations between the town councils and the factories to improve working and living conditions.[39] From 1970 onwards, common projects were planned for five years in advance.

In 1967 Hans Spigath, vice-chairman of the state planning commission at the time, criticized co-operation between factories, VVB and local administrations as a poor substitute for structural decisions that should have been taken much earlier. However, he also admitted that collaboration had been successful with regard to single issues.[40] At the local level such agreements had a stabilizing influence. Routinization set in quickly as the factories set up commissions that drew up more long-term plans for the improvement of living and working conditions and for communal contracts.

When Honecker took power in 1971, he centralized social policy by making it a mainstay of his politics. Nevertheless, the structure of social policy stayed the same: Rubbel's eight sections were still used to define specific social and cultural needs within the population. State-owned factories remained important focal points of social initiative, specifically for their employees, who demanded from their employers more social initiatives, as in the 1960s. However, the realization of promises became difficult. Building capacities, for example, were almost entirely taken up by the state's housing programme, which meant that important improvement plans lagged behind. Also, it became ever more difficult in the 1970s and 1980s to obtain the necessary materials, such as those needed for example for the refurbishment of showers, toilets and changing rooms.

In 1967 investment cuts had already forced state-owned factories either to limit their programmes for the improvement of working and living conditions or fund for themselves the most vital projects. These cuts were hidden behind a new regulation which allocated to the Social and Cultural Fund, the main source of finance for the improvement of working and living conditions at the time not a certain percentage of the factory's wage bill any more but instead a linking of investment to profit.[41] In the difficult climate of the later 1960s and 1970s this was a disastrous decision for companies. In 1974 various state-owned factories encountered major financial difficulties and drastic measures to save money had to be introduced.[42] In most cases, this meant that individual projects were cancelled or delayed. In 1978, for example, the works director of the TRO asked the local SED organization for help. Building work was urgently needed to improve the provision of meals for workers.[43] The extension of the canteen and other projects had been put off repeatedly, a tendency that could not be hidden from the workforce.[44] Everyday experience stood in stark contrast to the officially propagated achievements of these programmes – a dichotomous conception of reality that marked the entire Honecker era. The consequences were reflected in an increase in staff turnover and sickness levels, beyond even the high levels of the early 1960s, which became clearly noticeable from the middle of the 1970s onwards.[45] The decline was most evident on the shop floor particularly with regard to the improvement of working and living conditions, which originally had caused some pride among the workers and emotional bonds to 'their' factory. With time, hopes for a better future were eradicated and replaced by lethargy and a primary concern for one's individual interests.

Summary

The improvement of working and living conditions was an issue long before 1964. In individual state-owned factories, efforts were made to make working life more bearable, even comfortable for the workforce. Here, at the epicentre of the East German state, some works directors had already introduced service industries, sports facilities and cultural activities to improve working and living conditions in the 1950s. However, before 1964 the funding of these measures was not ensured beyond providing workers with hot meals and foodstuffs, and even that could not be guaranteed. Even in 1964, when Ulbricht finally announced the state's new interest in social policy, only childcare and the building of accommodation were added to the central priorities regarding working and living conditions.

Nevertheless, the rehabilitation of material interest as one aspect of workers' motivation was a crucial step away from the ideology of the early years. The extensive and compulsory programmes from the middle of the 1960s onwards reflected a more complex approach to social policy, and indicated not only a greater commitment to social policy but also the possibility of it being acted upon. Furthermore, co-operation between state-owned factories and local communities increased and was formalized in contracts, which helped to redistribute resources and capacities, thereby allowing both state-owned factories and communities to be stabilized. This context gave the workforce grounds to make claims, to complain and to demand the improvement of working and living conditions, an opportunity that was taken seriously throughout the 1970s and 1980s.

Perhaps the most interesting aspect of the development of the programme for the improvement of working and living conditions in the middle of the 1960s was the interaction between individual managers and central authorities, which was accommodated by the changes that had been introduced with the economic reforms. Within the NES, works directors were given more opportunities to influence the situation within their specific factories, which some used, even beyond given or perceived limits. Their main aims were the reduction of staff turnover and sickness rates and an increase in productivity. At the same time, management teams reacted to the interests, demands and discontent of their workforce.

This case study has provided an opportunity to follow up the centralization efforts of the late 1960s and 1970s, which in one sense undermined individual initiatives but could also be taken to have forced less active works directors to follow a progressive trend. Similarly, changes in the financing structure of the Cultural and Social Fund in 1967 and the creation of *Kombinate* tended to limit individual initiatives.[46] However, new ways had to be found to deal with the unpredictability of the planned economic system in the GDR from the late 1960s onwards. Possibly, this was one of the causes of the strong shift towards the semi-legal dealings with which management teams tried to keep production going throughout the late 1970s and 1980s. When resources became scarce the need to organize materials and accommodate exchanges with other factories outside the central plan became more dominant in the daily struggle to maintain production.

Furthermore, we have seen with regard to Rudi Rubbel that the role of works directors was crucial to long-term economic success. Helmut Wunderlich at the TRO was similarly well connected and was equally successful in getting the factory back on track for economic success. His former employees at the TRO also remember him as an outstanding leader with a tendentiously authoritarian manner, who got things done and could not be matched by his successors.[47] The initiatives of a successful works director were never directed against central economic policy. Rather, it was important to realize resolutions that had been presented at party conferences or plenary sessions of the ZK SED. The crux of the matter was how these central decisions were translated into real measures and, at this point, a good works director would be able to inject his or her own agenda, as we have seen with regard to Rudi Rubbel. There are many more examples of such creativity that ensured a factory's success.[48]

Also, social circumstances were relevant to the long-term development of a state-owned factory. The BGW, for example, employed a very high percentage of women whilst the TRO employed primarily men. This had a strong impact on their social initiatives. Especially in the 1960s, when great efforts were made to recruit women into full-time employment, social provisions were huge assets in the labour market. Of course, the labour market in the GDR was centrally controlled. Nevertheless, especially in the 1960s, workers still tended to leave their place of work quickly if dissatisfied with their circumstances. Also, female employment was not yet an established norm and, therefore, special efforts were necessary to convince women and their husbands that female employment was both acceptable and practicable.

Similarly important, however, was the type of production or service offered by the factories. Products that could be exported to Western countries and be sold expensively for hard currency received more support, be that in terms of investment, getting deliveries of materials or building capacities, than other sections of industry that were less profitable. These privileged companies were then able to build up a more complex framework of social benefits and institutions for their workforces. Even a short spell of advanced status could bring progress within the lucky factory that would improve social provisions for many years.[49]

To some extent, the developments of the 1960s prepared the ground for long-term attitude changes in the East German population. In particular, the extensive programmes for the improvement of working and living conditions influenced attitudes and resulted in a tendency to stay with one factory from qualification to retirement. Expectations that were directed at the management and, from the 1970s onwards, increasingly at the state regarding social policy rose dramatically in this period, outlasting even unification in 1990 and, for some time, even experiencing a revival in the early years of the twenty-first century when the economy of unified Germany was encountering massive problems.

The next chapter will focus on a state-owned factory that was newly created in the 1960s in a formerly rural area, thereby providing a comparative case to the two Berlin factories considered so far. The EVW enjoyed high economic and political status throughout its existence, which had a noticeable impact on its development in the 1960s and 1970s.

Voices

H.B. (born 1945): female, skilled worker (finished school at 15):

> In 1962 I finished my qualification course at the BGW and was given a contract starting from 1 September 1962 to work as a production worker in the department *Allgebrauchslampe*. I worked there for two, and later three, shifts. We had 18 days paid holiday. We also went to work on Saturdays ... Then came the time when brigades were created; our brigade was called *Rosa Luxemburg*. Every brigade created a wall newspaper. I was not involved in politics but designing wall newspapers – that was my hobby. Nobody was as enthusiastic about this as I was. I would enjoy it even today.
>
> Mostly, I worked as a *Spannerkraft*. This was working on a production line and everything had to be done faster, faster, faster. The breaks were very short ... In summer, when temperatures outside were very high, it was unbearable in the departments, sometimes up to 60°C. Then we got a replacement, ran up the stairs to the showers and then we came back already sweaty again. What was always motivating was the BGW's radio station, but it only started at 9am ...
>
> When the plan was in danger towards the end of the year, the machines were run faster and it was difficult to keep up with the new speed. During the ten minutes' break time in which the machines were closed down, we had to work one minute longer at the beginning and the machines were started anew one minute earlier. There was often not enough time to reach the canteen, where a long queue of people was already waiting to be served.
>
> Actually, it was a good time there at the BGW all in all.

E.K. (born 1920): male, Technical Director (finished school at 16, engineer's diploma), member of the SED 1948 to 1990:

> *Remembering Rudi Rubbel*:
> The demands on the BGW increased continuously ... Finally, it came to a stage at which the ministry ordered the replacement of

the works director. At a meeting of the entire management team, a representative of the ministry took leave of the old works director and the new one was introduced. Comme il faut, a member of the management also had to say a few words of farewell. Because I was the vice-director, I had to do it. I did it as I thought fit. I praised his work, mentioned what had been achieved and done together. At the end, I thanked him for his work for the BGW and wished him all the best in his new position. When the meeting had dissolved and we sat together a few minutes longer, my new boss said to me: 'That Heinrich Müller did not fulfil his tasks and you even thanked him for it.' I did not answer but I thought that this would become difficult, respect for a human being and manners do not seem to mean anything to [Rudi Rubbel].

The new boss had been given the *Nationalpreis* when he was still a welder, was highly respected at the ministry and, so he told me himself once, he had taken on the position at the BGW only under the condition that nobody would interfere with any of his measures ... His professional work, backed up by the ministry, was decidedly good and successful. He brought the plant to the fore again and carried through the reduction of the exaggerated demands that had been put on the BGW, which the former works director could never have achieved. He worked far into the night to prepare a new production plan and we, his closest associates, had to keep up with him ... The new boss knew everything that was happening at the plant, even that which he should not have known. It did not take long before a colleague told me that the new boss, after a glass of beer, had indicated that he had informers in every section of the state-owned factory. In his position as a works director, he needed to know everything that was going on at the BGW.

B.R. (born 1949): male, technologist (finished school at 18, engineer's diploma):

Another view on Rudi Rubbel:
Plain behaviour was typical of Rudi Rubbel; there was never before him and certainly not after him such a works director, who was so attached even to simple workers and employees! Sometimes, it happened that he went through the plant in his blue overall during the days before Christmas and everybody whom he met, he wished everybody a Merry Christmas. Many colleagues did not even know who he was. Also, in the case of averages on the production lines,

he would suddenly stand behind the mechanics to get information on the spot ... When Rudi Rubbel died in a car accident, we were really sad!

E.W. (born 1930): female, administrative staff (finished school at 14), member of the SED 1975 to 1989:

Normal life:
We did not know any other life and made a home for ourselves [in the GDR]; however, we did not let others interfere. Within my work group I felt very secure, everybody looked out for everybody else. Problems were discussed openly.

Changes over time:
After the border was closed (1961), there was an economic upturn. People worked better and there was more to buy. In the middle of the 1970s, things became generally worse. An increase in productivity became the main priority. Demand for consumer products grew and could not always be satisfied.

E.U. (born 1934): female, skilled worker (finished school at 16):

Up to 1975, even 1980 we had the impression that the economic situation had got better, slowly but steadily. Then, however, things got worse. Poor material from delivery firms made everyday work harder. Stoppages and repairs had an impact on one's salary. At meetings, workers were not listened to any more or were hardly heard, so that a lack of interest ensued and the number of participants at such meetings declined even more.

4
Erdölverarbeitungswerk Schwedt: Privileged Within a Shortage Economy

The East German economy offered opportunities for differentiation within a fundamental similarity that was shaped by the inherent deficiencies of the system and the application of central policy. As shown by the *Erdölverarbeitungswerk Schwedt* (EVW) in particular, central policy had an impact on all state-owned factories at all levels. In comparison to the two Berlin factories already discussed, the case of the EVW will highlight the specific position of a new and privileged economic unit located in an industrially underdeveloped area. Both the implementation of central policy in a high-status factory and the inclusion of regional administrative bodies in the process are factors that will be particularly addressed.

The status of a state-owned factory was linked to both the priority of its products and its propaganda value. Status determined access to limited resources. In many state-owned factories, such as the BGW, production was hindered by old equipment that was not adequate in terms of technological standards or simply the lack of raw materials. In contrast, the EVW had high political and economic priority. It was privileged primarily because of its task of processing valuable crude oil coming from the Soviet Union, which would then bring in much needed hard currency. Accordingly, the EVW was provided with new equipment, attracted a young, qualified and enthusiastic workforce and, at least in comparison to other plants, enjoyed a fairly regular supply of raw materials.

Characteristics

In November 1958 the first Chemical Programme was launched in Leuna. It was intended to double production in the chemical industry by 1965. Although the campaign had already failed by 1961, one lasting outcome was the foundation of the EVW in Schwedt in the *Uckermark*, an almost entirely rural area. This tiny town is located near Frankfurt/Oder and close to the Polish border, which was important for the plant's access to the oil pipe that was being built to bring crude oil from the Soviet Union to the GDR and other Eastern Bloc countries.

When construction of the new plant began in late November 1958 the circumstances were difficult. Builders and technical staff from the whole of the GDR were sleeping in temporary housing, even tents, and were dealing with less than desirable sanitary conditions whilst working long hours. As early as May 1959, the EVW became a central youth project, which meant that the FDJ accorded priority to mobilizing its members to join the construction work. Many young people, members of the FDJ or not, contributed to a very enthusiastic atmosphere at the plant, which was based on the feeling of adventure offered by the strenuous working conditions but also reflected, at least to some extent, the conviction of building a better future for everybody.[1] The enthusiasm associated with the original socialist idea was seldom realized in the East German dictatorship but, arguably, it surfaced at least fleetingly in projects such as the construction of the EVW.

Control and privilege

The official inauguration of the EVW was delayed by the hard winter of 1962–3 as well as by disorganization and a lack of building capacity, which led to the involvement of central authorities and, eventually, the replacement of works directors. In July 1963 a working group of experts, members of the EVW's management team and representatives of eminent economic institutions, was formed under the presidency of Rainer Birthler, holder of the *Nationalpreis*. This *Zentrale Anfahrstab* (ZAST) was commissioned with the task of speeding up construction work and, for some time, was continuously present at the building site. It had the power to fast-track decisions, proposals and suggestions directly to state institutions higher up the hierarchical ladder; this was a huge advantage in a system marked by an expansive bureaucracy that was defined by a pronounced reluctance to take on responsibility.[2]

In August 1963, the chemist and party member Werner Hager took on the position of works director at the EVW. His main task was to meet the official deadline for the commencement of operations, which had become as much a political as an economic necessity. In addition, from autumn 1963 to April 1964, member of the Politburo and president of the VWR Alfred Neumann kept a close watch on progress in Schwedt.[3] On 18 December 1963, Walter Ulbricht visited the EVW to officially inaugurate the oil pipe in spite of the fact that production did not start for another four months.[4] With some delay, trial runs began in April 1964 and on 1 July 1964 regular production runs commenced.

Stabilizing the workforce

After this difficult start, major problems surfaced again in 1965, when staff turnover rates became very high. In some departments, turnover reached 14 per cent, averaging 11 per cent over the entire workforce.[5] In the same year, 1519 new employees were recruited but 703 left the plant without what were officially deemed 'acceptable reasons', meaning that most of those resigning left for personal reasons such as a persistent lack of suitable accommodation and kindergartens, or of cultural and service facilities.[6] Also, high staff turnover rates may well have been caused by other issues such as low salaries and bonuses, especially compared to Berlin.[7] Although bonuses and higher wages were of primary interest to most workers in any state-owned factory, in the face of limited funds management teams looked for alternative methods of satisfying workers' demands and increasing the workforce's interest in high productivity. In late August 1965 Hager ordered the first analysis, which connected the employees' zest for work directly with the provision of flats and industrial goods.[8] Accordingly, an early but limited version of the plan for the improvement of working and living conditions was drawn up. This contract between management and workforce regulated practical issues such as public transport between Schwedt and the plant.[9] Hager implemented these improvements against the wishes of the BPO of the EVW.

In spite of a new emphasis on such issues by central decision makers, which had been discernible since the Council of Minister's resolution in May 1965 at the latest, the EVW's party organization strongly criticized the growing tendency towards a discussion of working and living conditions as irrelevant and politically incorrect as late as September 1965. At a party meeting on 21 September 1965, an open discussion of working and living conditions was refused outright: 'Is it not embarrassing for the relevant economic functionary, for the relevant trade union functionary to include such issues in a protocol recording the plan discussion for 1966?' The link between productivity and working and living conditions, apparently, was not yet recognized by SED functionaries at the EVW. Furthermore, even the occurrence of such discussions was seen to reflect 'considerable ideological weakness among the colleagues who chaired these meetings'.[10] This, of course, was a harsh condemnation which, coming from the EVW's BPO, would have created some unease among the criticized functionaries. Nevertheless, the plan discussions for 1966 were dominated by questions from the workforce concerning childcare, provision of workers with meals, foodstuffs and fruit, and the building of a swimming pool. Certainly, these topics had been on the agenda for years, but by then the workforce had become more inclined to put forward related demands.

The attitudes and growing self-confidence of workers played no small role in this development. Even in an extremely controlled environment, as existed at the EVW, workers had some influence. For example, they were able to insist on the assurance of their bonuses before even starting on one of the many initiatives to increase productivity. In 1965, for over two months, workers delayed a campaign because bonuses had not been secured, as an official report pointed out:

> The realization of the scheme of 2.8.1965, conceived by the main section, could only be begun from 18.10.1965 onwards because, up to that date, the ÖAW section [Economic Work Competition] had been unable to confirm the availability of monetary incentives for this campaign. From that day, workers could be won over for the realization of this campaign and have developed great activity.[11]

The management seems to have been relieved that the workers decided to take up the campaign once the question of the monetary incentives had been resolved. Also, conditions within the EVW were criticized in 1965, when a building that had been planned for social provisions was struck off the plan. After protests from the workforce, however, the works director decided to reinstate the original building plan.[12] The larger patterns of the East German economy were not entirely unmarked by traditional working class culture although these may have become less visible in the late 1960s and 1970s.[13]

In the middle of the 1960s, the improvement of working and living conditions seemed a promising solution to many economic functionaries, and with time even central decision makers supported this strategy. At the beginning of August 1966, the *VVB Mineralöle und organische Grundstoffe* provided the EVW with detailed information about a programme for the improvement of working and living conditions for 1967; this became part of the annual planning procedures.[14] The structure proposed by the VVB was a precise copy of the structure drafted by Rubbel for the BGW.

Co-operation with local communities

Based on state orders, regional administrations and local factories had been working together since the early 1960s to ensure sufficient recruitment of workers and, specifically, to draw in more women and to expand childcare facilities. In the middle of the 1960s co-operation was extended even further and included the improvement of working and living conditions in general.

Such annual agreements between Schwedt's town council and the EVW existed from 1966 onwards.[15] In this particular case, it was the works director Hager who had put pressure on the town administration to agree to and comply with plans for the improvement of living conditions in the area.[16] Hager still focused on the basic needs of his workforce, demanding a specific number of flats and childcare facilities in order to attract more workers to the plant. Nonetheless, provisions were still seen to be lacking in 1967, and reports to the EVW's BPO suggested that the workforce found working conditions acceptable but were unhappy with the provision of accommodation, shopping, childcare and cultural facilities in Schwedt. Again, it was pointed out that salaries and social benefits offered by the EVW could not compete with other chemical plants and therefore staff turnover rates were rising.[17] In response, projects such as shopping facilities, healthcare centres, sports facilities and cultural schemes in the town centre were instigated. These benefited the entire area as building capacities were shared and, in many cases, the EVW provided the necessary finances.[18] From 1968 onwards, contracts between state-owned factories and their local communities became an official requirement. Accordingly, the EVW sported its first community contract in 1968, even though co-operation with Schwedt's town council had shaped living conditions in the area for some time prior to this arrangement.

Throughout the 1960s and 1970s Schwedt profited immensely from its connections with the EVW. The town's population increased rapidly from about 6500 in August 1950 to over 19 000 at the end of 1964, 34 000 in 1970 and over 52 000 by 1982.[19] Accommodation blocks, along with social and service facilities, were built to accommodate the needs of a predominantly young population. They included hospitals, kindergartens, schools, shopping centres, cultural houses, theatres and a public swimming pool. A new town grew up during this period and, to a great extent, this was due to the presence of the petrochemical plant, which offered jobs and facilities for vocational training and utilized its capacities and finances for regional requirements. In comparison to the two Berlin factories that have been described previously, the EVW was carrying the socio-economic responsibility for a large area.

The differences between state-owned factories in industrial areas such as Berlin and those in the provinces, however, went beyond those of socio-economic duty. Specifically, closely controlled, new economic units of high economic and political importance such as the EVW provided ideal conditions for the implementation of central policy, as state and party functionaries clearly accorded it high priority. Nevertheless, even in this environment, the workforce was able to defend its interests.

Central control of the EVW

Throughout the 1960s and 1970s, the EVW's management team was consistently intent both on realizing central policy and working closely with the SED.[20] For example, as a result of a marked turn towards technology and science during the economic reforms, highly qualified economic functionaries had been put into important positions within the East German economic system without consideration being given to their (often lacking) SED membership. This enabled these functionaries to circumvent direct party control, supplying them with a comparatively wide area of responsibility within their positions. The Politburo was forced to deal with a situation whereby leading economic functionaries, especially works directors, were showing increasingly independent tendencies whilst essential economic projects were blocked by dogma and bureaucracy at the intermediary level. This dilemma was solved by ordering that leading functionaries should be politically and economically qualified. In March 1966 seminars were started at the Central Institute for Socialist Economic Management to train leading functionaries according to the new planning and management methods.[21] Considering that central policy generally took some time to be realized in state-owned factories, Werner Hager at the EVW reacted very quickly. As early as May 1966 he decided that all leading functionaries should be required to attend the district's party school.[22] A close alliance between the EVW's works directors and central decision makers marked the development of this high status plant throughout the 1960s and 1970s. This also meant that central control of the EVW was particularly rigorous, even severe.

Beyond the implementation of general policies, central authorities also interfered directly in the management of the EVW, sometimes even without the prior knowledge of the works director. Towards the end of the 1960s it was decided centrally to import entire fertilizer units from England and France. The works director was not involved in this decision, only informed of it.[23] Disagreements with the foreign firms and a lack of building capacities delayed the erection of the new units for some years, leading to the EVW's prolonged failure to fulfil its plans. The replacement of the works director Hager with Werner Frohn was also linked to this disastrous project.

Official interpretation blamed Hager for a lack of interest and engagement in relation to the new units. Allegedly, there had been 'serious flaws' in dealings with the workforce at the EVW, particularly on the part of the management:

> The management team of the EVW took up its responsibility for the commencement of operation of the fertilizer plant extremely inadequately and only after long critical discussions ... Especially the assumption of a wait-and-see attitude and a lack of individual responsibility among a number of members of the management team hindered the mobilization of the workforce.[24]

It appears that this had a negative impact on the general mood and on staff turnover rates at the EVW.[25] The EVW's case was even mentioned at the ninth meeting of the ZK SED.[26] One result was that the BPO became involved in order to reach 'ideological clarification'. In 1969, Schwedt was provided with its own local SED group that was meant to guide the EVW's BPO more effectively.[27]

In addition to the official view, there is another perspective to be considered here – that of those involved at the EVW. Interestingly, Werner Hager had already been quietly substituted in 1968 although his ultimate successor replaced him officially only in 1970. Hager explains this time gap as resulting from more than his stance on the fertilizer unit. In 1968 he had had an outburst at a meeting of the ZK SED, of which he was a member due to his position at the EVW. At the meeting, he complained openly about the handling of the foreign project at the central level. In addition, he criticized the East German economic system in general and, which was probably worse, the *Rat der gegenseitigen Wirtschaftshilfe* (RGW), in Western countries known as COMECON. According to his recollections, there was no direct reaction at the meeting. Afterwards, however, he was quickly sent off to a party school for one year (1968–9) and was then allocated a less exposed position as a sectional director at the *Leuna-Werke* where he stayed until 1990.[28]

Apparently, fundamental problems and a critical attitude rather than a lack of management skills may have been responsible for both the situation at the plant and the replacement of leading functionaries in the late 1960s.[29] However, the changes in personnel did not bring any immediate relief to the EVW, which continued to struggle with high turnover rates, low productivity and irregular deliveries of crude oil from the Soviet Union in the late 1960s. In addition, uncertainty affected the workforce, which had heard rumours that the EVW would be made part of a *Kombinat* but was not given any information on these plans for some time.[30]

The *Petrolchemisches Kombinat* (PCK) was founded on 30 December 1969. One day later, the *VVB Mineralöle*, which had controlled the EVW, was dissolved and the new *Kombinat* was directly subordinated to the Ministry for Chemical Industries. From 1 January 1970 onwards it contained four major factories and eight additional sections comprising about 30 000 employees altogether. The EVW became the parent unit within the PCK because it produced almost half of the conglomerate's production and offered a high research potential. It was also the most modern and, in spite of the internal problems caused by the fertilizer unit at the time, the most productive unit and had already introduced data-processing. Frohn became the new works director of the EVW and, thereby, General Director of the PCK in March 1970. Frohn occupied this position until 1990. From October 1970 onwards there was an upwards economic trend at the plant. However, this was only possible because beforehand reductions had been introduced into the plan, which allowed the EVW to seem more productive.[31]

To change economic plans was not unusual within this apparently very rigid economic system. Specifically under Honecker, it became almost more important to seem successful than to achieve success. Privileged factories such as the EVW, which was a political symbol of the East German system's technological and economic progress, needed to be seen to be successful. Nevertheless, the question as to the soundness of the planning system needs to be asked. In the following section, the shortfalls of economic planning at every level of the economic system will be traced.[32]

Economic planning – a farce?

The planning process was never satisfactory – often reality undermined not only a plan's realization but also its inception. Major faults in the latter arose through inaccurate statistics, impractical expectations and the sheer impossibility of predicting both international and domestic economic developments. The deficiencies of central planning led management teams to hoard resources, both material and employees, produce quantity rather than quality, focus on particular products which may not even have been saleable in order to fulfil inflexible plans, and even to falsify accounts in order to avoid costly fines or obtain more favourable plans.[33] Mostly, economic plans were a farce and the way they were handled at all levels of the East German economic system, from the SPK down to individual factories, made them even less useful. In the following section, the difficulties from the level of state-owned factories up to central decision makers will be described in some detail by tracing the issue vertically from the EVW to the Politburo.

In the files of the EVW examples of the shortfalls of central planning can be found throughout the 1960s and 1970s. Early in 1963, for example, one report stated that economic performance had been satisfactory in the previous year. However, it also commented that 'in reality the results that were claimed had been achieved only in part'.[34] In the same year, the EVW's canteen had been able to reduce losses dramatically in only one month but it was suspected that this success was not based on a 'real footing'. Rather, recipes had been changed and the necessary measures of ingredients had been reduced.[35] Also, the files contain descriptions of how to distort statistics by accounting for the moving of a train wagon not within the cost section but in a different category, namely steam and energy, which would then turn a loss into a neutral figure or even a profit.[36] For 1963 there are various instances throughout the file where management attempted to get aspects of the plan changed because it could not be fulfilled. Independently of real performance, it was of the utmost importance to at least seem to have reached planned targets, even if these targets had been reduced again and again over the year. In many cases, central institutions quietly condoned such methods and, thereby, undermined all serious consideration of the plan.[37]

In June 1965 Günther Wyschofsky, at that time vice-chairman of the SPK's Department for Chemical Industry, informed Erich Apel of difficulties between the *VVB Mineralöle und organische Grundstoffe* and the EVW with regard to the plant's economic progress. Apparently, the VVB had repeatedly given ad hoc orders without considering the economic consequences for the EVW. Often, the decisions of the VVB's general director had been forwarded to the works director by telephone without providing written confirmation. This had led, at least in one case, to disagreements as to the content of such an order. Also, the criticism was made that planning methods were not flexible enough, that is to say operational changes in the plan took too long, going from the state-owned factory to the VVB to the Council of Ministers before a decision could be reached. In addition, the VVB was working with plan figures that differed from those used by the EVW. Wyschofsky concluded his report by stressing that the contract system 'in practice was of no relevance' to the EVW, at least in relation to one of its major contractors, the *VEB Minol* and the VVB. This meant that there was no agreement on the volume of mutual supplies between these two important companies and there were no fines for failing to comply with contractual agreements. In fact, their co-operation had become plan-less. Suggestions were made to deal with some of the issues addressed by Wyschofsky but without even touching the fundamental problems of the central planning system.[38]

Also, at the SED's seventh party conference in December 1967 examples were presented which described serious shortcomings in state-owned factories. Besides complaints from workers with regard to their exclusion from the management of the production process, the workers also warned the SED of 'a growing atmosphere of resignation, lack of interest, lack of perspective'. It was pointed out that in general 'as before, habits and customs persist, which can be compared with a dogmatic and formalistic stance on planning'.[39] Apparently, the reforms intended by the NES were not reaching the grassroots, nor were they realized by management teams or at the intermediary level of the VVBs.

In 1970 the SPK's internal SED organization criticized the planning commission's working methods at that time: 'In the SPK, we have the typical phenomenon that decisions are made without a realistic appraisal of the possibilities that the functionaries have for their realization, both quantitative and qualitative.'[40] The negative impact of such decision making was pointed out: disquiet among the workforce and dissatisfaction with the constant hectic pressure that was leading to 'a tense mood, a certain gallows humour and sarcastic opinions about non-existence of clear directions'.[41] Joachim Oelschlägel from the SPK made a similar point when he wrote to Günter Mittag, member of the Politburo responsible for the economic sector, on 27 November 1970. In complicated economic and political circumstances, just months before the removal of Ulbricht from his post, the SPK was trying to prepare the central economic plan on the basis of a Politburo decision of 8 September 1970. However, this proved immensely difficult according to the SPK:

The plan has been drawn up from above and there is no guarantee that a lack of balance will not occur at the level of the *Kombinate* and factories, which is not visible from above and which would diminish the reality of the plan.[42]

In addition, it could not be ascertained whether the lack of balance between end producers and supply industries had been solved. In fact, the SPK thought the high increases planned for the export of products to be unrealistic. Furthermore, actual work on balance sheets had been reduced to an 'unacceptable minimum', not only in the SPK but also in ministries.[43] Central planning was in dire straights at the end of Ulbricht's reign. However, Honecker also seems to have been unable fundamentally to improve the situation after he came to power in 1971.

In a Politburo discussion towards the end of 1971 Honecker made clear that what was needed, in his opinion, was a plan that would conform to reality. The East German economy should work according to a feasible plan. In this way, the authority of central decision makers would be re-established. With a view to the problems discussed above, this would have been a sensible approach.

However, Honecker did not specify how this great goal of central planning, namely realistic plans, was to be achieved. Fundamental changes to the economic system were not planned and, therefore, the basic shortcomings of central state planning still shaped reality at the grassroots. Furthermore, Honecker made clear that standards of living should not decline; rather, state reserves should be used to import the necessary raw materials and better technologies. For Honecker, this was 'a question of the authority of the party and the government'.[44] Nevertheless, in 1972 the planning process was still as capricious as in the 1960s, as one report from the Department for Economic Management of the ZK SED pointed out:

> Proposals for the plan from state-owned factories and *Kombinate* are sometimes rejected without discussion until they agree with central planning. The VVB and the *Kombinate* then feel forced to pass on the discrepancies contained in the plans to subordinate factories or *Kombinate*.[45]

Towards the end of 1972 problems were escalating. The year was about to finish with a deficit in the state's coffers of 5.2 billion Marks, mainly because of the additional expenditure needed for Honecker's social programme. The solution suggested was typical of the book-keeping of the entire East German economic system. The deficit could not be financed with funds intended for 1973; therefore within the SPK it was suggested that funds from 1972 should be used. That meant that the central planning commission was playing with figures to cover up financial problems. Apparently, this had been done before.[46]

To turn back to the EVW: one last example will highlight the continued deficiencies that undermined economic planning and the fulfilment of plans at every level of the East German economy. In June 1973 the Department for Rationalization and Investment of the ZK SED assembled a collection of facts on the situation in Schwedt. It concluded that the main causes of insufficient effectiveness were faulty planning and balancing of material funds 'starting with the SPK then to the ministry and down to the VVB and the *Kombinate*'. The unrealistic appraisal of available resources was blamed along with the lack of a balanced scheme for the long-term development of the chemical industry and, finally, an inadequate grasp of industrial complexities.[47] To summarize this assessment: central decision makers did not necessarily know what was going on at intermediary levels of the centralized system, not to mention their lack of insight into economic realities at the grassroots. Nevertheless, economic plans were decided upon centrally up to the end of the GDR and little could be done by management teams to avoid pressure from central authorities to comply with them, even if these plans were clearly unrealistic and ineffective from the outset. However, some state-owned factories were in a better position than others when dealing with central authorities, as will be shown in the next section.

Achieving success within the centrally planned economic system

Works directors at the EVW were in a special position. First of all, they headed a high-status factory, which meant a great deal in terms of material supplies and allocation of financial funds and capacities. The EVW was one of the few factories which dominated the structure of its industrial sector, primarily because of its importance for the GDR's foreign trade. Other factories of lesser status within the East German economic system were repeatedly forced to delay or cancel crucial investment projects in order to finance major developments elsewhere, such as the petrochemical plant at Schwedt.[48]

High-status factories offered other advantages too, as Ingrid Deich has pointed out in an excellent study of social efforts in East German factories.[49] In particular, investment in social, medical, sports and cultural facilities tended to be higher than in other factories, often based on their easier access to material capacities and other examples of privileged treatment by central authorities. In the East German shortage economy, despite the equality slogans so defining for socialist societies, both these aspects determined the real situation on the ground. In the GDR, and particularly so from the 1960s, social policy was directed at four chief goals: mobilizing labour; expansion of the employment of women; an increase in productivity; and the creation of a qualified and stable workforce. The close co-operation between state-owned factories and their local communities, as has been described above, was crucial to the development of necessary facilities and, thereby, the improvement of working and living conditions. In turn this ensured, at least in theory but often also in practice, a more productive and compliant workforce. Good food at the canteen, a modern flat and sufficient childcare facilities went a long way towards workers' satisfaction in the East German state, where all these things continued to be in short supply up to the 1980s. High-status factories were in a much better position to alleviate difficulties in the procurement of such envied goods.[50] The EVW belonged to this small group of the privileged, which also increased the status of the plant's works directors.[51]

An additional factor with enormous economic and political implications for the EVW and its leading functionaries was the works director's automatic membership of the ZK SED. In the 1970s and 1980s there were six *Kombinate* with a seat and a vote on the ZK SED: *VEB Kombinat Robotron; Kombinat Schiffbau; VEB Kombinat Carl Zeiss Jena; Werkzeugmaschinenkombinat 'Fritz Heckert'; Kombinat Textima;* and the *PCK Schwedt*.[52] Werner Hager, as works director of the EVW, had been a member of the ZK SED and, according to his own description, had used his position to criticize economic policy in front of leading SED members. When asked about his dealings with the EVW's party secretary, he pointed out his privileged position that offered direct access to the ZK SED and, based on this, a networking potential that would never be equalled by any BPO.[53] Hager, nonetheless, was toppled by central authorities, as has been seen, and could probably count himself lucky that he did not suffer any other hardships.[54]

Werner Frohn, in contrast, was successful in using his position to make the PCK economically more viable in the 1970s. In 1969 and 1970, shortly before Ulbricht was replaced by Honecker, many attacks were made on Ulbricht's policy of giving privileged treatment to specific industrial sections at the expense of all the others.[55] Nevertheless, this prioritizing seems to have hardly changed under Honecker, at least not with regard to the EVW. Even so, in the 1970s other factors may have become even more important for the success of a state-owned concern, primarily personal networks and connections reaching up to the highest echelons of the economic and political hierarchy. Frohn, for example, owed much to his seat on the ZK SED but at least part of his achievement was based also on his good relationship with Wyschofsky, Minister of Chemical Industries.[56] Another important aspect of his success was his close co-operation with a competent local SED functionary. Jochen Hertwig, first secretary of the SED district organization, had been a member of the ZK SED since 1954 and showed no fear of confronting even Mittag, who was not known for his mild temper.[57] On the basis of these connections, in the late 1970s Frohn managed to start a major economic campaign which benefited the PCK throughout the 1980s.

The slogan *'Weniger produzieren mehr'* (Fewer people produce more) described this initiative, started at the EVW with the aim of reducing the number of people needed to work the plant. Productivity was intended to increase despite using fewer employees. This project was born mainly as a result of the constantly dwindling supplies of labour in the GDR. This problem was not linked to a particularly low population count but to both the deficiencies of the East German economic system and political priorities. International studies from the 1970s and Knortz's recent research on the PCK initiative have shown that reasons for the perceived lack of labour can be found in an East German employee's primary interest in higher wages and bonuses. However, even after wage reform in the late 1970s and early 1980s, individual performance counted only for 20 to 30 per cent of an employee's wages, thereby undermining motivation.[58] Furthermore, the East German economic system suffered from a clash of goals; it was difficult, if not impossible, to link higher productivity to full employment, an ideological mainstay of the East German socialist system.[59] Political dodging diluted economic logic. This was the fundamental fault line running through the entire economic history of the GDR, and has to be made primarily accountable for the East German state's eventual bankruptcy.[60]

However, at the PCK, Frohn was able to introduce an initiative which radically reduced the number of essential employees at the plant in Schwedt, although for the reasons mentioned above it did not take off in the East German economy apart from a few exceptions.[61] In order to make the point that it was possible, in favourable

conditions as present at the EVW, to introduce major structural innovations from the bottom up, Knortz stresses that the scheme originated with Frohn and not the ZK SED or the local SED administration,
as had been stated officially and also by Frohn in his dissertation on
the project in 1980.[62] The aim was to reduce staff by 15 to 20 per cent
whilst, as Frohn felt the need to insist, averting the suspicion of 'soft
plans', that is to say, having originally claimed a higher need for staff
than was really necessary. Apparently, up to 600 positions within the
EVW had not been filled at one time or another.[63] Frohn managed to
cut 637 positions in the new units, which had already been approved
by central planning but then did not need to be utilized. However, the
fact that these 637 positions had been approved did not mean that
this number of people were available for work. Where to get these
people from? 'Nobody could tell us that!' as Frohn put it.[64] The basic
idea of *'Weniger produzieren mehr'*, therefore, was to determine real
requirements more precisely rather than looking for simple but less
efficient solutions. These savings measures were possible at the EVW
Schwedt primarily because the plant was expanding, which meant
that new positions were simply filled by those people whose place of
work had been rationalized. Nobody was made redundant and, even
more importantly, everybody could stay at the EVW. In this way, the
guarantee of work was not touched. Other factories found it much
more difficult, not to find inessential positions perhaps, but to relo-
cate affected staff.[65]

Frohn's initiative provided good results for the EVW, even as the
GDR's economic situation was growing more difficult. Naturally, as the
primary recipient of crude oil from the Soviet Union, the oil crisis
affected the plant considerably. Production was adjusted to accommodate declining supplies. Also, during the 1970s the EVW was ordered to
start producing consumer goods, as was every state-owned concern in
the GDR. This was certainly not an economically efficient way of
organizing the production of consumer goods but, within the remit
given by Honecker, the EVW was quite successful with its production
of furniture made from plastic.[66] Generally, it can be said that the EVW
was probably one of the more flourishing socialist concerns within the
East German economic system, this fact certainly being linked to its
high-status position and the initiative of some dedicated individuals
such as Werner Hager and Werner Frohn. It was one of the very few
plants which continued to exist after 1990. It is still in existence today
(2006) although much reduced in size and belonging to a private
company.

Conclusion

All five factories that are being discussed in this study showed a direct, although often delayed, reaction to central policy such as the brigade movement, the creation of *Kombinate* in the late 1960s, renewed vigour towards the end of the 1970s, and the introduction of data-processing into factories. In this sense, the upsurge in the number of brigades in 1967 was a direct reaction to the eleventh plenary session of the ZK SED, supported by a resolution of the tenth meeting of the BV FDGB in 1966, which called for a new mass initiative on the part of the workers.[67] Similarly, all factories started to prepare for the introduction of computers around 1967. Most used this opportunity to restructure and simplify administration. In turn, the need for both computers and simplification was related to the integration of factories into larger structures such as *Kombinate* between 1969 and 1970. Even more relevant to the East German population was the improvement of working and living conditions, which has been examined in detail in the previous chapter. As has already been indicated repeatedly, to most working people the big issues were linked primarily to new types of wages, bonuses and the improvement of working and living conditions.

Each of the themes indicated above offered a case in point of how trade unions, ministries and groups of firms in specific sectors directed by the VVB translated highly ideological party conference speeches and subjects discussed at the plenary meetings of the ZK SED into smaller issues and tangible measures applicable to factory structures. Such examples of the implementation of central policy are, however, noticeably less easily traceable in the archival material of the Berlin factories. In the BGW and the TRO decision processes and problem solving were more dependent on individuals and often give the impression of having been applied ad hoc. In comparison to the EVW in particular, the Berlin factories seem cluttered and disordered, less controlled but also less controllable. At the TRO, positively chaotic conditions existed throughout the 1960s and 1970s, which are reflected in the available archival material. These state-owned factories were beset with greater structural deficiencies, which often delayed or made impossible an efficient implementation of central policy; such chaos had a direct impact on management style and workers' behaviour.

In contrast, the EVW in Schwedt was a new, highly privileged factory, which profited from its high status throughout its existence. The advantages of status, however, were linked inseparably to close control from central authorities, which was unique in its extent when compared to the other factories under scrutiny in this study. Nevertheless, the EVW's special position enabled it to be successful. Even within the incompetence of central state planning, the EVW was able to achieve comparatively high economic efficiency and provide extensively for its workforce.

In the next chapter, another newly established factory located in the district of Frankfurt/Oder will be examined in detail. It will be shown that, in comparison to the EVW and in spite of a similar location, foundation date and initial political priority, the HFO underwent an entirely different experience from the outset.

Voices

K.G. (born 1922): male, chief accountant (finished school at 16, higher education), member of the SED since 1964:

> I was working at the *VVB Mineralöle Halle* to which the EVW belonged at the time. My first experiences with the EVW were negative because the documentation we received from the EVW was often incorrect. The workforce was still inexperienced in many areas but nevertheless we were left with the mess. When the VVB was dissolved in 1969 and the PCK was created with the primary factory in Schwedt, many of us were shocked as we had little trust in this state-owned factory. Nevertheless, I went to Schwedt because the new job was tempting. Many experienced colleagues from the VVB also came along ... the Kombinat PCK became a model enterprise of the GDR. It was fun working there. Co-operation within the work group and with the workforce was very good.

H.B. (born 1939): female, high-level administrative staff (finished school at 14, engineering economist), member of the CDU from the middle of the 1970s onwards:

> *Creating a new plant from scratch: 1959*:
> My primary task within the Department for Material Economy (*Materialwirtschaft*) was to obtain furniture for the accommodation of the builders such as tables, chairs, beds, lockers, mattresses and bedding ... Mostly at the weekend, when we did not travel home, we, the administrative staff, furnished the accommodation blocks because builders came from all over the republic. Furthermore, we helped [with] the clearing of trees or digging of ditches.

The best time of my youth in Schwedt was when we were lodging in the flats of the newly built accommodation blocks. We were all young people who had come to Schwedt from a variety of regions and towns in the GDR ... We met in these flats after work and on Saturdays; we had parties, we talked and we helped each other when somebody had personal problems. It was a wonderful team spirit.

Conflict and solution:
I took care of my career myself in discussion with those responsible, when it concerned the employment of a woman in managerial positions even without being a member of the SED. At that time, I had an understanding boss. I was always able to impress with my professional abilities, even though it was not easy for women in the GDR ... I remained absolutely consistent regarding my position to the CDU and the Church. Here, I did not submit to the pressure from my superiors and had to accept disadvantages in my career, for example it was harder to climb the career ladder, salary increases were denied to me by my supervisor, because I was not a member of the SED ... My husband had massive problems because of my links to the Church and the CDU. We got to know each other in the early 1970s. At that time, he was a high-ranking officer of the national armed forces (NVA). It was made clear to him that his career would be finished if he continued his relationship with me. He gave up his position in the NVA in 1973 and started a new career in the economic sector. It was also important to me that I had contact with my relations and friends in West Germany. We would have had to give these up entirely. I always refused.

Ministry for Security:
I knew that the Stasi existed in the GDR. I did not know that they were present that much and had such a strong influence on the lives of the citizens of the GDR. In the factories there was a special Department for Security, which was directly subordinated to the works or general director. These people worked closely together with the Stasi. Also, the chief personnel officer worked together with the Stasi. I did not notice directly that there were many employees in the factories who informed on their colleagues for the Stasi. At the PCK, this must have been especially bad as so many foreign firms were working in its region.

I first had contact with the Stasi in the 1960s. At that time, the head of the Department for Security asked me if I wanted to be his secretary, then I would become an employee of the Stasi. Naturally, I refused that straight away. He threatened that he would make sure that I would never become a director's secretary at the EVW. Nevertheless, I had a good career. One only had to be steadfast.

[In the course of this career] co-operation with the Department for Security became necessary for me and my staff ... It was sometimes asked of me to describe personal impressions and behaviour patterns of specific employees of foreign firms. I tried to avoid that with excuses that I made up ... The head of the Department for Security was one of the first of those who got a job at a US firm and immediately started to earn good money again. He had all the information about foreign firms and their products. In GDR times, these had been [called] the bad capitalists!

Normal life:
Regarding this, I want to say that I would not like to have had to go without my time in the GDR.

E.H. (born 1940s): female, head librarian (university education):

I would say about myself that I was neither a victim nor a perpetrator. As a girl, whose father did not return from the Second World War and who, as a refugee, had very moderate prerequisites, I was able to follow a path in the GDR which enabled me to learn my favourite profession, later even to study. That was all possible without support from a family; it was this GDR that made it possible for me.

5
Halbleiterwerk Frankfurt/Oder: Falling Behind the Times

It is necessary to consider carefully the type of state-owned factory analysed and the circumstances of its location and history. These factors had a major impact on any factory's status and therefore its potential for success. They also shaped the problems encountered by the management, influenced its productivity, the social benefits offered to the workforce and, generally, the factory's position within the East German economic system. It does not do just to look at large state-owned factories with top priority productions in large industrial towns when trying to describe the realities of working life in the GDR.[1]

State-owned factories that were built up from scratch in the countryside or in very small townships had no reliable and appropriately skilled workforce to rely upon. A pronounced lack of both experience in industrial work and the mental and physical discipline and stamina required when working in a factory made it difficult to organize production efficiently. Issues such as recruitment, qualifications and housing for employees could hinder productivity even in the long term. However, some new factories benefited from an entire set of new machinery and attracted a young and enthusiastic workforce, such as the EVW, and were envied for it. Others, such as the *Halbleiterwerk Frankfurt/Oder* (HFO), were provided only with old surplus equipment and were forced to train up former housewives and other women, who had previously worked in different industries. There were not just huge differences between established and new factories but also between newly established state-owned factories.

Characteristics

Similarly to the EVW, the HFO[2] was founded in 1958. The production of electronic semiconductors started in 1960. Just as at the BGW, the factory was subordinate to the *VVB Bauelemente und Vakuumtechnik*.[3] In reaction to international technological developments, at a national conference on electronics in April 1960 demands were made to increase the production of semiconductor modules by 350 per cent by 1965. To the benefit of the HFO, the sixth party conference in January 1963 reinforced this trend by resolving once again to intensify the production of semiconductors. The increasing political priority of the HFO probably also prompted a two-day visit of a working group of the East German parliament, the *Volkskammer*, to the factory in June 1963. By that time, however, the HFO was already encountering massive production problems.

Internally, an impression of inefficiency dominates the archival material relating to the HFO. The conflict commission, for example, criticized the fact that directives from the works director were not realized promptly: 'It should be noted that in parts of our factory it takes an unusually long time for directives from the works director to be carried out in all parts [of the factory].'[4] The HFO was less privileged but also less tightly controlled than the EVW, despite its similar situation in terms of history and location.

A new factory in the storms of the NES

The HFO was an East German pioneer in the production of semiconductors and encountered problems linked to the application and exploration of new technologies. For example, the initial production hall (an old school building) was not really suitable for the production of tiny objects susceptible to dust. Technical equipment was unsatisfactory and the supply of raw materials unreliable. Also, the new workforce directed towards the HFO was mostly unqualified. Those employed were either former housewives or, in the early 1960s, women who had been forced to leave their former places of work at a textile factory that was being closed down and, later on, unqualified Polish women. In terms of technological staff, the VVB tended to send inexperienced graduates to the HFO. This did not make the situation easier for the management, which had to deal with an entirely new production line.[5]

Perhaps unsurprisingly, from 1960 the HFO had been unable to cover costs, thereby incurring financial debts that the central bank was forced to cover.[6] In 1963 the works director at that time, Rudi Schmidt, a former director of the VVB, was reprimanded by the VWR for unsatisfactory management.[7] The VWR decided to install a representative of the VVB to ensure better methods of work organization at the HFO.

Also, for a period of two months from August to October 1963, a deputy replaced the works director. Underlying problems such as a lack of qualified staff, however, were not resolved for some years.[8] Repeatedly, plans were fulfilled in terms of sheer numbers but not with regard to the assortment of modules required by the HFO's plans.[9] Furthermore, in October 1963 the VVB came to the conclusion that accounts handed in for September 1963 had been falsified. Instead of the 90 per cent plan fulfilment that had been reported, only 1.4 per cent had realistically been reached.[10] The VVB threatened to involve the VWR to clarify the situation and ordered the creation of a working group under the leadership of two VVB functionaries to develop a scheme setting out the future of the HFO.[11]

Nevertheless, in 1964 the HFO was merged with the *Institut für Halbleitertechnik* in Teltow (IHT) and put under the management of the HFO's works director Schmidt, who had been so sharply criticized in 1963. The IHT was a research centre specializing in semiconductor technology that had already been working with the HFO for some time, but neither institution had been very successful individually, nor had they managed to co-operate effectively.[12] In July 1965 a new works director (Krahl) was introduced. He only stayed for two years before being replaced by Elmar Sommer.

Sommer was born in the late 1920s, had become an engineer in 1950 and was accepted into the SED in 1952. After that, he worked for the *VEB Bauelemente der Nachrichtentechnik* in Grossbreitenbach for nine years, first as technical director and then moving up to the position of works director. From 1962 he was employed in leading positions within the section for semiconductor technology by the *VVB Bauelemente und Vakuumtechnik* before becoming Director for Plan Realization (*Plandurchführung*). The VVB then sent Sommer to Frankfurt/Oder. At that time, the HFO had just managed to catch up with its economic plans again.

In December 1966 not only had all plan conditions been fulfilled but the first stage of the HFO's expansion had been successfully completed. Therefore, Sommer's arrival cannot be directly linked to a particular failure of the management team. Possibly the VVB decided in 1967, at a time when expansion was about to demand a great deal of organizational skill, to bring in one of its own specialists. In November 1967, in response to central decisions at the seventh party conference, the production group Semiconductor Technology was created, of which the HFO became the primary factory.[13] Sommer continued as works director into the 1980s in spite of economic problems at the HFO. He even became general director of the newly created *VEB Kombinat Halbleiter-werk* Frankfurt/Oder in 1969.

Before turning to the creation of the *Kombinat* and its consequences for the HFO, however, some other factors that defined work at the HFO need to be considered. In the following section, the employment of Polish workers at the plant will be highlighted. In turn, this will provide a useful link to the working and living conditions at the HFO, an issue that, as has been pointed out repeatedly, was of the greatest consequence for the workforce of any state-owned factory.

Polish employees at the HFO

In the year of Sommer's arrival in Frankfurt/Oder, in 1967, a major challenge to the organizational skills of the new works director was posed when a whole new group of employees was introduced to the HFO. In March of that year, 35 Polish women started work at the factory. It was the beginning of a long-term employment strategy, which benefited both the factory that had always had difficulties in meeting its workforce requirements and the Polish employees, who had little chance of getting a job in Poland at that time. Earlier, in November 1966, 26 Vietnamese had also come to the HFO for temporary practical work placements that also included some teaching. Although there was a continuous stream of Vietnamese working at the HFO from then on, the co-operation with Poland was more extensive.

Other state-owned factories, such as the EVW and the TRO, also employed Poles from the middle of the 1960s onwards but not to the extent of the HFO. Foreign nationals who came to the GDR to work were not an unusual phenomenon at that time, the earliest agreements being drawn up in the early 1960s, often under the cover of promising these people vocational training.[14] Especially with regard to Poland, this was a necessary stipulation, as the experiences of the Third Reich were still too close to avoid altogether comparisons with forced labour, even under these favourable circumstances. In 1989 about 93 000 foreign workers were employed in the East German economy. Of those, 52 000 were Poles, a number which does not include commuting workers many of whom were working at the HFO.[15]

Poles working at the HFO were mostly unqualified women, who entered into a contract which promised not just fair wages and equal treatment to German employees but also vocational and language training, and social benefits which included childcare facilities, holiday camps for their children and cultural events organized in their Polish home towns. In 1968, publishing a summary of the HFO's newspaper in Polish was considered in order to encourage integration.[16] By June 1972, 733 Polish employees were working at the HFO. This was about one fifth of the workforce, which amounted to 3716 employees on 31 December 1971. Most of the the Poles were female (670), lived in Poland and commuted across the border by bus.[17] The experience of foreigners in the East German economy differed widely, often at least partly depending on their nationality. Polish people employed by the HFO remember their treatment by management and colleagues differently, ranging from accounts of discrimination to close personal relationships that lasted beyond 1989.[18]

One issue that caused particular tension throughout the 1970s and 1980s was the Poles' practice of buying large quantities of consumer goods that were rare in Poland. East Germans, who felt their own provision of consumer goods to be less than adequate without Poles buying *en masse*, resented this situation.[19] These goods were often used to supply relations and neighbours, who were struggling to survive in a much more severe shortage economy than the GDR.[20] Some, however, sold their booty for profit in Poland, thereby augmenting their already comparably comfortable income, part of which they were paid in GDR currency.[21] The reaction of Poles in Słubice, where many HFO employees lived, was sometimes almost hostile. One account describes anger, grounded in memories going back to the Second World War, that was revived by the daily confrontation with compatriots who had accepted work in the GDR:

> We well remembered the times when our compatriots and relatives were carried off to do forced labour in the Third Reich and were treated there as slaves. We felt it to be beneath our dignity to work in Germany. Nevertheless, day by day we lived alongside those who had taken on jobs there because material temptations were more important than patriotism.[22]

Poles working at the HFO tended to describe such accusations of a lack of patriotism as pure envy.[23] Nevertheless, Poles employed by the HFO were confronted with an ambivalent situation not only in Frankfurt/Oder but also in their homeland.

One positive impression, repeatedly mentioned in memory reports from Polish employees, was the modern working conditions[24] and extensive social provisions at the HFO.[25] Obviously, such praise was seen in contrast to Polish conditions at that time. By East German standards the HFO was not a model factory. Nevertheless, it had had a programme for the improvement of working and living conditions from 1965 and had introduced projects that catered directly to the needs of its primarily female workforce.[26]

Management demonstrably aimed to strengthen the emotional bonds of its Polish employees and, even more so, of the citizens of Frankfurt/Oder to the HFO, giving much attention to the improvement of cultural provisions on offer in the area. The hope was that by organizing cultural events and celebrating important anniversaries, families would eventually settle down and provide a steady stream of workers for the HFO. Staff turnover had been very high up to 1967 and, therefore, both the management of the HFO and local administrators felt that improvements in the social, cultural and sports sectors had to be introduced. This strategy seems to have been effective: staff turnover rates sank from 1967 onwards. Also, the number of people living in Frankfurt/Oder rose steadily, particularly in the 1970s. In the 1950s, shortly after the devastation caused by the Second World War, the population of the area was as low as 52 800, rising slowly to 58 000 in 1964–5. By 1970 a figure of 62 000 had been reached, which had gone up to 81 009 by the end of December 1981.[27]

Of course there were various reasons for the pronounced rise in the population of the area. However, the most influential causes were based on socio-economic developments linked to efforts by the HFO to improve working and living conditions in Frankfurt/Oder. From 1968 onwards the structure of the plan for the improvement of working and living conditions changed to the eight sections first introduced by Rudi Rubbel.[28] It seems that the HFO was brought into line with the official model, possibly following the appointment of the new works director Sommer who, as a former functionary of the VVB, would have been attuned to official requirements.

The allocation of investment, raw materials and building capacities – and not only with regard to the programme for the improvement of working and living conditions – depended to a great extent on central authorities. The concept of status and its relevance to individual factories has already been discussed at some length.[29] Such considerations certainly also applied to the HFO, which lost much of its political priority due to a temporary loss of interest in the development of microelectronics at the central level in the early to mid 1970s.[30] In addition, another major change, the HFO's integration into a *Kombinat*, had a strong impact on the factory's position. In 1969 the *VEB Halbleiterwerk Frankfurt/Oder* was created. The HFO became the primary unit within this conglomerate.

Changing circumstances: the creation of *Kombinate* and its impact on the HFO

The creation of larger economic units took place in stages in the GDR. The first major drive happened in the late 1960s. The second, more extensive attempt was made in the late 1970s resulting in 133 centrally led *Kombinate*.[31] The creation of such large conglomerates of factories included a dimension which was relevant to social policy issues and specifically to the improvement of working and living conditions. In the following section, the experience of a parent unit will be compared to the difficulties that inhibited the progress of subordinate factories.

The experiences of subordinate factories within a larger *Kombinat* differed greatly, although a combination of practical problems and loss of influence seem to have prevailed. One report written up for Mittag explained that the administrative workload increased massively with the creation of the *Kombinate*. The *VEB Werkzeugmaschinenkombinat 'Fritz Heckert'*, for example, had built up a separate management team comprising some 280 people.[32] Another report on discussions between a department of the ZK SED and management teams in Mühlhausen and Dresden presented a selection of opinions from 1972. Conversely a feeling of neglect or even exploitation dominated the wide range of circumstances. Some felt that the interests of smaller factories received more attention within a *Kombinat* than in a VVB. One works director pointed to some practical problems such as the co-operation between mass organizations such as the FDGB, FDJ or the SED and the individual factories, which was still difficult at that time. Most opinions given were critical of the status of individual units; they demanded that the independence of state-owned factories should be increased as 'many factories, functionaries and workforces felt demoted [in the new conglomerates]'.[33] In the case of one factory, a representative claimed that it was being worn out on purpose by the *Kombinat*.[34] Also, in groupings where the management of the *Kombinat* and the parent unit were the same, there had been instances where either the primary factory was left without guidance or the general director of the *Kombinat* collapsed from overwork.[35] Experiences varied but there was certainly a danger of subordinate factories losing control within a large conglomerate and equally the parent unit could suffer from the overwork experienced by the general director – the HFO underwent both sets of circumstances and both worked to the disadvantage of the factory and its workforce in Frankfurt/Oder.

Turning into a *Kombinat*

A *Kombinat* could incorporate economic units with differing levels of productivity, numbers of employees, financial positions and so on. It could combine factories that were located far apart from each other. The *VEB Möbelkombinat Deutsche Werkätten Hellerau*, for example, was spread across five districts with seven state-owned factories, 135 sections and production units. It encountered massive organizational problems in 1973.[36] The basic idea was to encourage the concentration of processes. In order to achieve a reduction in costs, intensive production and an effective use of resources, factories were bound together that either belonged to a similar industrial sector, that is to say were producing similar things, or formed a vertical line of co-operation partners, combining all the units needed to manufacture a specific final product.[37] Sometimes, factories that were 'left over' as a result of this concentration were also thrown together and given the title of *Kombinat* independent of any economic considerations.[38] Central planning expected that working and living conditions and spending on their improvement would be averaged out within the new bigger economic units.

The formation of *Kombinate* in the late 1960s may well have been a reflection of the SED's attempt to regain control of and regulate the political tool called social policy. At the same time, it may have been intended to bring less successful state-owned factories up to a certain level of achievement, both in terms of economic success and the provision of social benefits for their workforce. Mittag, in contrast, suggested in hindsight that the primary intention of the Politburo under Honecker's leadership had been to reduce the influence of local party functionaries on the factories.[39] However, this assertion is difficult to reconcile with the increased politicization under Honecker, who had shown a marked interest in increasing the influence of the SED at every level of society since the late 1960s. In the late 1970s centralization efforts lay at the heart of the campaign, which led to even greater inflexibility and a further reduction in competition.[40]

These conglomerates, which could be quite large, incorporating tens of thousands of employees, were unable to extend the stabilizing bond between individual factories, towns and workforces to include the entire *Kombinat*. In 1973 one report had already been drawn up by a department of the ZK SED, after a meeting with general directors from Berlin, which pointed to negative consequences for sociological developments within these enormous units. It stated that 'Concentration processes are causing a diversity of sociological and social problems.'[41] Also, in 1980, the FDGB noted a 30 per cent increase in conflicts in factories. Most conflicts and threats of giving up trade union membership originated in state-owned factories affected by the creation of *Kombinate*.[42] Related difficulties also characterized the experience of the HFO.

The *VEB Kombinat Halbleiterwerk Frankfurt/Oder* contained four factories in addition to the HFO. It existed from 1969 to 1977, a period defined by a variety of tribulations and few successes. Before the creation of the *Kombinat* and also in the early 1970s the HFO had already proved itself unable to fulfil the plan. In fact, structural changes relating to the HFO's position as the parent unit within this conglomerate had brought new problems for the struggling factory. In particular, the need to achieve a convergence of working and living conditions between the various parts of the conglomerate and the HFO's responsibility for related regional developments were given high priority.[43] In the first blueprint and model for the future *Kombinat*, the HFO management had already indicated that one of the main goals would be to reach a uniform standard of socio-economic attainment. However, this task seems to have overtaxed the HFO, which was meant to take charge and oversee related activities in all sections of the conglomerate. In 1970 co-operation with individual factories had consisted primarily of discussions with regard to the preparation of the *Kombinat*'s economic plans.[44] Also, a central fund for cultural and social projects had been established.[45] No practical results had been achieved. The reasons for this unsatisfactory progress were found to be a lack of suitable functionaries at the HFO. Accordingly, changes in personnel became the aim.

The attempt to fill management positions with new people was not just linked to a lack of qualifications, as may have been appropriate and necessary in the face of the administrative challenges posed by the structural complexities of a *Kombinat*. Rather, a distinct drive to increase the influence of the SED within the HFO was the central concern from the late 1960s. The focus on economic considerations, which had been the priority during the economic reforms, had caused some neglect of political education; at least that was the view of specific factions within the SED leadership. This interpretation, arguably, lay at the heart of the reorientation prompted by Honecker's growing influence in the late 1960s and his taking power in 1971.

Within the HFO, this approach was supported by the BPO. A report drawn up for the BPO in January 1968 had asserted the workforce's pronounced reluctance to get involved in political mass organizations or attend courses on Marxist–Leninist ideology. Both production workers and technological staff had expressed little desire to familiarize themselves with Marxism–Leninism. The report also highlighted major shortcomings in the activities of the trade union and FDJ functionaries.[46] In reaction to the changes in the political orientation of the Politburo, but also acting on this report, the BPO intervened. In August 1968 talk at a BPO meeting had been of the need to exert more influence on 'the unity of politics and economics'.[47] Two months later, shortly before the new *Kombinat* was founded, the BPO strongly criticized the works director Sommer and his management team for not adhering to party decisions. Party decisions, in this case, applied to the economic management of the HFO. Sommer was given specific advice as to the organization of work and it was even demanded that research on a specific transistor should be speeded up.[48] In the same year, consideration was given to publishing the HFO's newspaper *Kristallspiegel*, edited by members of the SED, not twice monthly any more but every eight days 'to improve political-ideological work'.[49] The BPO also planned to start a discussion of the HFO's economic problems within the *Kristallspiegel*.[50] The self-confidence of the BPO was clearly on the up again and stood in stark contrast to the earlier aims of the NES, which had intended to subdue the interference of SED functionaries in economic decisions. By 1972, at a time when Honecker was already in power, the HFO's director for social economics suggested various replacements, including one sectional and three departmental heads, in order 'to increase the influence of the party'.[51] In conclusion, it was stressed that the 'leading role of the SED needed to be enforced' within the HFO.[52] Honecker's strong orientation towards recentralization and increased politicization had reached the new *Kombinat* very quickly.

In general, the position of the general director of the *Kombinat* and works director of the HFO seems to have been rather shaky at that time. In 1972 Sommer complained to the general director of the VVB that various functionaries of the VVB and also its general director had interfered in the running of the *Kombinat*. Without the knowledge of Sommer, they had given orders to the works directors of the other factories in the conglomerate. Apparently, this had not been a one-off incident but had happened repeatedly. In one example given by Sommer, works directors had been told by the general director of the VVB to prepare parts of a scheme for the development of the region up to 1980. Sommer had not been informed of this order.[53] Economic and organizational problems also hampered progress throughout the early 1970s in relation to projects linked to the programme for the improvement of working and living conditions.[54]

The implementation of this programme was becoming a real burden to the HFO in the middle of the 1970s. In 1975, for example, a report claimed that there were insufficient resources available for the projected plans for 1976 and 1977. The standard reached so far would not be maintained if there were no changes such as passing on responsibility for childcare facilities to the regional administration. Obligations within the region were getting too much for the HFO. It was also suggested that the VVB should be informed and adjustments to the funds that had been allocated to the *Kombinat* be demanded. These should include consideration of the varying standards of working and living conditions in the various factories and not just be calculated according to the number of employees.[55] The funding of the *Kultur- und Sozialfonds* had changed from being linked to net profits in the late 1960s to being entirely decided upon by the institution next in rank, that is to say the VVB.[56] In 1977 a summary concluded that the funds for 1976 had not been sufficient, as predicted in 1975, and those for 1977 were 'more [deficient] than ever'. The VVB provided 4 216 000 Marks whilst 5 873 800 Marks were required. The VVB was strongly criticized, especially as it had promised to provide solutions, and it was decided to lodge a complaint with the minister about the general director of the VVB in relation to this problem.[57] In the case of the HFO, the allocation of finances was leading to levels of funding that were insufficient to uphold the standard which had been attained in the late 1960s.

The difficulties experienced by the HFO in the 1970s were reflected to some extent at least by the ups and downs of staff turnover. Figures for staff turnover increased in the 1970s, although the high levels of the mid 1960s were not reached again. The highest rate had been 21.2 per cent in 1965, which had declined to about 11 per cent in 1967.[58] In 1972 turnover had risen to 13.4 per cent[59] reaching 16.8 per cent in 1974[60] and declining slightly to 13.4 per cent in 1976 and 15.3 per cent in 1977.[61] The reasons for leaving the HFO that were given by the workforce varied: they included difficulties in finding accommodation; a person's partner moving to another town; financial benefits in a new position; and personal considerations. Sometimes those departing were more openly critical of their old jobs at the HFO and mentioned unsatisfactory work assignments.[62] Similarly, rates for sickness leave had been between 5 to 6 per cent in the early 1960s, which was above planned figures. They stayed below those planned for in the second half of the 1960s. In the 1970s, however, with between 7 to 8 per cent, illness rates again exceeded the plan, which had already calculated for higher levels of sickness than those reached in the 1960s.[63]

The creation of the *VEB Kombinat Halbleiterwerk Frankfurt/Oder* had turned out to be a disaster for the HFO in the longer term. In particular, the need to achieve a uniform level of attainment, specifically regarding standards of working and living conditions, had proved an impossible task for the management of the HFO. In particular, the works director Sommer had been unable to deal with the administrative and economic challenge of achieving success in the face of declining investment and a reduced status under the new government. Honecker's initial lack of interest in developing microelectronics had long-term consequences for both the HFO and the East German economy in general.

Losing control: being a small part of a large *Kombinat*

The problems encountered in the early and mid 1970s were partly blamed on the HFO's works director,[64] whose career suffered noticeably during this period. From August 1973 Sommer's position as general director of the *VEB Kombinat Halbleiterwerk Frankfurt/Oder* was occupied by a replacement for some time. In September 1977 the *Kombinat* had again seemed unable to meet the obligations set by its economic plan, and in October the Politburo decision of 21 September 1977 – to create the *Kombinat VEB Mikroelektronik Erfurt* (KME) – had been made known to the HFO's management team.[65] Effectively demoting Sommer, in 1978 the HFO was integrated into the KME under the leadership of Heinz Wedler.

Wedler was born in 1927, had taken part in the Second World War and had been badly wounded. In the newly founded GDR, he studied engineering until 1952. Only 11 years later, after finishing his doctorate, he became works director at the *VEB Uhrenwerke Ruhla*, a firm with a long history of successful international competition with the renowned Ruhla clockworks.[66] In 1967 this factory had been turned into the *VEB Uhrenkombinat Ruhla* before being changed into yet another *Kombinat* in 1978, of which Wedler also became the general director.[67] The careers of both Wedler and Sommer ran along similar lines for some time before 1978, when the HFO lost its position as a parent unit and Sommer was demoted from his position of general director. However, Sommer was neither able to compete with Wedler's academic qualifications nor had he been successful in handling the task of leading an entire *Kombinat*, nor again did he establish a working relationship with the responsible VVB's leading functionaries. Apparently, he had been unable to fill the positions of both works director of the HFO and general director of the *Kombinat* sufficiently well to keep both running smoothly. This was not an unusual experience although other state-owned factories fared better.[68] Nevertheless, within the KME Sommer remained the works director of the HFO.

The new conglomerate, as its title suggested, was geared towards microelectronics and was a direct result of the Microelectronics Programme, which was launched in June 1977 in reaction to developments on the international market. In particular the oil crisis of 1973 made it clear to the East German Politburo that a country without sufficient natural resources would need to focus its economic efforts on technological advances. Ulbricht, of course, had realized this much earlier and the programme was an attempt to resume related initiatives that had been begun in the 1960s but had been stopped when Honecker came to power in 1971. The decision to invest in microelectronics, although crucial, was taken with some delay when seen in an international context.[69] In addition, the initial programme needed to be implemented again in 1979 as not much had been achieved in the first two years. Nevertheless, up to the early 1980s the GDR managed to prevent a widening of the gap in international advances in related technologies.[70]

The Microelectronics Programme should have catapulted the HFO to the forefront of political and economic priorities again. Semiconductors were crucial to microelectronic products. Taking into consideration the research section in Stahnsdorf and the HFO's production halls in Markendorf that had been opened in 1966, Frankfurt/Oder offered great potential for the further technological development of semiconductors. The HFO would have benefited in terms of the allocation of investment funds. However, this seems not to have happened. The integration of the factory into the *Kombinat* in Erfurt worked against such considerations, although the KME as such was prioritized by central authorities in terms of finances and supplies. The decision of the Politburo in June 1979 had led to structural changes in the central investment policy. In 1977, the Ministry for Electronics and Electrical Engineering was given 6.2 per cent of the entire investment in the East German economy. This figure rose to 7.4 per cent in 1979. The *VEB Funkwerk Erfurt*, the parent unit of the KME, received an investment of 31.8 million Marks in 1977, increasing to 55.8 million Marks in 1978, 71 million Marks in 1979 and 101.4 million Marks in 1980.[71]

This is not to say that the HFO declined within the KME. On the contrary, the number of its employees continued to grow from about 5000 in 1978 to 8000 in 1989. It was made responsible for the entire export of microelectronics and had to provide a large selection of circuits for the whole East German economy. However, from the time of the integration into the new microelectronics *Kombinat* the initiative seems to have been surrendered to the management of the KME. Meetings with the works director at the HFO became noticeably more calm and passive compared to the hustle and bustle of the period up to 1978.[72] Also, financial resources and capacities for research were redirected towards the parent unit in Erfurt and one other part of the KME, the *VEB Zentrum für Forschung und Technologie* in Dresden. Frankfurt/Oder was disadvantaged with regard to investments in the HFO and the Frankfurt/Oder region.[73] One document from 1979, which described the consequences of the Politburo decision on the Microelectronics Programme of June 1979 for the HFO, demanded an increase in productivity and rationalization, regarding both the number of employees and material resources. Much space was dedicated to technological questions but no mention was made of additional investment in the plant.[74] Again, this course of action was entirely legal, as decisions on the apportioning of resources within a *Kombinat* were up to its general director, who also had full responsibility for the success or failure of his economic strategies. Furthermore, in this special case, central policy aimed to develop Thuringia, particularly Erfurt, Suhl and Gera into the GDR's leading centre for microelectronics, and therefore directed investment towards this area.[75]

It also has to be said that Dresden had much more to offer than Frankfurt/Oder, both in terms of technological progress and ongoing research in relation to microelectronics. For example, the presence of the *VEB Kombinat Robotron*[76] provided the KME unit *VEB Zentrum für Forschung und Technologie* with an invaluable co-operation partner in relation to research on microelectronics, as both were working on similar technological problems. Within a shortage economy, resources had to be carefully distributed and were never sufficient to satisfy all needs. In comparison to the units in Erfurt and Dresden, which were at the forefront of research, Frankfurt/Oder was, by the late 1970s, only able to provide the services of a crucial supply industry rather than having an impact on technological progress. Naturally, this had an impact on the status of the HFO and, thereby, on its position within the East German economic system and access to the privileges on offer to those state-owned factories that were deemed to have high political priority.

Conclusion

The HFO's early experience had been defined by organizational difficulties caused by its pioneering role and by the usual shortfalls of the centrally planned economic system such as unreliable supplies of materials and a lack of suitable employees. The latter problem at least was solved by the employment of Polish women from 1967, although economic success continued to be a rare experience at the plant in Frankfurt/Oder. Again and again problems occurred but, nevertheless, working and living conditions were improved in co-operation with the regional administration. By the late 1960s, the HFO was building up a reliable workforce with a low turnover rate although it continued to struggle with economic difficulties.

The creation of *Kombinate* in the late 1960s and in the late 1970s had a marked impact on individual factories such as the HFO that, up to their integration into a larger conglomerate, had operated under the guidance and control of the VVBs but as a single unit. Structures changed dramatically and affected both management and workforce, which suddenly were forced to deal with their new position either as a subordinate or primary factory of a much bigger and diverse entity that in its individual segments was often spread far and wide across the country. The need to level out standards across the *Kombinat*, also with regard to working and living conditions, proved difficult and some-times counterproductive in the long term, not only for the HFO.

In comparison to the other three state-owned factories analysed so far, the HFO was much less well positioned to avoid the pitfalls of the East German economic system. It was not located in Berlin and had no responsibility for the use of any immensely valuable natural material such as crude oil, neither was the HFO convincing in its economic per-formance. All these points taken together meant that the HFO was strongly dependent on economic policy and the changing political climate which steered the economy. Central planning in the East German shortage economy meant that scarce resources were allocated not equally but according to a factory's economic and political prior-ity. The HFO enjoyed some status early on, when it was considered to be part of the Electronics Programme but lost this strong position relatively quickly. Economic difficulties encountered by the factory throughout the 1960s were perpetuated by the HFO's installation as the parent unit of the new VEB *Kombinat Halbleiterwerk Frankfurt/Oder* in 1969, whilst its integration into another *Kombinat*, KEM, in 1978 finalized the HFO's loss of privilege. Nevertheless, the HFO remained part of a high-status *Kombinat* and, thereby, benefited at least partly from political prioritizing.

Another state-owned factory that experienced the leading edge of political prioritizing even less than the HFO was the CFW, which will be analysed in the next chapter. Even more so than with factories situated in Berlin or the Frankfurt/Oder area, the CFW's location in the province of Potsdam delineated its primary focus. The social projects of the plant's management and, linked to this, co-operation with regional administrations, was crucial to the CFW, its workforce and the surrounding area.

Voices

The experience of Polish women at the HFO will be given priority in this selection of memory reports.[77] Not only did they work at the HFO in large numbers but their experiences provide the reader with a point of view that differed from that taken by East Germans, who had no worries about employment and basic provisions. In Poland, everyday life had been marked by economic and political crises since the late 1960s. Especially in the districts close to the border between Poland and the GDR, many were without employment and shops were empty. The HFO offered a lifeline to those Polish women who were lucky enough to be selected for employment.

The following two excerpts describe the awe experienced on first arrival at the plant and the importance of employment at the HFO to Polish women and their families.

B.B. (female, arrived at the HFO in September 1971):

> The first impressions ... were simply marvellous. The town [Frankfurt/Oder] was clean and smart. Large shop windows, different shops caught our eyes. The area around the HFO was interesting, modern buildings, large spaces, everywhere light and air, the huge car parks full with cars. We were impressed.

V.W. (female):

> My family was revived when I was working in the GDR. I earned good money, it was enough for everything: eating, drinking, clothing, beautiful things which not every Pole could buy, rent and other things. For me, the GDR was the second USA ... Many of my fellow countrymen and women were envious and ill-disposed towards us women from the HFO... Today, many declare that during the time of socialism, there was only friendship between Germans and Poles that was ordered by the state. That is not true; I experienced that

quite differently in those many years ... They were wonderful years, good times at the HFO in Frankfurt/Oder in the GDR.

Work at the HFO is remembered by many but not all, as has been shown in this chapter, as 'one of the best times of their lives': apparently the relationship with German colleagues was good and superiors are mostly remembered as kind and fair. Many Polish women insist that they were treated as equals although some voices describe their experiences in less positive terms.

J.D. (female):

> We were respected by our supervisors. They did not distinguish between Polish and German workers. For them, reliability, good work and work discipline was important ... During training courses and meetings, our opinions were always asked for even though we were simple production workers ... Today, I remember this period as the best and most beautiful time of my life.

C.M. (female):

> Generally, we had very good relations with the Germans. During the time when I was working for the BGL, good working relations predominated. When I, as a representative of my colleagues, asked for help for our brigade, we were always given assistance; at least others tried to help. Naturally, there were problems sometimes, where are there none? They were resolved together with the supervisor or head of department and us ... After public holidays sometimes some colleagues had to be sent home because they were hungover. Then, the supervisor acted very generously, very humanely, he wrote a houseday [*Haustag*, paid day of work to do household chores]. That was possible! Regarding work, our opinions were always asked.

B.B.: (female, arrived at the HFO in September 1971)

> We did not receive any social support from the HFO although we paid the same contributions as our German colleagues. I looked at German colleagues, who used the advantageous social welfare benefits, with envy ... I absolutely have to mention the collegial relations in our factory. Many different contacts and friendships developed and were kept. Polish and German colleagues were nice

and agreeable. I can say the same about the economic functionaries ... Outside the factory, sometimes it was different.

Apparently, experiences within the HFO and outside differed noticeably, as has been indicated above. Nevertheless, the memories of the Polish employees at the HFO tend to stress good relations with their German colleagues, and fair and equal treatment at least until 1989. During the upheaval and eventual German unification, as East Germans became scared of losing their jobs and the HFO was dissolved, even Poles who had worked at the plant for decades experienced some hostility. However, German–Polish support networks and individual friendships between former colleagues continue to exist even today.

V.W. (female):

I am grateful to the women from the Democratic Women's Union in Frankfurt/Oder for their many donations and for the opportunity for joint excursions or invitations to a concert. The donations are distributed here in Słubice among the former Polish employees of the HFO and help again and again. That gives the lie to those who maintain that our friendship had been ordered ... I rather believe that this friendship was desired by the state but not ordered. In this way, I have seen it, in this way I approved of it and today I am convinced that it was right just so.

6
Chemiefaserwerk Premnitz: Creating a Home for Thousands

Having discussed four state-owned factories of differing or changing status, this chapter will turn to another type of experience: the state-owned factory in the provinces that never had either political priority or a predominant position within a *Kombinat*. For the *Chemiefaserwerk Premnitz* (CFW) the combination of two factors, its low status in the context of the East German economic system and its high value for the Premnitz area, will be considered in detail and in relation to both central policy and the economic difficulties of the plant in the 1960s and 1970s. To cover a variety of experiences within the East German state, state-owned factories of less consequence in provincial areas need to be analysed as they were confronted with different issues and problems from high-status factories, especially with regard to their management's priorities and networking potential and to the work-force's attitude towards the plant. The CFW[1] in Premnitz can be seen as a prime example of the problems encountered in such a context.

Characteristics

The CFW succeeded an established firm which produced artificial silk and had existed since the early twentieth century. In the late 1920s this firm had been integrated into the *IG Farben* concern. The CFW became state-owned shortly after the end of the Second World War and expanded dramatically during the 1960s. In that period it became ever more important as the major employer not only for Premnitz, which was given official status as a town in 1962, and Rathenow, the nearest bigger town, but also many villages in the surrounding area. The population of Premnitz grew from about 8700 in 1960 to 11 700 in 1970 and 12 000 in 1979. Of those 12 000 citizens, over a third were employed by the CFW, which altogether numbered between 7000 and 7500 employees in the 1970s.[2] The special position of the CFW as the major employer in an otherwise predominantly rural area accorded it responsibility for and influence on the communities in which its workforce was living.

The chemical industry in Premnitz was of comparatively low status within the East German economic system in spite of the Chemical Programme of 1958, which had catapulted forward other plants such as the EVW. Also, the management of the CFW had no far-reaching connections that might have advanced the interests of the plant within the economic or political hierarchy of the GDR. In addition, the CFW was located in the province of Potsdam, in the midst of a fundamentally rural area and, therefore, did not command the Berlin bonus of plants such as the BGW and the TRO. To summarize, from the outset the CFW was not predestined to have a privileged position within the East German economic system.

Nevertheless, there were various phases in the 1960s and early 1970s when the CFW accommodated large investment projects which furthered its modernization and expansion. In spite of some economic importance accorded to the production of chemical textiles throughout the period in question, the CFW's position could not be compared to that of other plants within the East German economy such as the EVW, with its primary responsibility for crude oil, or the TRO, with its production of large transformers. The comparatively low status of the CFW was reflected in the plant's works directors and their connections. As has been pointed out before, a works director's networking ability and political influence were crucial to any state-owned factory in the GDR and although the CFW's long-term director, Hermann Danz, was an able manager, who steered the plant through the ups and downs of the 1960s and 1970s, he was never what one would have called a top functionary. He was not in the same league as Rudi Rubbel, Helmut Wunderlich or Werner Frohn. As will be shown, this had some impact on both Danz's position within the plant and his dealings with regional administrators.

On the other hand, the CFW was of major importance to its workforce and the surrounding area. This strong position was built up throughout the 1960s and continued up to the demise of the plant in the 1990s. Even beyond 2000 Premnitz and its population are marked by the fact that a large proportion of the town's citizens worked at the plant for many years during GDR times. In particular, the social and cultural efforts of the CFW's management from the 1960s helped to attract employees and created an almost homely feeling for thousands. In contrast to state-owned factories located in areas that offered a range of employment opportunities, as was the case in Berlin and to some extent even in the area of Frankfurt/Oder, the focus in and around Premnitz was dominantly on the CFW. Furthermore, Danz seems to have accepted his role wholeheartedly and, with hindsight, felt that the financial and material investment in the improvement of working and living conditions in the region was an essential feature of his management. Economic considerations regarding the cost of such actions, which would have been at the forefront in a market economy, were not dominant in his consideration of the CFW's interests.[3]

Social effort in Premnitz

In 1960 the CFW employed 6981 people, of which roughly half were women. At the end of that year an analysis of the situation within the state-owned factory noted that social facilities 'were not keeping up with demands' because of the CFW's rapid development. In the plans of the local administration up to 1965, no childcare facilities were planned and little thought was given to issues of accommodation and the building of hospitals.[4] With regard to the high percentage of female employees, these considerations should have been given high priority. At that time, however, local administrations received hardly any funds that they could dispose of at their own discretion. In this situation, the CFW was forced to take on most of the responsibility for the development of working and living conditions in order to ensure a stable workforce for its production. Accordingly, in 1961, a major childcare facility within the factory, which would accommodate children during the week, was planned by the management of the CFW. This was to be funded entirely by the state-owned factory but was deemed necessary to keep female employees.[5] The plan had to be delayed until 1963 because of a lack of funds. Nevertheless, the CFW was socially and culturally active throughout those early years; it organized dances for its workforce and provided a borrowing service for nappies, a laundry service, a shoemaker and the possibility of private repairs for household appliances. It also provided shops for selling textiles, paints and lacquers, plants and fruit. The major problem throughout was the lack of finance, as the district administration was unable, and possibly unwilling, to support these efforts.[6] In May 1961 the budget for social and cultural projects was already proving to be insufficient to cover the costs of all these services, forcing management to look for alternative sources. It even considered the use of finances that actually belonged to the budget for technical improvements. This kind of shifting of resources between budgets was not unusual although it was at best only a semi-legal practice in spite of the fact that, according to the law, the district administration was responsible for the building of cultural and social facilities.[7]

Up to the middle of the 1960s, such efforts were primarily based on the needs of female employees in order to allow them to stay in full-time employment. In 1963 the concept of material interest was still mostly linked to wages and bonuses rather than, as was conceived from the middle of the 1960s onwards, to the improvement of working and living conditions in order to improve productivity by complying with the workers' more general expectations and demands.[8] This changed slightly in 1964 in reaction to a decision of the Council of Ministers on the reduction of sickness rates. In consideration of this ruling, the CFW management discussed the preparation of a programme for the improvement of working conditions.[9] In a process similar to those that have been described for the other state-owned factories at the centre of this study, the management of the CFW tried to reduce high staff turnover and sickness rates by investing in working conditions, child-care and accommodation for its employees. This process was intensified by desperation: by 1965, a shortage of employees was endangering continuous production. In some sections, highly-qualified engineers were kept busy with organizing transport equipment and road signs because there was even a shortage of secretaries and auxiliary staff. At the same time, qualified technologists were also in short supply, leading to even greater problems in keeping up production.[10] The plant's management had a vested interest in making working and living conditions in Premnitz more attractive and in ensuring sufficient childcare and service facilities. The range of related programmes became much broader in the middle of the 1960s and, crucially, they became part of the general plan. By this means, most of the voluntary character that had been attached to these projects was removed. Planned projects had to be accounted for; they became more controllable.

In 1965 the CFW prepared its first plan for the improvement of working and living conditions. In the following year the programme was implemented for the first time as part of the BKV.[11] In 1967 a central commission and sub-commission for the realization of party and government resolutions on the improvement of working and living conditions was set up. In the same year the first measures to secure a rise in productivity were introduced, based on measures suggested by the seventh party conference of the SED, such as the five-day working week and an increase in holidays. From 1969 onwards, long-term plans were prepared for the period from 1971 to 1975. Routinization had truly begun when, in May 1970, a directorate for the improvement of working and living conditions started work with a sectional chief, five main departments and 13 subdivisions.

Danz accorded great importance to the improvement of working and living conditions. In 1970 he stated solemnly: 'Concern for the people is taken to be the most important measure of every leading functionary's political consciousness.'[12] Following up this admonition with practical measures, the management's performance was judged by their concern for the workforce and was to have direct implications for the allocation of bonuses.

Management at the CFW

Hermann Danz was born in 1924 and had become a member of the SED in 1949. He was qualified in economics and had previously been employed at the *VEB Chemiefaserwerk* Schwarza, where he had worked his way up the career ladder until he became works director at a comparatively young age. At Schwarza he had made it one of his main principles to maintain close contact with the workforce. After his transfer to Premnitz he was unable to follow this up to the same extent because, according to his own account, he was kept extremely busy by both the problematic situation within the CFW and the planned expansion and modernization of the plant in the late 1960s.[13] Danz took up his position at Premnitz in 1967 and was to stay into the 1980s.

Before his placement there had been some problems with the previous works director, Karl Kaiser. In 1965, for example, a report of a department's SED organization (APO) complained bitterly that management was forgetting to order essential materials or basic equipment such as cramp-irons, which then had to be manufactured one by one although it would have been much cheaper to order the required amount.[14] Kaiser also failed to prepare the application for investment funds to the complete satisfaction of the SED BL and its first secretary, Baum. As a result, the planned starting date for the project had to be delayed.[15] Baum accused Kaiser and his management team not only of 'serious shortcomings' but also seemed especially annoyed about their reluctance to take full responsibility for the problems that had been encountered. Baum spoke of arguments 'that doubted the scientific character and usefulness of long-term planning as a management tool'.[16] This was the end of the road for Kaiser. Nevertheless, he was praised by Danz[17] and is still remembered by the workforce as an efficient works director with much authority. Also, at least some of the delay had been caused by higher institutions such as the Ministry for Chemical Industry and the VWR. It seems a distinct possibility that Kaiser was forced to take the blame for failings higher up in the hierarchy of the East German economic system and thereby lost his post.[18] Considering the many problems that oppressed the East German economy throughout the 1960s and 1970s, this was probably not an exceptional case.

When Danz first arrived at the CFW he commented on the substandard conditions in quite strong words. In a summary on 17 December 1967 he pointed out: 'I am fully prepared to recognize everything that's good but, on the other hand, I cannot help thinking that, in some sections of the plant, the Second World War ended only two weeks ago.'[19] He complained about dirt and filth in the production halls. In his opinion: 'The last few days and weeks have shown that we are neither in control of production nor the technical equipment, nor the technologies, nor the fund for repairs, nor economic results at any time.'[20] Seemingly, the situation at the CFW was catastrophic at the end of 1967.

Danz was confronted with another major problem; the CFW's long-standing party secretary, Erich Dorn. Dorn made it difficult for the new works director, according to both archival material and accounts from various former employees. He had been at the plant for many years before Danz's arrival and had his own opinions on how to manage the CFW. In contrast to the constellation of works director, and party secretaries at the other plants under discussion in this study, Danz was not particularly influential whilst Dorn has been described as authoritarian. Perhaps his personality type, but probably also the changes in the late 1960s, which promoted SED influence on economic decisions, conspired to turn Dorn into an opponent rather than a supporter of the works director, at least in the early years after Danz's arrival.[21]

One explanation for the party secretary's attack on Danz, besides personal animosity, personality characteristics and an overly politicized attitude, may have been Dorn's perception of the works director as a weak target. Danz's position was under threat at various times. In 1971, for example, only one year after the CFW had been integrated into the *VEB Chemiefaserkombinat Schwarza*, suddenly and without warning, he was replaced on an order from the general director.

The reason for this decision can be found in the delays that had been incurred with regard to expansion projects at the CFW. By the middle of 1969 the delay had already provided cause for criticism from the VVB as the projects were almost 30 per cent behind the planned realization of investment.[22] Such delays would have undermined the production plan for years to come. Furthermore, from the middle of January 1971, the CFW had been unable to fulfil its sales plan, which had led to liquidity problems. Financial obligations towards suppliers and the *Kombinat* could not be met as debts of between 25 and 30 million Marks had accumulated over the years.[23]

However, when he was replaced in 1971 Danz complained bitterly to the general director in Schwarza:

> Contrary to all principles of socialist management, work and co-operation you decided, without exchanging one word of discussion with me or co-ordination and in my absence on 8 February 1971, to dispense with my services as works director and appointed party member Giese as acting works director.[24]

Danz had even been threatened with disciplinary measures but without letting him know exactly what he should expect. Nevertheless, shortly after his complaint, he was reappointed to his post.

In 1973, Danz again came under attack. In January at his office he was handed a letter from the BPO, which was extremely critical of his management style. It stated that 'the management team and every individual member of it have not taken on full responsibility for all political and economic tasks at the CFW.' Also, the BPO lamented, misdemeanours were not being punished and questions of principle were not being discussed enough.[25] The party secretary was thus accusing Danz of being lacking in both ability and authority. In his letter of reply Danz pointed out, rather meekly, that he was overloaded with work and did not have enough time in spite of committing himself to long working days and having 'practically no weekends'. Also, he argued that he had come into the CFW at the start of an expansion phase when the management team was undergoing a fundamental change of personnel. Danz affirmed that economic functionaries were primarily political executives[26] and that the decisions of the plant's SED organization, the BPO, were binding, would be put into action and their realization controlled.[27] He stressed especially that party principles were the foundation of all work at the CFW.[28] To summarize, the works director was retreating on to safe ground by expressing a strong allegiance to the SED rather than denying the allegations that had been made about his work. Although Danz was able to fight off this attack, the circumstances of this exchange were neither amiable nor conducive to co-operation in the future.

Besides internal problems, Danz also encountered difficulties in his dealings with regional administrations, even though co-operation had advanced greatly since the early 1960s, especially regarding the improvement of working and living conditions. Nevertheless, it was crucial to the CFW, its workforce and the Premnitz area that support from both state and party administrations of the region be assured.

Co-operation with administrative bodies of the region

Up to the late 1960s co-operation with regional administrations had been less than satisfactory for various reasons. Social and cultural projects most often had to be financed by the CFW, with only limited support from the local or district administration. This had been exceedingly difficult for the state-owned factory, which exhausted and even exceeded its budget a number of times in order to feed the insatiable beast called 'the improvement of working and living conditions'. Regional administrations were divided into government agencies and representative bodies of the SED. Good relations had to be maintained with both, although in terms of personnel and tasks, related institutions often overlapped. In this section, the difficulties of a works director at a less important plant, who did not command the political influence and economic capacities of a high-status firm in getting support from district organizations, will be highlighted. At the same time, however, the pressures on those state and party organizations, that were bound to comply with central decisions and accommodate local needs without access to essential resources, have to be considered in order to show both sides of the coin. The CFW was reliant on support from local and district administrations of both party and state with regard to various issues. One important aspect was social and cultural activity. Another was the close co-operation required for the realization of the investment project at the CFW.

In 1969 the CFW's co-operation with the local party organization had progressed so far that a joint letter was sent to the SED BL in Potsdam: it demanded more interest in, and action for, Premnitz and its people. Danz and the local administration had prepared a long-term plan which would have benefited both the plant and the area. This plan was designed to secure support at district level, which was crucial in terms of ensuring the necessary capacities. In addition, the agreement of the

SED BL was needed according to law, which put responsibility for the planning and building of social and cultural facilities on the district administration and not the state-owned factory. The CFW was only allowed to improve facilities that already existed.

In November 1969 Danz met with the SED BL to discuss current problems with regard to the major investment project at the CFW. The discussion of the project on 18 November 1969 in Premnitz focused on two points in particular and was closely related to the previous clash between Danz and Baum in August of the same year. Once more, Danz stressed that the improvement of working and living conditions 'is to be seen as a particular main focus and for this scheme an extensive programme or agreement between the administrations of the locality, the town and the CFW already exists. A positive reaction from the district, however, has been missing up to this point.'[29] In response to this statement, Baum admitted that the needs of the population required consideration:

> We are dealing with the largest investment project of the [German Democratic] Republic here in Premnitz. That generates not only economic but ideological questions. When the programme was prepared, the point of it was to create conditions with the help of that investment that would, among other things, satisfy the needs of the population.[30]

In a discussion in Potsdam, however, Danz was told to expect no such support from the SED BL. In December 1969 the first party secretary of the BL asserted 'that the district was not even thinking of agreeing to a binding contract. Contracts of this kind would mean an attempt by the local administration to patronize the district.'[31] The figures for the plan for 1971 to 1975 had not yet been given out and, therefore, the district felt unable to commit itself to any long-term programme that would set down obligations in terms of finances and capacities. Also, the hierarchical order was to be kept at any cost, even though the initiative was essential for Premnitz and the CFW, which was struggling with high staff turnover rates and a shortage of employees at that time. The plant's expansion plans were at stake. That seemingly final refusal, however, was not the end of the matter.

By 1970 the CFW had begun very close co-operation with local government agencies, which even included the ideological and professional training of all teachers and educational staff with support from the plant and the delegation of pedagogic staff to schools in

Premnitz.[32] In 1970 legal changes to community politics replaced the annual community contracts, from 1968 to 1970, with agreements for five years in advance, and later even for a decade.[33] By 1971, 35 employees of the CFW represented the interests of the state-owned factory in Premnitz. Of those, seven were town councillors. Many community groups combining representatives of the town and of the CFW were working on issues such as accommodation and childcare.[34] In the same year, contracts with eight towns and communities were drawn up. In addition, the plant had some influence on local politics, with 85 local representatives amongst its employees.

Although such influence was unable to guarantee the fulfilment of the plans, the regional strength of a state-owned factory could put pressure on local government which, in the face of insufficient funds from central sources, was forced to rely on the financial and institutional prowess of local industry.[35] This situation was a concern for central authorities. In the late 1960s and early 1970s legal changes were introduced that were intended to strengthen central influence on, and standardization of, social initiatives.

There were no fundamental changes in programmes for the improvement of working and living conditions visible from 1966 onwards until 1980; even the same structure was kept. What changed towards the late 1960s and early 1970s, however, was the close co-operation with local government administrations. This trend was part of an increasing standardization of the programmes for the improvement of working and living conditions and, possibly, a method employed to ensure the centralization of related projects in state-owned factories. An increase in co-operation and changes in legal conditions also meant that town councils became more self-confident and demanding during the 1970s, as legal rulings had ensured that they were included in the planning process. With regard to the CFW, this proved to be in the interests of the plant, whose works director had tried for some time to expand co-operation with local and district administrations. The rapid establishment of commissions and later the directorate also reflected this strong concern for the improvement of working and living conditions for the workforce and their families, wherever they worked and lived. Linked to the focus on working and living conditions was a growing influence on regional developments and the rise of stability. It is remarkable, however, that these processes took place in spite of the concerns of the party's district organization in Potsdam.

The case of the CFW, in spite of the almost ideal picture it presented of the implementation and routinization of central policy, also gives an indication of potential differentiation. The management team's interest in Premnitz and the surrounding area was neither a special case nor did it represent the norm. The same can be said of the clash with the SED at the district level. It was one of the possible experiences of a state-owned factory of little political or economic influence within the East German economy. For other state-owned factories, such as the HFO, co-operation with local administrations for the provision of social and cultural facilities was less successful. As has been pointed out in the previous chapter, the HFO had great difficulty in keeping up its support for related initiatives and even exceeded its budgets when trying to do so in the 1970s. The 1970s was a demanding decade for most state-owned factories, not to speak of private firms.[36]

Surviving the 1970s: the containment of decline

As has been pointed out in relation to the trials and tribulations encountered by Danz, the CFW was forced to deal with a variety of problems throughout the early 1970s. It is only to be expected that these reflected upon working conditions and were felt by most of the workforce. In July 1972, for example, a discussion about the situation in the new production halls was held with a member of the ZK SED. A whole list of complaints was presented, which indicated that criticism had accumulated over some time without being addressed sufficiently by the CFW's management. One major criticism was that the '*Sozialist-ischer Wettbewerb*' had been badly organized in the new production halls and that this had led to egalitarianism that was not conducive to productivity. For example, the best workers were not recognized and the supervisor had to be begged to give an evaluation of the contest. To explain this interest, it is necessary to know that it gives an indication of what kind of bonuses the workforce could expect. Workers also felt that they were insufficiently informed by management and that those who were working on innovations received no support. Furthermore, it was alleged that serious tensions between female workers and their mostly male supervisors had built up. It was demanded that more female supervisors should be appointed, who were expected to have a better understanding of women's needs. In addition, there was criticism with regard to transportation from and to work and in relation to the provision of meals. In conclusion, the BPO was criticized for its obvious lack of knowledge in relation to the real situation in the new production halls. The accusation of 'serious shortcomings in political work', at the end of the report, was the appropriate condemnation to ensure at least some reaction higher up in the economic and political hierarchy.[37]

In addition to the list of issues put forward by an embittered workforce in 1972, another major problem was the implementation of the programmes for the improvement of working and living conditions under Honecker.

Honecker's explicit use of social policy as a political tool changed the position of state-owned factories with regard to the implementation of the improvement of working and living conditions. Crucially, the regime restricted the social initiative of the factories' management teams by propagating the importance of and, coincidentally, taking on the responsibility for, the standard of living in East Germany. At the same time, the redistribution of investment and a lack of capacity forced state-owned factories to either limit their programmes for the improvement of working and living conditions or provide funds for only the most essential projects. The HFO's trade union organization, for example, complained in 1972 that the plan for the improvement of working and living conditions was being treated as an onerous appendage to the economic plan and not the crucial part that it was supposed to be.[38] This situation was exacerbated in 1974, when various economic units encountered major financial difficulties and drastic measures to save money had to be introduced.[39] In most cases, this meant that social or cultural projects were cancelled or delayed. In contrast to repeated demands to reveal the results achieved through the plan for the improvement of working and living conditions, requests to make public the decline in funding under Honecker were suppressed. The consequences for a state-owned factory and its workforce were reflected in an increase in staff turnover and sickness levels.

The development of the *Kultur- und Sozialfonds*, which funded most social and cultural projects, highlighted this decline. At the CFW, this fund stagnated at 8.2 per cent of the plant's income from 1974 onwards.[40] In 1962 it had been at a very low 1.2 per cent, which had risen to 4.6 per cent in 1965, rising noticeably in 1967, only to decline again in 1968. 1969 and 1970 saw an increase, the fund reaching 6 per cent of income in 1970.[41] Under Honecker it reached 7.5 per cent in 1973 and then stayed at 8.2 per cent until at least 1976. In 1974 complaints were made with regard to insufficient funding and disastrous working conditions, leading to high turnover rates in the weaving section.[42] Furthermore, in 1975 the CFW's programme for the improvement of working and living conditions was not secured financially.[43] In that year, central orders kept investment to an absolute minimum.[44] One year later, a report to the management team stated that there was some need to catch up on social policy and the building of accommodation blocks that had been neglected previously.[45] By 1979 the state-owned factory was unable to support the regional administration financially, in spite of central policy demanding co-operation; apparently this had already been a problem in the previous year.[46]

These trends correlated closely with developments at the HFO Frankfurt/Oder, which was allocated 2 per cent of its general income for the *Kultur- und Sozialfonds* in 1961. This was more than usual and only possible because of special permission, which the VVB revoked the following year.[47] An increase in funding in the middle of the 1960s can be assumed, although there are no exact numbers provided in the archives. Nevertheless, in 1971 the HFO had to deal with various cuts in investment funds. In December, a cut of 20 million Marks threatened the realization of social measures.[48] In 1974, the HFO ran into financial difficulties by spending too much on the improvement of working and living conditions.[49] From 1975 onwards, just as was happening in Premnitz at the same time, the HFO recorded that the allocated budgets were insufficient even to keep up those levels of working and living conditions that had been achieved in the previous decade.[50] Its complaint, and demands for further money made to the VVB, did not yield any improvement to the HFO's financial situation.[51] This decline was reflected in a comment from a brigade's diary, which noted in 1978 that it had taken three years of repeated demands for the improvement of working conditions in a specific production hall to take place. They also linked the draughty and cold working environment to high levels of sick leave among women working in that specific hall.[52]

Levels of sickness and turnover of staff began to increase again in the 1970s. In the early to mid 1960s both turnover and sickness rates had been higher than planned for by most firms. In the 1960s this had been a major factor prompting individual works directors to invest in the improvement of working and living conditions, with the result that both turnover rates and sickness leave tended to decline in 1967. The CFW, for example, recorded a rate of 5.11 per cent sickness leave in 1966 but only 4.86 per cent in 1967.[53] In 1969, however, rates had risen beyond planned figures again, reaching 5.77 per cent in 1969 and 6.58 per cent in 1970 (partly caused by a bout of flu). For both years, a rate of 5 per cent had been planned. In addition, turnover rates had reached a very high level, between 16 and 20 per cent per annum by 1969.[54] Interestingly and perhaps typically for the Honecker period, from 1971 onwards planned rates were higher, at 5.95 per cent and 6 per cent in 1972 and 1973 respectively, and therefore able to accommodate real rates (up to 5.98 per cent in 1973). The plan was being fulfilled even though rates had risen continuously for some years, as one report rightly pointed out in 1974.[55] In 1978, 6.53 per cent and in 1979 a high count of 6.72 per cent were reached.[56] Clearly the situation at the CFW was acute by the end of the 1970s.

In addition to the turnover rates and levels of sickness that have been cited above, a continuous lack of resources, technical disruptions and breakdowns at the plant undermined the production process. The works director was carefully wording his appraisal of the situation when he pointed out that, in spite of these hindrances, performance had turned out to be 'positive'.[57] This kind of positivist language reflected habits that had developed over many years of pressure to succeed, or at least to be seen to be successful in spite of obvious problems. It prevented open discussion and constructive criticism whilst presenting a false picture of economic achievement, which many recognized and resented for what it was: empty propaganda slogans.

It is apparent that Honecker's approach to social policy not only led to overspending centrally but also, from the middle of the 1970s onwards, to dangerous levels of indebtedness, which historians have recognized for some years now.[58] In addition to this, it is crucial to acknowledge the consequences of the redistribution of investment and capacities that were introduced very early in Honecker's reign. By undermining the social projects of state-owned factories, their stabilizing role within the economic and political system of the East German dictatorship was severely limited. Furthermore, stagnation and decline were encountered by most economic units in the late 1970s and were clearly communicated to the workforce through deteriorating working conditions, interrupted production processes, drastic savings measures and a noticeable lack of progress, both in terms of technology and productivity. The order of the day had become the containment of decline; the enthusiasm that arguably had lingered throughout the 1960s finally fell apart.

Conclusion

The CFW was one of the many state-owned factories of lesser status within the East German economic system. This had an impact not only on its dealings with local and district administrations but also on its standing in relation to institutions higher up in the economic hierarchy such as the VVB or, later, the management of the *Kombinat* and the Ministry for Chemical Industries. Within and without the CFW, its works director had a much weaker position than, for example, Werner Frohn at the EVW. This was highlighted by the attitude of the CFW's first party secretary and the discussions with Potsdam's SED BL. Nevertheless, the state-owned factory commanded some influence in and around Premnitz.

Social and cultural activity at the CFW was especially important to its position in the region. Besides being the one and only major employer in this primarily rural setting, the plant in Premnitz put a great deal in terms of finance capacities and effort into the improvement of working and living conditions during the 1960s. To a great extent, this strategy had had economic motives as it was intended to reduce high staff turnover rates and sickness levels in the middle of that decade. At the same time, it also encouraged a strong, almost emotional, bond between the CFW and its workforce, which even seems to have outlasted the plant's closure in the 1990s. It became more difficult in the 1970s to keep up this social and cultural effort at the CFW – a trend that was typical of most state-owned factories. As a result of the shifts in investment and the lack of capacities caused by Honecker's unity of social and economic policy, state-owned factories encountered difficulties in maintaining their programmes for the improvement of working and living conditions, although co-operation with local administrations improved after the late 1960s. More so than high-status factories, the CFW had already felt the full force of these changes in the early 1970s, leading to rising staff turnover rates and high levels of sickness by the middle of the 1970s. Throughout the 1970s, economic achievement became more difficult for the plant.

In one sense, the CFW is a perfect example of the struggles of a low status, provincial state-owned factory, which takes on responsibility for the social context in which it is situated and, thereby, achieves some standing within the local area. In contrast to high-status plants, the CFW's production of artificial textiles was economically less important than the processing of crude oil, with all the consequences for wage levels and central investment. Social activity at the CFW was even more necessary to ensure a steady supply of workers as wages were low and alternative employment in Potsdam or Berlin not entirely out of reach. Furthermore, investment in social and cultural projects tended to exhaust the plant's financial and material possibilities, certainly more so than seemed to be necessary in Berlin, Schwedt or even Frankfurt/Oder, which benefited from central investment policies. In addition, the CFW was made part of a large *Kombinat*, the *VEB Chemiefaserkombinat Schwarza*, but was never a primary factory. Therefore, the plant was dependent on the decisions of its general director not only regarding the allocation of funds but also in relation to economic decisions. The CFW was not particularly neglected but neither did it receive the attention of central authorities that would have been required for long-term economic success within the East German economic system.

The differences between state-owned factories, which have been described in five case studies, will provide the frame in which to view the next chapter. Much attention has been given to conflicts between central authorities and management teams, which were often based on either the shortcomings of central policy, or changes to central policy, or an inability, and sometimes unwillingness, to implement central policy. Also, it has become apparent that state-owned factories had to deal with a variety of problems over the years, the extent of which depended on the individual characteristics of every single concern, its location, status, workforce and managers. Accordingly, the solutions demanded or sought differed widely and were closely linked to the specific potential of every factory. In the following chapter, the focus will be primarily on conflicts that occurred within state-owned factories. Internal tensions flaring up among the workforce or in relation to the management's expectations and decisions will be central to the analysis.

Voices

J.G. (born 1947): female, supervisor (finished school at 16):

> When I came to the CFW in Premnitz in 1964, this was still a self-sufficient world. There were 7500 employees. The factory maintained a nursery (garden centre), a butcher, a piggery, a hospital, two dentists, a laundry, childcare facilities, cultural centres, sports facilities, a large accommodation block for apprentices, a school for vocational training, a library, a bath house, five canteens and so on... The CFW had flats [for its employees] and financed almost all sporting and social initiatives for the town of Premnitz ...
>
> The CFP slowly lost its independence after its integration into a *Kombinat*. The workforce noticed these changes because decision making processes took longer. Also, funds were provided less generously. It was noticeable that decisions were made elsewhere. The plan figures were set higher and higher every year although the necessary technical preconditions did not provide for such growth. Technical equipment that had been installed was only serviced and repaired. There was no investment or modernization ...

Within our family, we talked a lot about the CFW even after work. Each family member knew about the job, the colleagues and the working environment of the others and could come to his or her own conclusions. That did not mean, however, that we were always of one mind. In the nearly 30 years that we worked at the CFW together, work and private life were often indistinguishable. It was not just 'earning money', it was life.

S.D. (born 1931): male, chemist (chemist diploma), member of the NDPD since 1950:

Social relations and politics:
My relations with the workers were good; I came from a working class background myself. However, management became more difficult with a diploma of vocational training or higher education as one was qualified beyond the working class. When I criticized or even punished a worker's omissions or misdemeanour too severely, according to his opinion, then he would go to the SED or the trade union and would ensure that I was disciplined for anti-working-class behaviour or for being bourgeois.

Normal life:
Every society has its 'rules of the game'; those of the GDR were clear, could be calculated and were severe but consistent.

The party [SED] got involved in everything, it was omnipresent and ruthless. Open attacks were hopeless and dangerous. One could avoid some things secretly and with cunning (rules of the game). For example, I saw how one party secretary refused to allow a party member to attend the funeral of his mother because there was a party meeting scheduled. The misuse of power by some party functionaries was to some extent obvious but no party member dared to intervene.

U.L. (born 1945): female, technologist (finished school at 16, chemist diploma):

I was already a member of the FDJ and the DTSB [German Gymnastics and Sports Union] at school; as an apprentice we were immediately asked to join the trade union and the DSF [Union of German–Soviet Friendship]. The contributions we had to pay were very low and therefore one did not mind joining. In my mind, they would have 'worked' on us until we said 'yes' anyway ... Membership of the SED was for many engineers the path towards a rapid career. I was and still am satisfied that I was then and remain today without a party membership ...

What annoyed me, for example, was the 'School of Socialist Work'; the themes were impossible, therefore one tried to make the best of it. For the theme 'Soviet working methods' only the title was read out; for the remaining time, I showed slides of a journey along the Black Sea coast. This was possible within a small work group at a factory producing artificial silk.

P.H. (born 1931): male, engineer (university education):

One tried to avoid conflicts.

7
Conflicts and Solutions

This chapter will consider two main issues in order to highlight the kind of conflict that might have had an impact on everyday working life in state-owned factories, and what solutions were offered to deal with the problems encountered by the workforce or the management. In the first part of the chapter, some attention will be given to general problems that were encountered. For example, the workers' attitude to work and working primarily for bonuses rather than for socialist ideals was discussed repeatedly throughout the 1960s, leading to some changes in central policy under Honecker. But also, sheer exhaustion, especially among female employees or the highest echelons of business management, were issues of concern. In addition, theft and financial fraud were recurring problems that had to be tackled. In the second half, special focus will be put on the type of problem that was made into an issue by the workforce. Helke Stadtland has described some of the major areas of conflict that affected the relationship between workforce and management from the late 1940s, such as working time and wages.[1] Working and living conditions also received great attention. Throughout this chapter, methods to solve problems will be discussed. Here, two major trends are discernible. On the one hand, educational measures were implemented to encourage the socialist consciousness of the workforce and, thereby, stimulate productivity and maintain social peace. On the other hand, punishment and criminalization were used to deflect or avoid conflicts. This latter method was not, as may perhaps be assumed at first glance, employed only by management or central authorities to suppress defiant workers. Rather, even among colleagues, for example in brigades, group pressure could be enormous and was often used to subordinate wayward individuals. Both sections will have to consider change over time in order to do justice to the changing importance of problems and the different approaches to the finding of solutions.

Renate Hürtgen has argued that management increasingly tried to individualize protests and keep them out of the public domain if at all possible.[2] Apparently, the basic rules of the game, such as avoiding publicity, acting spontaneously rather than planning strikes, and focusing on non-political issues, had already been learned by the late 1950s, enabling the workforce to avoid open confrontation whilst still voicing its concerns.[3] Furthermore, Hürtgen suggests that by the 1970s workers' interests were put forward individually, for example by using petitions, rather than as a group.[4] With time, strikes almost entirely disappeared from the factories.

However, even in the 1970s and 1980s, collective forms of opting out or refusing to accept changes to working conditions still existed. Higher norms or lower wages, different working hours or reductions in social benefits were issues that workers felt strongly about and dealt with by concealed resistance, such as holding back innovative work methods in order to prevent an increase in norms. Also, improvements that had either been promised by the management or were central policy were rigorously demanded by the workforce.

To illustrate these more antagonistic aspects of working life, a variety of specific cases that occurred in these five state-owned factories will be described in order to highlight the various conflicts and solutions encountered by the separate workforces and management teams. Although general factors, applicable to most economic units within the East German economic system, will be shown, much attention will be allotted to more specific issues that were, perhaps, relevant only to one of the state-owned factories under consideration. This will enable the reader to differentiate and will make it possible for the author to combine general concepts with individual experiences. It will be argued that conflicts, and the solutions applied to conflict situations, were not only largely dependent on central policy; they were also delineated by the characteristics of each individual state-owned factory and they changed over time. In summary, it is unhelpful to generalize on the subject of conflicts and solutions. Rather, differentiation and a continuous development marked the experiences of the workforce at least as much as more general trends.

Before launching into the main questions outlined above, it is crucial to stress that the origins of conflict varied immensely. For one thing, according to Alf Lüdtke who devised the concept, the *Eigen-Sinn* of the production worker was based on priorities that differed from the main concerns of economic, party or trade union functionaries. It seems only a logical conclusion that conflicts and attempts to solve them diverged widely depending on both origin and context. *Eigen-Sinn* could affect every part of any state-owned factory in many different ways.

Eigen-Sinn

Eigen-Sinn describes a state of mind focused solely on individual interests; it becomes paramount to ensure an advantage for oneself or a small group, such as a brigade, within the circumstances of everyday life.[5] The difference between *Eigen-Sinn* and power needs to be stressed: *Eigen-Sinn* stays within given limits or limits stretched just enough to allow for the realization of individual interests, but not to challenge boundaries outright. To give a simple example: the smoking of a cigarette or eating a sandwich whilst working on machines is generally forbidden in factories, for safety reasons mostly but also to ensure high productivity. A worker who smokes or eats in spite of such rules gains an advantage because the act gives him or her a little comfort during a strenuous working day. However, workers will try very hard to avoid detection when defying the limits set by the management. They do not challenge the rules; just try to bend them according to their own interests. Nevertheless, *Eigen-Sinn* is a political act and can be very powerful, as Lüdtke and others have pointed out.[6] Arguably, it forced economic, social and cultural adjustments in the GDR during the 1960s and 1970s and brought about the collapse of the idealism within socialism.

Eigen-Sinn can also been described as a problem of competing standards, suggesting that the concept can be applied not only to one specific group of people, such as workers in a state-owned factory, but also to all layers of a population both within and without a factory environment.[7] The individual interests of a production worker simply differed from those of the works director. Officially, the rules were set by the works director and would be tested by the workforce, which would try to make itself comfortable within the given circumstances, if these were not too trying, without starting a revolt. The rules of the game were delineated by compromises intended to suit both parties. Often, however, both sides would carve out their own small space in which individual interests could be realized.

In addition, the position of an East German employee differed from his/her counterpart in Western societies because of ideological tenets. In the GDR the right to work was guaranteed by the constitution.

Within Marxism–Leninism, the working class occupies the primary role in terms of political progress. At least in theory, workers in the East German economy should have had great influence on both structures and proceedings within state-owned factories, of which they were co-owners. These basic principles, in combination with some of the shortcomings of the centrally planned system, such as soft norms, strengthened the self-confidence of workers. Perhaps this was one reason why individual East German workers were not reluctant to exercise *Eigen-Sinn* to define their own space within their immediate surroundings, the borders of which were controlled by responsible functionaries, as Thomas Lindenberger has pointed out. Crucially, however, East Germans were prepared to defend their space even beyond these borders and against a higher authority.[8] It needs to be stressed that these borders were easily permeated and that the East German population seems to have delighted in approaching the highest political authorities in order to demand a solution to their individual problems. The relationship between the East German population and the East German state was certainly more complex than suggested by an approach that limits the impact of workers' *Eigen-Sinn* to the shaping of somebody's individual space. It can be argued that the East German working population significantly influenced central policy.

In the following sections, general problems, the specific concerns of the workforce and methods to solve problems will be analysed in relation to the arguments laid out above. In this way, attention will be drawn to general trends, the differences between the individual state-owned factories, and changes over time. This approach will help to focus on the everyday experiences of the workforce. It will also accommodate a consideration of the power of the workforce within the centrally planned economic system of a socialist state.

General problems

One general problem that was an issue throughout the period under scrutiny was people's attitude to work. Marxist–Leninist ideology relies on a strong conviction that the workers, once they have been enlightened about their class affiliation and the role of the working class as a progressive force, will begin to work not solely for their individual interests but for the betterment of a socialist society as a whole. In this model, according to these tenets, a marked difference to capitalism can be seen. In the latter everybody is working solely for their own good and the proletariat is, for the most part, not even conscious of its slave status or of being exploited by the owners of the means of production – that is to say, anybody employing wage-labourers and making a profit from their business. Therefore, the main priority of the East German Communist Party was to create so-called 'socialist personalities': people who were willing to contribute selflessly to a better future for all. Everyone was expected to fill a position in a socialist society, whether as a functionary or a production worker, to the best of their ability without asking much in terms of financial or material rewards in return. The planned economic system was intended to support these notions by distributing resources, labour and profits according to the needs of the people's state. The economy was crucial to the success of the socialist state; productivity was a catchword for both Ulbricht and Honecker, although their methods differed.

In spite of these theoretically honourable aims of the socialist state, the practice was much more problematic. On the shop floor, achieving high productivity proved difficult. In most state-owned factories, employees were driven by material interests, not ideological fervour. Ulbricht recognized this in the early 1960s by allowing managers to use financial and material bonuses to reward superior efforts. Also, highly qualified staff benefited from changes in the wage system introduced during the NES period. In addition, the new drive to improve working and living conditions was intended to encourage employees at all levels to work more productively. In the 1970s Honecker set much store on a similar tactic by offering higher standards of living in the hope of achieving an increase in productivity. However, employees remained reluctant to invest more effort than was necessary for them to receive a good wage. The wage system already included many bonuses as a standard and therefore proved not very efficient in encouraging higher productivity. Also, strenuous working conditions and interrupted production processes undermined enthusiasm, although it cannot and should not be denied that most employees tried to make the best of very difficult circumstances.

Nevertheless, wages, working conditions and attitudes to work were a constant source of conflict between the workforce and management. In many cases, both sides blamed the other for difficulties in keeping up productivity, citing a lack of work ethics or organizational inability as the main reasons for interruptions to the production process. In particular, brigade diaries from the early 1960s, in spite of all the source problems attached to this medium, tended to illustrate such everyday conflicts vividly.[9] For example, in 1961 the first document referring to the problems of the brigade 'Käthe Kollwitz' at the BGW remarked on the rejects brigade members had been producing. They promised to solve this problem. However, the brigade also insisted: 'In our opinion, we should also expect a new style of work from our economic functionaries and colleagues working in the purchasing department.'[10]

Conflict resolution?

Alongside management efforts to improve the supply of materials, recruit more people or offer training courses to the workforce, complaints were also often ignored or, in some cases, political pressure was exerted to suppress criticism. In the early 1960s, after some initial enthusiasm that was visible in brigades' efforts to make management aware of their everyday problems on the shop floor, individual production workers and entire brigades gradually reached the conclusion that the slogan '*Arbeite mit, plane mit, regiere mit*' (Work together, plan together, govern together) was nothing more than political propaganda and not applicable to reality.[11]

On the other side, central authorities were quick, sometimes too quick, to blame economic functionaries for not responding more readily to workers' complaints, although the problems encountered in factories were often not of their making, as for example when wages were kept low, materials were not supplied or old machines could not be replaced for lack of finance or capacity. The argument central authorities liked to put forward when they were made aware of problems in state-owned factories was that 'political and ideological work' with the workforce had not been sufficient. Tensions had arisen not for practical reasons but because of a lack of political knowledge; functionaries had failed to enlighten workers about the ideological background of any problems or new central policies, and the workers could not therefore be blamed for complaining.

In 1962, for example, a report by the industrial trade union *IG Metall* on tensions in a Berlin factory, *VEB Bergmann Borsig*, highlighted a combination of the problems described above. The report related partly to complaints about low standards of living and partly to the plans of the government to introduce a six-day working week. The workers were angry not only about these two larger issues but also complained about transportation, the provision of meals and social care. They also felt that they had no influence at all on central policy decisions, the criticism being that workers were never asked about their opinions, and that the trade union was not at all supportive on these questions. Furthermore, they voiced their reluctance to say any more 'because the

Stasi would come to get us'.[12] In this particular case, people had actually refused to work for a few hours – a situation to which central authorities tended to react fairly quickly.[13] There was, therefore, a real threat that the Stasi would get involved, which would not have been in the interests of either the workers or the responsible functionaries. Functionaries at all levels had to tread very carefully to avoid full-blown conflicts that could have turned into a strike or, at least, a walkout.

Since 17 June 1953 strikes had been greatly dreaded by the political elite, which therefore put much pressure on economic functionaries at all levels to ensure that conflicts would not be allowed to escalate. This was what happened at the Berlin factory. The criticism from the central authorities was that political work with the workforce had been neglected and, thereby, unnecessary tensions had been caused.[14] To combat this problem, the SED presence in the trade union was to be increased, some replacements were to be made to strengthen political influence and, in the future, the selection of functionaries was to be made more carefully. The problems at the heart of the workforce's complaints were not dealt with.[15] Neither the angry workforce nor the factory's functionaries received support; no measures were implemented to solve the practical problems that had been highlighted by the strike. Rather, political pressure within the factory was increased.

It does not seem surprising then that a strong tendency to solve problems internally without the involvement of central authorities emerged, and that *Eigen-Sinn* was given so much space within state-owned factories. Solutions to such general conflicts were mostly looked for in the shape of compromises, often in the interests of the workforce.[16] Dismissals were used only very rarely as a punishment, at least from the middle of the 1960s, partly because of a lack of labour and partly because of political considerations. For management it was extremely difficult to enforce redundancy because the law required the employer to provide a substitute place of work suitable to the abilities of the person in question.

Other issues linked to work discipline were unnecessary sick leave, arriving at work too late or causing work accidents because of non-adherence to health and safety measures. Members of the offender's brigade were responsible for dealing with these problems. In some cases, mostly those the brigade felt unable or unwilling to deal with, or those that dealt with repeated or serious misdemeanours, the conflict commission was involved to decide on the legal aspects and possible punishments or educational efforts that were to be applied. For example, if a colleague was repeatedly late for work, not interested in fulfilling his norm and had not responded to offers of help or pressure from other members of the brigade, the case could be passed on to the conflict commission. In one such case at the TRO, a wayward worker was moved into a different department and it was recommended he should be encouraged to further his qualifications.[17]

Conflict commissions had to be set up in every factory with over 200 employees.[18] Their members were elected by the workforce and were given the task of solving minor conflicts caused by employees of any position. These conflicts, however, did not have to be solely related to his or her place of work and otherwise may even have gone to a proper court.[19] For example, a car accident involving an employee could be dealt with by the conflict commission as well as disagreements over wages, contracts or other issues affecting both management and the workforce. In the follow-up to work accidents, especially those that resulted in a financial loss for the factory, the colleagues involved would be heard by the conflict commission and, if found guilty of negligence, had to repay all costs. However, the conflict commission was generally quite lenient and tended to adopt an educational role rather than focusing on severe punishment.[20]

Theft, or the changing priorities of *Eigen-Sinn*

As well as such general issues, other more specific problems occurred in every state-owned factory. Theft of material or equipment was one such issue, particularly in a shortage economy and within a political system that claimed to have introduced people's co-ownership for almost everything. For many it was only a small step to taking what could not be obtained easily in the shops. In many cases, theft of that kind was looked upon mildly by co-workers, who often had the same problems in finding essential goods. Sometimes, brigades would even cover for their members from higher authorities, even if money had been stolen from the brigade's own funds, and rather preferred to deal with the problem internally.[21] Although protection was a key role of the brigades, what was felt to be not acceptable was theft from colleagues, or other behaviour that undermined mutual trust and, thereby, the unity of the group.[22]

Lüdtke's concept of *Eigen-Sinn* becomes slippery here; the strict differentiation between theft from the state-owned factory and theft from colleagues could have been reflective of a simplistic attitude that pitted the state against society and vice versa. In Lüdtke's study of factory life in the late nineteenth and early twentieth centuries, theft from colleagues is described as a possible aspect of *Eigen-Sinn*. However, in the GDR, arguably, group dynamics played a greater role, thereby forbidding theft from colleagues more strongly than perhaps had been the case in the period from the German empire to the Third Reich.[23] In addition to posing a moral issue, it acquired political connotations.

Theft existed at all levels. One kind of theft was financial fraud, sometimes used by works directors and their accountants to cover up unfulfilled plans or unauthorized debt in order to avoid unpleasant encounters with the central authorities. In the 1970s and 1980s, semi-legal dealings with other state-owned factories were mostly used to procure essential materials and the increase of capacities in order to counteract rising economic problems. These transactions were also hidden in adjusted accounts. Such activities were in the interests of works directors or other economic functionaries concerned about being made responsible for their company's, section's or department's economic failure. Fraud of this kind was also beneficial to the workforce at large, seen in the short term of course. In the long term such unplanned activities wrecked even the last hope of central planning to calculate economic correlations accurately. In the short term, however, co-operation between state-owned factories in order to counterbalance the shortcomings of the East German economy ensured the workforce's bonuses, continued production and a relatively quiet life without interference from central authorities. Here, we are confronted with a complex pattern of political, economic and moral issues which were modified according to changing circumstances. The question that needs to be asked is not only what *Eigen-Sinn* is comprised of in different socio-political systems, but also how and why it is adjusted over time.

In the early 1960s the *Eigen-Sinn* of the workforce, from production worker to technological or administrative staff, focused mostly on achieving reasonable working and living conditions in very difficult circumstances. By the late 1970s, the workforce's open criticism of the 1960s had turned into a constant undercurrent of grumbling and a strong reluctance to get involved in any effort to solve problems. The experience of the previous two decades had taught most employees to deal with existing circumstances rather than to demand improvements and, possibly, risk criminalization in a situation which, by many, was seen to be hopeless. Economic functionaries felt equally inclined to reduce the possibility of open conflict by individualizing complaints and taking short-term measures to minimize tensions. Generally, functionaries dealing directly with the workforce, such as the foremen

(*Meister*), compromised with the workforce's smaller demands by, for example, offering more than standard pay for overtime or writing down more overtime than had actually been worked when necessary.[24] In this way, the production plans were fulfilled, often pulling in the workforce on short notice when long-delayed raw materials arrived at last, and the workforce was kept both working and quiet. In the long term, this attitude undermined the East German economy although such complaining seems a logical consequence of both the politicization of economic issues in the GDR and the state-owned factories' changing circumstances in the 1960s and 1970s.

Eigen-Sinn is a multi-faceted concept that is useful to describe the subtle powers of the East German workforce within state-owned factories. Moreover, it highlights the issues that were of importance to the working population, such as wages, working and living conditions, and the methods used to realize these primary interests within a socialist dictatorship. Increasingly during the 1960s and certainly during the 1970s, open conflict was avoided in favour of compromises, and expectations were geared towards possibilities based on the Communist Party's own ideological orientation and not unreasonable hopes. Within political limits, much was achievable by employing subtle methods adjusted to the fears and hopes of the socialist system.

Moreover, a case can be made for the notion that *Eigen-Sinn* adjusts to changing circumstances, both in terms of workers' interests and the methods employed. Naturally, industrial work exhibits characteristics that have not changed very much since the beginning of industrialization. The human being working on machines is subordinated to the rhythm of both the factory time plan and the machinery. Stealing some time for a cigarette or a break, generally during working hours, is still of supreme importance for many production workers even today and throughout the world. However, in the GDR's state-owned factories working conditions changed throughout the 1960s and 1970s, arguably, at least in part, as a reaction to the demands of the East German working population. As a result, workers' primary interests were adjusted: if basic working conditions improve, other issues move to the forefront of concern. Standards, therefore, can change. Also, methods to push through individual interests were altered in response, for example, to new legislation, economic restructuring such as that caused by the creation of *Kombinate*, or political re-orientation such as followed Honecker's rise to power, and also in reaction to changes in the roles of both trade unions and state-owned factories. Much has been said already about Ulbricht's economic reforms in the 1960s and

Honecker's policies during the 1970s. Particularly the improvement of working and living conditions has been discussed repeatedly in order to highlight changes in relation to both the position of the working population and the role of the state-owned factory within the East German economic system. By the 1970s, demands regarding working and living conditions were being voiced more forcefully than in the 1960s because legally binding rules had been established that could be called upon by the workforce. Although these rights were not necessarily realized, expectations had changed dramatically.

In summary, these rights were implemented in reaction to the *Eigen-Sinn* of the workforce, thereby undermining the idealism of the socialist creed. Also, the focus of *Eigen-Sinn* adjusted to changing conditions, thereby continuously applying pressure to the socialist system. *Eigen-Sinn* modified circumstances, and is therefore a political act, as Lüdtke has pointed out.

Work, politics and private life intertwining

In this section, it will be argued that the growing entwining of private, professional and political life led to a new tendency, whereby conflicts of any kind were avoided and, accordingly, solutions were not found. In the long term, an undercurrent of disillusionment, resentment and tension was established, which was based on cynicism towards the ideas of progress, social fairness and participation that reflected SED slogans of the 1960s. Particularly, membership of mass organizations and parties, but also of brigades, necessarily led to an individual's greater involvement in political structures. Also, the exposure of a person's private life to group dynamics and external control was increased by joining any political, cultural or professional grouping.

Changes to central policy, such as the aim to become autarkic in combination with the building of the wall in 1961, had a marked impact on everyday life in the state-owned factories. Practical implications were, for example, that materials either were not available or were replaced from other sources, and were often of lesser quality. This partly explains the great difficulties state-owned factories experienced in the first years of the 1960s in ensuring continuous production. In those years, many or most factory directors were forced to accept compromises with the workforce regarding norms, as was shown with the TRO, or made deals offering high bonuses to fulfil the plan at least on paper. In the BGW, for example, brigades were offered a high financial reward in the early 1960s if they managed to reach a certain output.[25] In this way, the plan would be fulfilled officially although only in terms of output, not cost. The workforce generally took up these offers cheerfully because it meant getting more money, and the management avoided conflicts. However, seen from the standpoint of economic efficiency such measures were clearly counter-productive.

In this context, the economic reforms were extremely necessary and unavoidable by 1963. At first, they highlighted and contributed to an already existing crisis and caused many factories to fail in fulfilling their plan. However, this also led to structural changes and created an urgent need and new motivation to improve the situation. From the middle of the 1960s onwards, a new discussion on norms began, from which it can be gleaned that the FDGB was unhappy to see that the economic functionaries, quite pragmatically, were prepared to forget about politics in state-owned factories and were primarily using the material interests of the workers to increase productivity.[26] In addition to this, the need to bind workers to their factory was recognized and social incentives were employed specifically to do this: childcare, FDGB holidays, hospitals and so on were all linked directly to individual state-owned factories.

Development within the factories showed various trends. With regard to the workforce, the connection between everyday life and work in the factories had clearly grown since the early 1960s, firstly building on the brigade movement and, secondly, from the middle of the 1960s onwards, on the basis of a conscious effort by the works directors to lower staff turnover rates by offering social, cultural and medical care to their workers. In various ways, work, politics and private life were inter-twining rapidly during these two decades. The strength which this bonding effort had achieved by the 1970s was reflected, for example, in petitions sent by wives of leading economic functionaries, who wrote to the works director to complain about their husbands working too much and spending too little time with their families. In one particular case from the early 1980s, the wife of an employee even asked for help with getting back her husband, who had begun a relationship with another woman. The answer was that the husband had been spoken to and encouraged to return to his wife but had refused to comply with the wishes of his superiors.[27] At that time, very personal issues seem to have become entangled with public life. This trend was accommodated by both the workforce, which was willing to use opportunities to enlist help from colleagues and superiors even regarding private concerns, and those willing to offer help beyond purely professional matters.

In addition, from the late 1960s a politicization of everyday life took place which also affected state-owned factories and their workforces. As has been argued in previous chapters, this trend increased the tensions between economic and political functionaries. The increase in political tasks, such as participation in party meetings and political education, had a negative influence on productivity.[28] Moreover, in reaction to this ideological onslaught, the majority of the East German population showed a marked reluctance to get involved in mass organizations, parties or even political functions beyond those perceived to be 'normal' and part of everyday life. 'Normal' in this context meant primarily that most people joined particular organizations almost automatically at certain crossroads in their lives: at a certain age or when taking up employment.[29] In contrast, joining the SED was considered much more carefully, as will be shown below.

Mass organizations and parties: getting involved in state structures

Although a very large percentage of East Germans were members of one or more of the various mass organizations, and thereby can be charged with getting involved in and upholding a dictatorship, subtle differences have to be acknowledged, both in terms of motivation to join such organizations and actual activity. In one sense, this behaviour can also be grouped under the heading of conflict avoidance, although the generally accepted mass organizations, such as the East German youth organization or the trade union, were perceived to be of little relevance to people's stance on ideology at the time. It can be argued that the indoctrination of the masses with the aims and principles of Marxism–Leninism through these organizations was not entirely unsuccessful.[30]

Independently of this and of greater relevance to most East Germans at the time, membership of mass organizations often provided benefits, such as entertainment for young people, educational courses (not just of a political orientation) and, offered particularly by the FDGB, cheap holidays. Mostly, participation in these organizations was necessary for leading a quiet life, in terms of not becoming noticed as potentially wayward or even dissident, even if activities were kept to the bare minimum.

People moved beyond such 'normality' by becoming a member of a particular party, especially taking up membership of the SED. Recruitment of members for the SED within state-owned factories, however, became difficult in the late 1960s as Kott points out in her study of Berlin factories.[31] Membership of the SED could advance one's career and, in the late 1960s, became a mostly unspoken of but generally known requirement for the more elevated posts, even within the economic sector. However, it also had much greater implications for an individual's political life.[32] Possibly, membership of mass organizations or any of the East German parties also changed attitudes to conflict resolution.

During the 1960s the number of members of mass organizations rose pretty consistently. Membership became routine. The East German population became increasingly involved in state structures and, thereby, more controllable. Similarly, the workforce became more disciplined during the 1960s, mostly with the help of soft measures such as bonuses, but also as a result of educational processes. Simply getting used to the rhythm of industrial work, particularly its strict time management, had a noticeable impact on the workforce in this decade. Factories which existed before the war, such as the TRO and the BGW, worked in a different way compared to new factories such as the EVW or very provincial factories such as the CFW. In the two latter cases, recruits tended to be either very young or come from an agrarian background, which meant that labour traditions were almost non-existent in these state-owned factories. Variations in the expression of *Eigen-Sinn*, as well as in the workers' emotional link to the respective factories and their work, resulted from such different characteristics and this forced works directors to establish priorities specific to their situation in dealing with their employees in order to ensure low staff turnover rates and high productivity.

However, active membership of parties, especially the SED, does not seem to have had a marked impact on behaviour patterns in relation to conflicts. By the late 1970s SED members seem to have been equally reluctant to bring problems to the attention of the party as non-members were, who generally showed little inclination towards open confrontation in the 1970s. Furthermore, some of the major mass organizations, such as the FDJ and the East German Women's Union (DFD), experienced a slump or, as in the case of the DFD, a stagnation in membership numbers in the late 1970s or early 1980s. This was dealt with by a recruitment campaign that mostly ignored the question of a potential member's (lack of) commitment.[33]

In contrast, SED members within state-owned factories may have felt more responsible for solving problems. Their membership of the SED exposed them to expectations and criticism from non-members, fellow party members and, probably, their own perception of an SED member's role. They were also in a slightly better position, in terms of both personal safety and status, to voice criticism, at least within certain limits and preferably within the party, and approach the right people or institutions to solve problems.[34] However, SED members were also closely scrutinized by their peers and were expected to adhere to a whole set of moral and political standards that were part of party discipline. In the case of misconduct, party proceedings would be instigated against the offending party member. During the proceedings, the party member in question would be heard and in most cases was given ample opportunity for self-criticism. Exclusion from the SED, which very often had dire consequences for the condemned's professional career, was the worst possible outcome of party proceedings.

Party proceedings took place at all levels of East German society, not only within state-owned factories but also within the Stasi[35] and at the higher levels of the economic, political and trade union hierarchy. In 1982, for example, the chief editor of the FDGB's newspaper *Tribüne* was reprimanded. Under the rubric 'Nuisances which bother us too', he had printed some selected quotations from the report of the Soviet Communist Party to its twenty-sixth party conference, which were deemed to criticize SED politics. A reprimand was only a fairly mild punishment, this being due to his profuse regrets. Nevertheless, he lost his post as chief editor in the aftermath of this affair.[36] Losing your professional position as a result of party proceedings was even more common than losing your cultural or political function,[37] which begs the question of the SED's primary purpose. It seems that party discipline was a useful tool with which to keep a hold even on party members in fairly high positions, even works directors, as we have seen with regard to Hermann Danz at the CFW.

In the later 1970s, at a time when many non-members were primarily interested in avoiding conflicts, SED members were also affected by the general disillusionment. According to statistics on party proceedings, the level of discontent was certainly rising in the late 1970s. In 1977 the SED's district organization in Potsdam, for example, noted an increase in proceedings in relation to subversive activity directed either at the state or the party. However, most of these cases were brought forward after an SED member had illegally left the GDR, which does not indicate that they had felt more comfortable in voicing criticism.[38] Nevertheless, it can be assumed that SED members were more likely to be scrutinized more closely than non-members with regard to their private life as much as their professional and political activity, and may have been more inclined to solve conflicts by using their membership as a tool and safety net. SED membership enforced a complex entanglement of public and private life, which was sought by the Communist Party but which at least some East Germans refused to accept.

Another path towards the growing interlacing of politics, work and private life was laid out by the brigade movement, which involved the majority of the working population. The following sub-section will consider the development of the second brigade movement in order to highlight the consequences for the conflict behaviour of the workforce. In looking at the collective spirit of brigades, a group of the East German population will be traced through changing times. It will be argued that individual interests were largely subsumed into the brigades' primary concerns during the 1960s but re-emerged somewhat in the middle to late 1970s as the brigade movement lost much of its initial meaning. Individualization grew in response to socio-economic changes that affected state-owned factories from the middle of the 1970s at the latest.

Brigades

The brigades were the immediate group for any employee, within which everyday problems such as working conditions surfaced most readily, were discussed and solved. Brigades could contain just a few members or, especially in the 1970s and 1980s, up to thirty and more colleagues. After the failure of the first brigade movement, which was dissolved by central authorities when it became too independent, the second brigade movement was started with some precautions in the late 1950s.[39] It was taken up enthusiastically by at least some groups of workers, who hoped to use it as a tool to find solutions for some matters of common interest, such as the improvement of working and living conditions, by drawing attention to problems affecting their working day.

The brigade movement in the 1960s and 1970s can be seen as a reflection of the advantages and disadvantages of 'normalization'. One advantage in this case was the growing stabilization during the 1960s, which in state-owned factories was partly accommodated by the creation of small groups of colleagues working together in the '*Sozialistischer Wettbewerb*' to achieve higher productivity. For individuals, brigades offered the security, protection and inter-personal relations of a social group within an immense economic unit. With time, some basic tenets of socialist society, such as team spirit and solidarity with those in need, seem to have shaped life in the brigades, at least to some extent. Brigade members depended on each other for high productivity, common cultural experiences and training measures, which were all part of the brigades' annual plans. The fulfilment of these plans meant bonuses and rewards. Within the difficult working conditions typical of the East German economy, co-operation between brigade members was necessary to fulfil plans of any kind; that some co-operation could quickly turn into group pressure on any wayward individuals, who refused to comply with the demands of the brigade.[40] Stabilization, therefore, was based on two aspects of the brigade movement, co-operation and control.

However, stabilization soon turned into routinization, especially because the initial enthusiasm of brigades was soon betrayed. Complaints about unsatisfactory working conditions, bad management and insufficient support from superiors hardly ever yielded long-term solutions. This was not necessarily because of ignorance or unwillingness on the part of management or central authorities, but often simply because the East German economic system would have had to be reformed fundamentally to eradicate some of the gravest problems. Not even Ulbricht's economic reforms were able to alter political control over economic processes – the basic fault line of the state-planned economy.[41]

From the middle of the 1960s at the latest, brigade members fairly quickly recognized the uselessness of their efforts, which ensured an adjustment of the brigade movement's initial role to existing conditions. Arguably, *Eigen-Sinn* prevailed over the SED's orientation towards societal co-operation according to the contemporary slogan 'From me to us', although this notion was not entirely lost on the workforce. Routinization meant that brigades continued to be used as a protective space and to discipline individual brigade members within this space.

By the late 1960s, brigade life had already undergone a change, whereby formalities required to comply with the rules of the *'Sozialistischer Wettbewerb'* were adhered to but lacked life and initiative. Brigades and their diaries, the *Brigadetagebücher*, became empty shells within which the whole set of ideological concepts attached to the brigade movement and the initial enthusiasm of the early 1960s had evaporated. Accordingly, the brigade diaries from the early 1960s are most interesting in their content. They list and discuss problems in the production process, within the brigade and with leading functionaries, and comment on political developments. They really provide a picture of what everyday life in the factories was like during that period. This entirely disappeared in the 1970s and 1980s and was replaced by many photographs, pictures and formalized descriptions of 'cultural events', ranging from evenings drinking with brigade members and their spouses to excursions and prescribed visits to the theatre. Criticism seldom occurred in diaries from the late 1960s onwards.[42]

In the late 1960s the reality for the brigades was dire. In a report on a survey conducted at the TRO in 1969 to determine the progress of socialist co-operation, the development of socialist consciousness and the emergence of socialist personalities, the conclusions were devastating. Participation in planning and management was described as under-developed. A lack of information regarding the wider economic issues within the company was criticized. The workforce was not given access to relevant information, which meant that they could not get involved in the solution of problems. This had a negative impact on the workforce's willingness to contribute to possible solutions, for example by taking up a training course. Also, debates and confrontations with colleagues were limited, and linked only to professional issues. Political work was non-existent and cultural activity insufficient.[43] All in all, the situation at the end of the 1960s was stamped by the experience of the decade: the workforce felt unable and unwilling to get involved in the search for solutions to problems. Conflicts were avoided if at all possible. Enthusiasm and activity beyond professional requirements was at a low ebb.

Parallel to this development, the diaries of all five state-owned factories under consideration show a clear politicization of the workplace in the 1960s, which was partly borne but also softened by the brigades. In the 1970s and 1980s political language was used routinely and political events were celebrated ritually. The brigades often included members of the SED; in many cases party candidates were delegated from within the brigades almost routinely in order to fulfil the brigade contract. However, their political influence on other members of the brigades should not be overestimated. The real importance of the brigades for their members from the late 1960s lay in their offer of a protective social network.

The trend towards the brigade movement's ineffectiveness was reflected in the inability of central authorities to give precise numbers of brigades in the 1960s, especially as some called themselves brigades without doing any of the things expected of them within the socialist brigade movement. In the 1960s no thorough control of the brigades was possible, as leading functionaries were not in a position to even say who and how many people belonged to a specific brigade and what this brigade was actually doing. By the 1970s this tendency had advanced further, in the sense that exact numbers were more readily available but they were no guarantee of activity in the counted brigades beyond sheer formality.

In the late 1970s, Semmelmann described the '*Sozialistischer Wettbe-werb*' as a 'more and more formalized' movement without any life of its own. Open confrontations were avoided and compromises sought at all levels to ensure at least continuity of production. This, however, kept productivity low and aggravated latent conflicts of interest between the management and the workforce, as shortcomings tended to be hidden or ignored rather than attempts being made to solve problems. In Semmelmann's view, this gave more room for the material interests of the individual workers, which became increasingly independent of the interests of both the state-owned factory and society in general.[44] In the final years of the 1970s, the workforce was focused on norms, wages and difficulties that could undermine their earning potential. Any contribution beyond these issues was seen as not worthwhile and useless: any changes would boomerang and result in negative consequences for their individual interests without solving problems.[45] At that time, very few traces were left of group dynamics, co-operation and mutual support.

What did remain was a sense of 'normality' attached to the brigade movement, or any of the mass organizations, which incorporated both personal and professional networks and was entangled with the politics of the socialist state and the ideological tenets of the Communist Party. By the end of the 1970s it felt 'normal' to most of the East German working population to be part of a brigade or mass organization, to enjoy the benefits of a closely-knit social group, to deal with the shortcomings of central planning and to avoid open confrontations about deficiencies that were deemed (on the basis of many years of experience) to be insoluble within this particular political system.

Conclusion

Eigen-Sinn has been an important concept in this chapter. It has been used, and expanded, to describe the interrelation between central policy, the grassroots and changing economic and political circumstances. Seen chronologically, *Eigen-Sinn* in the early 1960s clashed with the needs of state-owned factories. Soft measures such as the improvement of working and living conditions and the brigade movement were used increasingly to discipline the workforce. With the economic reforms, the rehabilitation of material interest accommodated *Eigen-Sinn* more easily as the workforce's demands were taken into account more readily by works directors who focused on stabilization and high productivity in a changing economic environment. As a result of these efforts, by the late 1960s and in the 1970s, workers were at least outwardly more disciplined, as the focus of *Eigen-Sinn* shifted from straightforward production issues to dealing with the daily grind in state-owned factories. By then, professional and political issues had become closely entwined with private concerns. During the 1970s at the latest, routine handling of both political and economic expectations on the basis of individual interests had been established in an attempt to accommodate the complexities of working life in a state-owned factory.

To summarize: in the 1960s, the rules of the game were set out and learned. The majority of the population did not seriously question these rules again until the mid 1980s in spite of political and economic problems. Rather, open confrontations were avoided for various reasons but primarily because there seemed little hope of fundamentally changing the political or economic system. Also, the East German population became more involved with state structures throughout the 1960s and 1970s. The ideological tenets of the Communist Party were transmitted and had at least some impact on East Germans, even if only as an undercurrent of long-term indoctrination. In the 1980s it was to be the new head of the Soviet Communist Party, Mikhail Gorbachev, who questioned the status quo and thereby encouraged East German people to challenge the established system.

To highlight the findings of this chapter, an excursus into the work of the Stasi and its unofficial collaborators, or IMs, will follow. Whilst this excursus will give the reader an impression of another type of conflict resolution used by the East German state in state-owned factories, it will also stress the state's growing interest in avoiding open conflicts, the breadth of information available to the Stasi, and its influence on company culture.

Excursus: spying for the Stasi

One method of conflict resolution and control was the Stasi's employment of IMs. With regard to surveillance of state-owned factories and the exercise of influence over their management or individual employees, the Stasi had official representatives, who were known to all staff and maintained close contact with the works director. These officers of the Stasi were present at the factories to deal with political provocation and suspected sabotage. With the information collected from the works director or in any other way, they prepared regular reports and, in some instances, they could be approached for assistance by using their connections when the delivery of urgently needed material was delayed or unobtainable. All in all, these official Stasi officers were part of any state-owned factory's daily routine and were almost treated as colleagues. In addition, however, IMs were recruited from among people who were already working at the factory.[46]

IMs worked secretly. Their identities were known only to the Stasi. They spied on colleagues, often providing detailed descriptions of their attitudes, utterances and way of life. Even more dangerously, these reports were often tainted by the IM's personal views and preferences. This could lead to extremely subjective assessments that put individuals in great danger if the Stasi decided to class the person in question as suspect or politically unreliable. In the following section, the career of one such IM will be traced to highlight the extensive knowledge base of the Stasi and how it was used.

The IM who will be described had been working at the TRO for some years before he was recruited by the Stasi. He was born in 1927 and had served as a sailor during the Second World War. After recovering from serious injuries, he became a member of the FDJ and, in 1953, of the SED. During the 1950s he was an active campaigner who was even sent to West Berlin and West Germany to campaign for the Communist Party and the East German state. He was repeatedly arrested for these activities by West German and West Berlin police. From 1954 to 1958 he was FDJ secretary at the TRO. Also, from 1957 onwards, he studied for over two years at a party school but, because of a lack of ability, did not finish the course. He also worked for the VVB and the Ministry for Electronics and Electrical Engineering in high administrative positions but lost his post at the VVB when he failed to meet expectations and was strongly reprimanded by his party organization. From 1961 onwards he was employed in a leading position at the TRO again.[47]

This person had been in official contact with the Stasi for some years, based on his position, before he was recruited as an IM. On one occassion before his recruitment in 1966, he had been proposed but was refused because of his personal characteristics, which included arrogance and a tendency to improvise, as well as a strong link to a family in West Berlin and his professional failure whilst working for the VVB. However, he was deemed keen to be recruited and was also in a position where he would be able to report on the entire management team of the TRO, and even influence them. Furthermore, he was described as a good organizer and had good insider knowledge of structures, power relations and the general mood at the plant. He was the ideal IM: talkative, reliable, committed to the SED and in a position which allowed him access to people, knowledge and all areas within the plant.

After his recruitment, this IM quickly started to report on conflicts relating to the management of the TRO, whereby he criticized the works director, Wolter, and the first secretary of the BPO, Schellknecht, for their dictatorial tendencies and incompetence. Schellknecht apparently dominated the works director, whom the IM accused of not taking any decisions without consulting the former. These two people were operating together against a weak trade union organization and the lower levels of the SED organization of the TRO. They ignored the wishes of the workforce, suppressed criticism and decided on management policy without consultation. In one case, a decision had been made on a fundamental structural change to the state-owned factory without even informing the APO. In response, some members of the APO contacted the ZK SED and the SED BL of Berlin, which reprimanded Wolter and Schellknecht, who were both party members and thereby obliged to refer to the SED even in questions of management. This case took place in 1967 when the role of the SED within state-owned factories was, in any case, a difficult issue. Here, however, it becomes clear what a multifaceted problem this could become on the ground. The works director and the head of the BPO co-operated against the lower ranks of the SED, which was then backed by Berlin's SED organization in their demand to be consulted on questions of management.

Of course, it always has to be remembered that this interpretation was based on the subjective report of an individual, who probably was taking sides in some respect and, therefore, cannot be counted as a reliable source. However, this excursus is interested primarily in the methods and insights of the Stasi and these were based on the work of their IM. This one report would have been cross-referenced with those of other IMs at the TRO but, based on the long career of this particular IM and the trust put in him by his supervisors, it can be assumed that he was deemed a dependable informer. Also, the reports prepared by this IM match the general outline of developments at TRO that can be extracted from other archival material.[48]

To give another example, Wolter was replaced by Wunderlich in July 1967 and it remains an open question whether the Stasi influenced that decision on the basis of the IM's reports. What the Stasi certainly did, however, was help the new works director to become established in his position. It asked the IM to compile assessments of every member of the management team and the problems within the plant. These were passed on to Wunderlich after the Stasi had added some of their recommendations on the most effective ways of dealing with existing problems and avoiding potential conflicts. Wunderlich, as has been described in Chapter 2, turned out to be a very successful works director for the TRO – again it cannot be determined if this was at least partly based on the information he received from the Stasi or entirely on his own abilities, as it cannot be established on what his decisions were based. According to the IM's reports, however, tensions subsided after his arrival at the TRO and the workforce was despondent when it was announced that Wunderlich would leave for another state-owned factory in 1971.

The IM's reports on the mood of the workforce increased noticeably in the early 1970s. When Ulbricht resigned his position as head of state, for example, the IM repeatedly described the reaction among his colleagues. In 1970 he noted a rumour that the West German media had alleged that Ulbricht was very ill and likely to die soon. The East German authorities did not deny these allegations, which most East Germans (at least those working at the TRO according to the IM) seem to have taken as an admission that this was the case. When Ulbricht resigned in 1971, therefore, most, if not all, first reactions acknowledged the old leader's achievements and expressed their appreciation of his need to retire to enjoy old age. Only when Ulbricht did not appear at the Party Conference did some lone voices indicate suspicion that Ulbricht may not have left his post as voluntarily as the new leadership had made out. Nevertheless, most supported Honecker as a representative of a younger generation who provided a better government than the old leader. When Ulbricht died during the World Youth Festival in 1973, one voice even expressed some annoyance that he could not have waited a few days longer and most agreed that the international event should not have been shortened by his death. Ulbricht's replacement, apparently, had been staged smoothly and without much interruption to the daily lives of the East German population, who wholeheartedly welcomed Honecker's extensive social policy in the first part of the 1970s.

Another important issue for the Stasi and the workforce in the 1970s, besides the leadership change, was visitors from West Berlin and West Germany. In 1972 Honecker had made a gesture of good will, as it was called officially, and allowed Western visitors into the GDR for holidays such as Easter. Interestingly, the reaction at the TRO was divided.

One part welcomed this decision and enjoyed visits from their relatives, especially the older colleagues who were visited by their children. Among younger employees, who were visited by their siblings, however, some displeasure was felt. Some were worried that people would be shopping so much in order to prepare for their Western visitors that provisions would not be sufficient. Many expressed anger that, because of tourist regulations, they could now be visited by anybody without being able to decide who they wanted to see. Others felt a growing alienation towards their Western relatives: over the years they had grown apart with little understanding of each other's problems and concerns. Most felt badly treated by relatives who brought few presents, ate a lot and looked down on their East German brothers and sisters. The gap between the two German states and their populations had widened considerably by the 1970s.

Another general source of annoyance was the behaviour of Polish workers in Berlin. The IM recounted a spontaneous discussion, which he overheard on the *S-Bahn*, the Berlin city railway, in May 1972. The report, which the IM wrote, pointed to some of the anxieties of the East German population which have also been indicated in Chapter 5. Mainly, there was anger because the Poles were buying provisions in bulk. Added to this was the opinion, voiced by two women but supported by much nodding from the other travellers, that Polish workers were not behaving in an orderly manner – appraisals that seem reminiscent of the racist propaganda of the Nazi dictatorship.

Within the TRO specifically, the 1970s seem to have been marked by some problems with the new works director, Friedrich. According to some of the IM's reports, Friedrich seems not to have been in control of his employees. In 1974 a case was reported in which the works director had been given and passed on to the VVB false accounts. Apparently, in spite of the figures given, the plan had only been fulfilled 95 per cent; a similar case occurred in 1978, in which it was the works director who was accused of falsifying accounts.[49]

The integration of the TRO into a *Kombinat* in the late 1970s was also an issue. Rumours had existed long before this actually happened. They were voiced with much concern regarding the status of the TRO within such a conglomerate, as it was generally expected that the primary factory would neglect the needs of subordinate factories. This fear dominated the general mood for some time although the IM denied any disadvantages regarding his own work within the new *Kombinat*.

The late 1970s, nevertheless, were marked by some discontent among the workforce. In December 1979 the IM reported on a discussion within the management in reaction to the eleventh meeting of the ZK SED. Apparently, for some time management had been inadequate at the TRO: 'It is now a daily occurrence that, to some extent, orders are not followed.' Furthermore, the IM was of the opinion that the lack of discipline at that time was largely due to the appalling organization, the constant changes to the plan and the chaotic state of production. He thought that much would change for the better if only people stopped glossing things over. The workforce was unhappy not only with the obvious difficulties regarding work organization and the procurement of materials and provisions for the population, but even more with the attempt to deny realities.

This particular IM worked for the Stasi from 1966 to 1989, received many financial rewards and was even allowed to travel to West Berlin repeatedly in the 1980s. He was deemed reliable and truthful by the Stasi; his reports were considered very useful. Looking at the above excerpts of his work, they seem to be faithful, detailed and informative, if also subjective, accounts of daily life at the TRO that helped the Stasi to gain in-depth knowledge of the internal power structures, company culture and selected employees of the TRO. This information could have been used to influence decision making and ensure control over individuals. Furthermore, it has to be remembered that the IM, whose reports have been recounted in the excerpts above, was only one of many at every level in every factory in East Germany. In Schwedt, for example, over 320 IMs were at work in 1976.[50] It can be taken for granted that the Stasi had both the information and the opportunities to make an impact secretly on everyday life in state-owned factories. In this context, throughout the late 1960s and the 1970s, the Stasi's main priority was to detect, dilute and solve conflicts, although its focus seems to have shifted from dealing with tensions linked to high-level management in the 1960s to observing the more general concerns shaping the attitudes of the workforce in the 1970s.

Conclusion: Normality in the GDR

It has been argued that daily life in state-owned factories and, thereby, the GDR as a whole was stabilized by changes in company culture during the 1960s. Particularly, standards of living became relevant to socio-political stability in this period and, as a result, reflected Honecker's policies during the 1970s and 1980s. To some extent at least, relevant modifications of central policy were based on long-standing workers' demands which were communicated to central authorities by intermediate functionaries, such as works directors and trade union officials. From the late 1960s onwards, policies slowly shifted in the context of a power struggle at the very top of the political hierarchy. In combination with international events and structural stagnation, these changes in the economic sector led to the GDR's increasingly precarious situation, both economically and politically.

Three factors came together to turn company culture into a political force. Firstly, the concepts and methods of the East German dictatorship were established and internalized primarily at people's places of work, where their daily lives came into direct contact with the Communist Party's principles and power. At the same time, many basic assumptions and aspirations were questioned, discussed and contested. Boundaries were tested to the limit and existing leeway was expanded but, in the course of this, there was also a close engagement with the expectations of central state and party institutions. Secondly, from 1965 onwards, state-owned factories took on responsibility for the improvement of working and living conditions. Efforts to improve workers' lives at their workplace and beyond were highly visible and, intentionally, recognizable to the workforce. With regard to major state-owned factories providing employment for an entire region, this growing care for their employees' well-being in the interests of higher productivity included a need to shape the regional setting. Thus, managers began to influence the daily lives of their workforce beyond mere work issues. By dealing with social issues, potential political conflicts were contained. Thirdly, large economic units such as *Kombinate* became more isolated and self-sufficient. Some turned into micro cosmoses that often extended to the local administration. Particularly the works director's networking abilities were of immense importance within this constellation. As a result, the workforce's loyalty was directed mainly at their factory and its director, who at least seemed to be in a position to represent their interests and fulfil their expectations.

Analysis of vertical relations from the bottom up to the highest level tends to suggest a greater influence from grassroots' interests on central policy makers than might be expected in a socialist dictatorship. Individual examples of company culture, however, need to be seen in the context of general developments, both political and economic.

Arrival in the everyday

In the 1960s the international battle of political systems led to the building of the Berlin Wall, the Prague Spring and, eventually, the beginnings of *Ostpolitik*. Early on, the Soviets put pressure on the GDR, which forced Ulbricht to stabilize the country by introducing economic reforms. These developments had a major influence on company culture and, as a result, on the grassroots of East German society, particularly in the economic sector but also with regard to socio-political processes. It has been shown throughout this study that after the building of the Berlin Wall in 1961 a normalization process within East German society can be traced in work and company culture. During the 1960s in particular, social norms developed that were suited to a socialist normality defined by the SED's promises and demands but not solely shaped by central authorities. Rather, the grassroots had an impact on East German realities.

Although reality differed from official propaganda, Ulbricht at least was never reluctant to discuss the economic difficulties facing East Germany. He built up the petition system to track and react to popular opinion. In the face of low productivity, high rates of sickness and turnover of personnel, social benefits were increased somewhat although economic progress remained the main priority. The five case studies on the experiences of state-owned factories in the context of the East German economic system have highlighted the drive for the improvement of working and living conditions, which became crucial to company politics in the 1960s.

A continuous interchange and communication between the work-force, company management and central institutions existed with regard not only to norms, salaries and productivity but also to social policy. This constellation had a major impact on the attitudes of the workforce. Furthermore, in the late 1960s and early 1970s, a strong drift towards standardization, institutionalization and centralization became noticeable in the application of policies, the replacement of state functionaries in the economic sector and the rising influence of SED functionaries in company management. As a result, public life and private concerns started to overlap in a way which became specific to the GDR but may have been typical of dictatorships.

Broken promises

When Erich Honecker came to power in 1971 he aimed to stabilize the GDR after the difficulties of the late 1960s. Repressive methods became more subtle as he aimed to improve the country's international status. An expensive social programme was introduced at a time when Eastern Bloc countries were being forced to compete in the world market. Low interest rates encouraged debt-funded growth in the early 1970s, a strategy which turned out to be disastrous in later years as the oil crises pushed up the price of crude oil. The Afghan War and the stationing of Pershing IIs in West Germany intensified the Cold War, whilst the signing of the Helsinki Agreement put pressure on Honecker to uphold human rights.[1] In this context, everyday life at the work place and at home changed for East Germans. After the initial euphoria of the early 1970s, economic problems became visible and were multiplied by Honecker's economic policies, which weakened the position of state-owned factories. The population was confronted with drastic saving measures, a massive lack of investment, and structural changes in the economic sector, all of which encouraged the use of individual strategies of adaptation. The SED's assurances seemed increasingly unrealistic in the late 1970s.

From the middle of the 1970s onwards, the population's early enthusiasm turned sour. In the factories, the lack of capacity resulted in apparent stagnation and, eventually, decline. In spite of positivist propaganda slogans, reality presented the East German population with shortages in all sectors. Everyday life included a constant search for consumer goods and the hoarding of money that could not be spent for the lack of wares, but it also meant social security in the form of low prices for basic food stuffs, rents and other necessities. Most East

Germans had come to expect these provisions and demanded they should be kept, always in line with official SED policy.[2] Even at times of economic crisis, such as during the late 1970s, the political elite did not dare to retreat on their increasingly unrealistic promises out of fear for the social peace. Polish developments in the early 1980s, in addition to the memories of 17 June 1953 upheaval, contributed to this stance.

Changing times

Stagnation caused frustration and lethargy in the late 1970s and the 1980s. Open criticism based on the hope of improvement almost disappeared in the face of apparent decline. In addition, since access to Western television had improved in the 1970s, West Germany in particular provided a constant, and very glossy, point of reference for people in the GDR. An entirely different value system found access to the GDR via radio, television and resilient personal ties. Bananas became a symbol of freedom (and liberated consumerism) for many GDR citizens, who could buy oranges only during the Christmas period. In this context, the socialist state's accomplishments were not only taken for granted but appeared very minor. In the early 1980s Ellen (19 years old) described an ambivalence which affected many:

> At first glance, one could say that socialism is better than capitalism. There are no unemployed, young people are provided with apprenticeships, we have stable prices and and and … But just once, I would like to enter a butcher's shop and right away get a ham or pork loin. That has happened to me once in the two years that I have been here in Gera.[3]

From the early 1970s onwards, Erich Honecker had to deal with criticism accusing him of encouraging consumerism among the population and, as a result, dissuading people from the higher purpose of socialism. In any case, the GDR proved unable to keep up with the products offered by the West. The availability (or lack) of consumer goods and economic success became more important than a concept of fairness and humanity.

Nevertheless, many accommodated their own wishes within the rigid framework, mostly by restricting their expectations of the future to a nice flat, a car and perhaps even a small garden. Kali, who was in his early twenties in 1989, saw his future in these terms:

I believe that I could have expected a secure and bearable existence in the GDR. In any case, I had prospects and the security to largely fulfil my (adapted) wishes ... a flat, an application for a car and buying the car ten years later, etc.[4]

This type of pre-ordained life-plan also caused frustration. One 18-year-old named this as a reason for his decision to leave: 'that was supposed to have been it? I had the feeling that my life was rotting away.'[5] The process of expatriation, however, could take years, there were no guarantees that it would be granted and it always caused great stress and anxiety. In some cases it meant the loss of jobs and even imprisonment. In most cases, fear of unemployment and failure kept people of all ages clinging to their protected lives in the GDR. The 17-year-old apprentice Imke voiced a common opinion in 1984: 'But I wouldn't like to live there [in West Germany]. Just want a look. Here, I feel safer.'[6] By the late 1980s this sentiment proved not sufficient any more to prevent mass emigration to West Germany.

The very late 1980s saw the beginnings of a movement that turned socialist normality upside-down although, in 1989 and as late as 1990, the thought processes of both intellectuals and activists within the citizens' movement still centred on concepts that would have continued the socialist experiment. The masses on the streets, however, demanded an end to experimentation with their lives in the name of a better future, which had been pledged repeatedly but never materialized in spite of much effort on the part of the working population. 'When, if not now?' Christa Wolf had asked at the end of her novel *Nachdenken über Christa T* (1969). At the end of the 1980s the same question was asked by people who saw their lives swept away by the shortcomings of a system that had pronounced great ideals but had proved itself unable to succeed economically. In moral terms, the Communist Party had also disappointed those who had supported the socialist ideas.

In the end, Western temptation and the collapse of the Soviet Union encouraged a reorientation towards unification with West Germany. In 1989 the regime collapsed in the face of combined pressure from mass migration, political upheaval and, last but certainly not least, its debt burden. Mass migration and behaviour patterns at demonstrations, nevertheless, were marked by the East German experience of the previous 40 years. Rather than open confrontation, candles were lit to make a quiet but strong statement of protest. Social norms acquired over such a long time could not be removed overnight. Most East

Germans had not even been aware of their 'socialist personality', which differed from official objectives. Over many years, the population had successfully adapted to a habitat which collapsed both suddenly and unexpectedly. The collapse of the socialist dictatorship in the GDR, German unification and the transformation process in the 1990s was marked by East Germans' 40-year-long experience of a specific 'socialist normality'.

Socialist normality

Socialist normality varied according to many factors: an individual's position within society; their place of work; the period under consideration; their age and gender; and their encounters with central authorities, to list only some of the most important ones. It was delineated by central policy and the actions of central authorities, but it was faceted by circumstances beyond the control of state or party institutions. Normality more often than not included having to do two things most astutely: deal with the difficulty of living in a shortage economy and handle ideological expectations. There was no single way in which people responded to the daily problems they encountered. It needs to be stressed that more than 16 million people lived over 16 million lives and have about 16 million different memories of their time within the East German dictatorship. This was normal in the GDR as it is normal in other countries.

Nevertheless, there were common experiences that marked the attitude of the individual and his social group. Class differences influenced opinions and behaviour at all times, as did gender roles. Generational conflicts had an impact on the workforce, just as any other aspect of daily life was touched by changes in social relations. In addition, probably every section of East German society was aware at some level of constant control; arguably an undercurrent of fear of the Stasi influenced behaviour patterns, even those of very young children. However, there was also pride and loyalty attached to the East German citizenship. The ideological goals of the SED attracted some support from the population, especially wider issues such as peace, solidarity and social fairness. However, in the late 1970s economic crisis and political stagnation encouraged individualization processes which, in the long term, replaced collective attitudes that had been built up in the 1960s. During the 1980s an entirely new outlook on social relations and political expectations developed, which became the basis of the sociopolitical upheaval that destroyed the GDR in the end.

East German society was shaped by compromise. It contained social-ist notions of collective life, basic ideals and practical values such as social fairness and guaranteed jobs, but excluded many of the SED's ideological tenets such as hostility towards Western imperialism. Norms and behaviour patterns were based to some extent on the SED's propaganda but also on traditional values. They had formed slowly in response to both given circumstances and growing expectations, but also out of a popular reluctance to accept wholesale resocialization. With time, norms were set in stagnating institutions, which distorted their original meaning. Both their rigidity and the notable difference between propaganda and everyday life prompted, at least in some parts of East German society, a backlash against both standardized biogra-phies and unsatisfying realities. By the late 1970s it had become clear that societal expectations of normality that had been introduced by the SED were not going to be fulfilled, and this led to resignation, frus-tration and a stronger focus on personal interests. Ensuing trends towards individualization undermined East German society in the long term.

Normalization: norms and normality in a socialist dictatorship

The building of the Berlin Wall in August 1961 changed life in the GDR. East Germans were confronted with circumstances beyond their control. In retrospect, the writer Günter de Bruyn described the over-whelming reaction of most people in his usual, eloquent and percep-tive way that does not speak of blame or guilt but of realities:

> To be able to live even as a prisoner, one had to try to live as if the prison did not exist. And the experiment worked, for most people even superbly. A few weeks after the building of the Berlin Wall ... many had already started to perceive the Wall as something natural and saw its positive aspects. One had a quiet life in its shadow. One didn't have to make a decision any more, to flee or not to flee; the provisional had acquired hard contours; the temporary seemed suddenly strengthened by the position of the West, which under protest had let everything happen, to become a constant feature. For the future, therefore, one needed to arrange one's life, to start families, to have children, to organize better accommodation and a garden for the weekends, to join the Party for career purposes, at least avoid unwanted attention and perhaps open up more to ideology; because it's uncomfortable living in constant political schizophrenia.[7]

In short, people had to adjust to given circumstances; they realized it quickly and managed it without much ado. In the process of adaptation, which could last a lifetime and led to ever more and finer nuances of behaviour, social norms emerged from the socialist value system propagated by the SED and affected most East Germans in one way or another.

According to Walter Friedrich, the director of the *Zentralinstitut für Jugendforschung* (ZIJ), social norms are

> demands on behaviour, which society or groups of any kind expect of their members. They direct behaviour and contain an expectation that demands will be followed although this expectation is not self-realizing. The realization of social norms follows from the evaluation and sanctioning of behaviour.[8]

Positive and negative sanctions make it possible to turn norms into behaviour patterns.[9] The SED's priorities were to create, firstly, an emotional link to the GDR; secondly, socialist internationalism; thirdly, a socialist world view; and, fourthly, hostility towards Western imperialism. In reality, however, social norms turned out to be more down-to-earth and of practical value. They were grouped around topics such as social fairness, gender equality and low costs of living, as well as education, professional training and work for everybody; all were based on the SED's socialist world-view.[10] An implicit acceptance of low-key political repression, which it was hoped would prevent the outright terror of the 1950s, was also present.

Reaching an understanding on such basic issues enabled communication. Furthermore, communication included a specific language, which reflected the ideological context of the East German dictatorship. It became part of an anticipated normality that developed in the 1960s and was still hoped for in the 1970s. Political acquiescence does not describe the situation adequately. Much more was going on in all sections of society. Specific behaviour patterns developed: the avoidance of open confrontation by accurately assessing the political implications of any situation; distrust of anybody who was not a close friend or relative, although even this was no guarantee against Stasi surveillance; careful positioning within political, professional and social structures depending on the individual's career aims; the use of a specific language to communicate effectively with governmental and party institutions, and so on. These methods allowed people to feel that they were shaping their own lives and that of their families in spite of an

intrusive system. They also learned to live with and exploit given circumstances, because socialist values and the promises made by the SED
had become part of the East German value system.

Routinization set in slowly, leading to the predictability of established structures which, even if they did not function efficiently, contained the possibility of working with, avoiding or exploiting given
circumstances. Routine stabilized East German society, at least in the
short term. In the long term, routine also carried a loss of meaning,
especially with regard to the political aims of the Communist Party.
Beyond any theoretical considerations of communist ideology, however, the more long-lasting outcomes of life in the East German dictatorship were specific values, such as social fairness, and behaviour
patterns as they were regularly demanded and employed in daily life.
They were a part of the survival strategies that structured and simpli-
fied everyday life; specifically and the learning and application of an
official language and behaviour towards state or party institutions.
Also, specific expectations were directed at the state, mostly regarding
social policy, such as the improvement of working and living conditions, the right to work, low prices and, more specifically, the provision
of cheap meals, vacations, and cultural and sporting facilities. By the
1970s these things were not just expected but demanded by the
working population.

The SED argued that socialist society, if it was to function at all,
required collective efforts to find solutions to its many shortcomings.
Many seemed to agree with that. Ulbricht's appreciation of the petition system as a valuable source of both information and legitimacy reflected this knowledge. However, the 1960s also marked the
beginning of a process of standardization and institutionalization.
It affected the education system, professional qualifications and state-
owned factories, even cultural activity, communication practices
and language. By the late 1970s, stagnation caused frustration and
lethargy. Open criticism based on the hope of improvement almost
disappeared in the face of apparent decline. Production workers at the
TRO, for example, explicitly expressed their reluctance to show initiative to make production more efficient.[11] They reasoned that their
experience had shown the futility of such attempts: '[To show initi-
ative] one would have to be an idealist or a fighter. That we are not as
we have been working too long at the TRO.'[12] At the end of the 1970s,
individualization was a growing phenomenon in the GDR. People's
interests increasingly focused on their individual needs, at least partly
in reaction to both routinization under Honecker, which further

reduced people's influence on the socialist project, and absurd propaganda that had nothing to do any more with lived realities.

Conclusion

Life in the socialist dictatorship was at least to some extent shaped by the working population which accommodated the Communist Party's expectations but also forced modifications of central policy. Over time, changes in normative behaviour accompanied the growing integration of state and society. Eventually, growing resentment against an overbearing state sparked off the search for individual fulfilment which undermined the Marxist principle of collective life. This led to the developments of the 1980s and, eventually, to the collapse of the GDR. The transformation process of the 1990s was marked by the fact that the GDR had been able to create a specific socio-political environment. In this socialist normality, East Germans had worked and lived in ways that differed from the lives of their Western brothers and sisters. Nevertheless, it had seemed 'normal' to most (but certainly not all) people in the GDR, which explains the ongoing phenomenon of nostalgia for a dictatorship that shot people for simply wanting to leave.

Normal lives?

In a survey of a vast variety of former employees of the five selected state-owned factories, one question in the questionnaire asked if a 'normal life' had been possible in the GDR. Fifty seven people responded, some enquiring what was meant by the admittedly extremely problematic term 'normal'. Of those 57, 32 were male and 25 female. The majority was born in the 1930s and 1940s, although the range of dates of birth extended to the 1920s and 1960s. Of the 57 people, only eight denied the possibility of a 'normal life' in the GDR, 18 described it as 'partly normal' and 31 claimed that a 'normal life' was possible in the East German dictatorship.

Notes

Introduction

1 Falco Werkentin speaking at the conference 'Staatsgründung auf Raten? Zu den Auswirkungen des Volksaufstandes 1953 und des Mauerbaus 1961 auf Staat, Militär und Gesellschaft der DDR', 20 & 21 April 2004, Potsdam.

2 See Walter Friedrich, 'Jugend und Jugendforschung in der ehemaligen DDR-Forschung', pp. 180–1, in W. Melzer, W. Heitmeyer, L. Liegle and J. Zinnecker (eds), *Osteuropäische Jugend im Wandel: Ergebnisse vergleichender Jugendforschung in der Sowjetunion, Polen, Ungarn und der ehemaligen DDR.* Munich: Juventa, 1991, pp. 172–83.

3 The German term 'Betrieb' cannot easily be translated into English. State-owned factory, company or business will be the favoured English equivalents in this study although none exactly conveys German terminology.

4 For a detailed discussion of the concept of 'institutionalization', see Silke Röbenack, *'Aber meistens einfach nur ein Kollege' Über die ersten Betriebsräte in Ostdeutschland.* Munich: Rainer Hampp, 2005, pp. 38ff. In relation to 'institutionalization', Röbenack also explores the issues of 'internalization' and Bourdieu's concept of 'habitus': ibid., pp. 54ff.

5 Ibid., p. 179.

6 Arim Soares do Bem, *Das Spiel der Identitäten in der Konstitution von 'Wir'-Gruppen. Ost- und Westdeutsche Jugendliche und in Berlin geborene Jugendliche ausländischer Herkunft im gesellschaftlichen Umbruch.* Frankfurt/Main: Peter Lang, 1998, p. 181.

7 For example on petitions, see Felix Mühlberg, *Bürger, Bitten und Behörden: Geschichte der Eingabe in der DDR.* Berlin: Dietz, 2004. On power politics within the SED, see Monika Kaiser, *Machtwechsel von Ulbricht zu Honecker. Funktionsmechanismen der SED-Diktatur in Konfliktsituationen 1962–1972.* Berlin: Akademie, 1997.

8 Hartmut Kaelble, Jürgen Kocka and Hartmut Zwahr (eds), *Sozialgeschichte der DDR.* Stuttgart: Klett-Cotta, 1994. See also Mary Fulbrook, *The People's State. East German Society from Hitler to Honecker.* Yale: Yale University Press, 2005.

9 For specific aspects such as the Prenzlauer Berg scene, see Christina Cosentino and Wolfgang Müller (eds), *'im widerstand/im missverstand?' Zur Literatur und Kunst des Prenzlauer Bergs.* DDR Studien, Vol. 8, New York: Peter Lang, 1995.

10 See Jens Gieseke, *Die DDR-Staatssicherheit: Schild und Schwert der Partei.* Bonn: BPB, 2000. See also Clemens Vollnhals, *Das Ministerium für Staatssicherheit – Ein Instrument totalitärer Herrschaftsausübung.* Berlin: BStU, 1995.

11 See André Steiner, *Die DDR-Wirtschaftsreform der sechziger Jahre – Konflikt zwischen Effizienz- und Machtkalkül.* Berlin: Akademie, 1999. See also Jeffrey Kopstein, *The Politics of Economic Decline in East Germany, 1945–89.* Chapel Hill: University of North Carolina, 1997.

12 See for example Annegret Schüle, *Die Spinne – Die Erfahrungsgeschichte weiblicher Industriearbeit im VEB Baumwollspinnerei.* Leipzig: Universitätsverlag, 2001. Sandrine Kott, *Le communisme au quotidien. Les Enterprises d'Etat dans la société est-allemande.* Paris: Edition Belin, 2001. See also various contributions by Renate Hürtgen, e.g. Renate Hürtgen and Thomas Reichel (eds), *Der Schein der Stabilität – DDR-Betriebsalltag in der Ära Honecker.* Berlin: Metropol, 2001. Peter Alheit and Hanna Haack, *Die vergessene 'Autonomie' der Arbeiter. Eine Studie zum frühen Scheitern der DDR am Beispiel der Neptunwerft.* Berlin: Dietz, 2004.

13 For a more detailed discussion of totalitarianism, see Jeannette Madarász, *Conflict and Compromise in East Germany, 1971–89. A Precarious Stability.* Basingstoke: Palgrave, 2003, pp. 5–8.

14 See for example Alf Lüdtke, 'Meister der Landtechnik oder: Grenzen der Feldforschung? Annäherungen an einen "Qualitätsarbeiter" auf dem Lande im Bezirk Erfurt', in Daniela Münkel and Jutta Schwarzkopf (eds), *Geschichte als Experiment. Studien zu Politik, Kultur und Alltag im 19. und 20. Jahrhundert.* Frankfurt/Main: Campus, 2004, pp. 243–57.

15 Peter Hübner, Jürgen Danyel, 'Soziale Argumente im politischen Machtkampf: Prag, Warschau, Berlin 1968–1971', in *ZfG* 9 (2002) pp. 804–32; Peter Hübner, 'Norm, Normalität, Normalisierung: Quellen und Ziele eines gesellschaftspolitischen Paradigmawechsels im sowjetischen Block um 1970', in *Potsdamer Bulletin für Zeithistorische Studien* 28/29 (January 2003) pp. 24–40.

16 Particularly the assertion that ordinary East Germans suffered from a 'false consciousness', an argument beloved by totalitarian approaches, is addressed here. It does not further an exploration of history in the sense of Ranke's 'as it really was'.

17 Jean Jacques Rousseau, *Du contrat social ou principes ou droit politique.* Amsterdam: Rey, 1762.

18 Mary Fulbrook, 'Arbeiter in sozialen und politischen Konfliktkonstellationen', in Peter Hübner, Christoph Klessmann and Klaus Tenfelde (eds), *Arbeiter im Staatssozialismus. Ideologischer Anspruch und soziale Wirklichkeit.* Cologne: Böhlau, 2005, pp. 347–56.

19 For a more detailed exploration, see Madarász, 'Normalisierung in der Diktatur? Potentiale und Limitationen eines Konzepts im Kontext der DDR-Geschichte, 1961–79', in Helmut Wagner (ed.), *Europa und Deutschland – Deutschland und Europa.* Münster: LIT, 2005, pp. 335–55.

20 Sarina Keiser, *Ostdeutsche Frauen zwischen Individualisierung und Re-Traditionalisierung – Ein Generationenvergleich.* Hamburg: Dr.Kovac, 1997, pp. 23–9.

21 Stephan Hermlin, quoted in Wolfgang Emmerich, *Kleine Literaturgeschichte der DDR.* Leipzig: Kiepenheuer, 1997, pp. 34–5.

22 Peter Hübner speaking at the conference 'Staatsgründung auf Raten? Zu den Auswirkungen des Volksaufstandes 1953 und des Mauerbaus 1961 auf Staat, Militär und Gesellschaft der DDR', 20 & 21 April 2004, Potsdam.

23 See, for example, studies by the ZIJ.

24 Stefan Hornbostel, 'Spätsozialismus, Legitimierung und Stabilität', in Hannah-Arendt-Institut (ed.), *Repression und Wohlstandsversprechen – Zur*

Stabilisierung von Parteiherrschaft in der DDR und der CSSR. Dresden: Hannah-Arendt-Institut, 1999, pp. 13–25.

25   Brigade diaries are notoriously difficult to use but can be very useful for tracing everyday issues on the shop floor, especially in the early 1960s. For a detailed discussion of their advantages and shortcomings, see Jörg Roesler, 'Das Brigadetagebuch – betriebliches Rapportbuch, Chronik des Brigadelebens oder Erziehungsfibel?' in Evemarie Badstübner, *Befremdlich Anders: Leben in der DDR.* Berlin: Dietz, 2000, pp. 151–66.

26   Comparatively little attention will be given to general developments within the East German trade union, the FDGB. In this area excellent studies already exist, see for example Wolfgang Biermann, *Demokratisierung in der DDR? Ökonomische Notwendigkeiten, Herrschaftsstrukturen, Rolle der Gewerkschaften 1961–1977.* Cologne: Wissenschaft und Politik, 1978; and Renate Hürtgen, *Zwischen Disziplinierung und Partizipation. Vertrauensleute des FDGB im DDR-Betrieb.* Cologne: Böhlau, 2005.

27   Liz Stanley, *The auto/biographical I.* Manchester: Manchester University Press, 1992, p. 10.

1   Economic Politics and Company Culture

1   See Sandrine Kott, 'Pour une histoire sociale du pouvoir en Europe communiste', in *Revue d'histoire moderne et contemporaire* 49 (2002) pp. 5–23.

2   See also related concepts, especially 'habitus' (Bourdieu, 1977) and 'structuration' (Giddens, 1984). For a concise discussion of related concepts, such as 'habitus' and 'structuration', and their links to 'routine', see George Ritzer, *Modern sociological theory.* London: Sage, 2001.

3   Steiner, *DDR-Wirtschaftsreform,* p. 556.

4   Heike Knortz, *Innovationsmanagement in der DDR 1973/79–1989. Der sozialistische Manager zwischen ökonomischen Herausforderungen und Systemblockaden.* Berlin: Duncker & Humblot, 2004, p. 186.

5   Detlef Pollack, 'Die konstitutive Widersprüchlichkeit der DDR. Oder: War die DDR-Gesellschaft homogen?', p. 116, in *Geschichte und Gesellschaft* 24 (1998) pp. 100–31.

6   For a superb analysis of international influences on East German economic policy, see Gareth Dale, *Between State Capitalism and Globalisation. The Collapse of the East German Economy.* Bern: Peter Lang, 2004. For development of theories regarding state planning in the GDR, see Peter C. Caldwell, *Dictatorship, State Planning, and Social Theory in the GDR.* Cambridge: Cambridge University Press, 2003.

7   Peter Hübner, 'Betriebe als Träger der Sozialpolitik, betriebliche Sozialpolitik', p. 735, in Bundesministerium für Gesundheit und Soziale Sicherung und Bundesarchiv (ed.), *Geschichte der Sozialpolitik in Deutschland seit 1945.* Vol. 8; Dierk Hoffmann and Michael Schwartz (eds), *DDR 1949–61, Im Zeichen des Aufbaus des Sozialismus.* Baden-Baden: Nomos, 2004, pp. 727–73.

8   Ibid., p. 756.

9   Ibid., pp. 757, 763.

10   Ibid., p. 773.

11   Peter Hübner, 'Der Betrieb als Ort der Sozialpolitik in der DDR', pp. 67–8, in Christoph Boyer and Peter Skyba (eds), *Repression und Wohlstandsversprechen*

– *Zur Stabilisierung von Parteiherrschaft in der DDR und der CSSR*. Dresden: Hanna-Arendt-Institut, 1999, pp. 63–74.

12 VVBs were positioned between the individual factories and the relevant ministries, in a liaising role but subordinate to the ministry and superior to the factory. Their influence declined again in the 1970s.

13 Steiner, *DDR-Wirtschaftsreform*, p. 65.

14 LAB, C Rep. 409–01 Nr. 54, Parteileitungssitzung 18.1.1965, p. 13.

15 Steiner, *DDR-Wirtschaftsreform*, pp. 555–6.

16 Philipp Heldmann, *Herrschaft, Wirtschaft, Anoraks. Konsumpolitik in der DDR der Sechzigerjahre*. Göttingen: Vandenhoeck & Ruprecht, 2004.

17 See specifically works by Peter Hübner, e.g. Hübner, *Konsens, Konflikt und Kompromiss – Soziale Arbeiterinteressen und Sozialpolitik in der SBZ/DDR 1945–70*. Berlin: Akademie, 1995; works by Jörg Roesler on the brigade movement, e.g. Roesler, 'Die Produktionsbrigaden in der Industrie der DDR. Zentrum der Arbeitswelt?' p. 154, in Kaelble *et al.*, *Sozialgeschichte*, pp. 144–70.

18 For an excellent study on trade union functionaries in factories, see Hürtgen, *Zwischen Disziplinierung und Partizipation*.

19 Werner Kaufmann, *Einfluss und Auswirkungen der neuen Technik auf die Entwicklung des Arbeitsvermögens der Werktätigen des Betriebsteils Leuchtstofflampe im VEB BGW*. University of Rostock (1966): unpublished, pp. 19–24.

20 BAB, DY 30 vorl. SED / 21069, Abt. Gewerkschaften und Sozialpolitik an Abt. Grundstoffindustrie, 10.5.1977.

21 The currency of the GDR was renamed various times: Deutsche Mark der Deutschen Notenbank (DM) 31.10.1951 – 31.7.1964; Mark der Deutschen Notenbank (MDN) 1.8.1964 – 31.12.1967; Mark der DDR (M) 1.1.1968 – 30.6.1990. The author will use the abbreviation appropriate to each period.

22 LAB C Rep. 409, Nr. 50, Vol. 1, Vorlage 14/75, 7.5.1975, pp. 4–6.

23 Kott, *Le communisme au quotidien*, p. 169.

24 Knortz, *Innovationsmanagement*, p. 207.

25 Hans-Hermann Hertle and Franz-Otto Gilles, 'Stasi in der Produktion – Die "Sicherung der Volkswirtschaft" am Beispiel der Struktur und Arbeitsweise der Objektdienststellen des MfS in den Chemiekombinaten', p. 133, in Klaus-Dietmar Henke and Roger Engelmann (eds), *Aktenlage – Die Bedeutung der Unterlagen des Staatssicherheitsdienstes für die Zeitgeschichtsforschung*. Berlin: Ch. Links, 1995, pp. 118–37.

26 See Kott, *Le communisme au quotidien*, p. 169.

27 See LAB C Rep. 411, Nr. 1339.

28 Example taken from the brigade diary of a brigade of administrative staff working at TRO; see Kott, *Le communisme au quotidien*, p. 169.

29 These efforts to save envelopes and postage were mentioned as a special and new achievement in the brigade diary of 1968, intended to contribute to a general effort to stabilize TRO. Six years later, in 1974, the decision was made to take on responsibility for the cleaning of the staff's places of work and the post-office boxes. See LAB C Rep. 411, Nr. 1339, Volumes 1 and 2.

30 For a notable exception to this attitude, see rationalization efforts at the EVW, which led to the campaign 'Weniger produzieren mehr' but remained a singular success; see Knortz, *Innovationsmanagement*.

31 See particularly Heike Solga, *Auf dem Weg in eine klassenlose Gesellschaft? Klassenlagen und Mobilität zwischen Generationen in der DDR*. Berlin:

Akademie, 1995. See also Johannes Huinink, Karl Ulrich Mayer *et al.*, *Kollektiv und Eigensinn – Lebensverläufe in der DDR und danach.* Berlin: Akademie, 1995.

32 Martin Kohli, 'Die DDR als Arbeitsgesellschaft? Arbeit, Lebenslauf und soziale Differenzierung', p. 49, in Kaelble *et al.*, *Sozialgeschichte*, pp. 31–61.

33 Kott, *Le communisme au quotidien*, p. 172.

34 See also Knortz, *Innovationsmanagement*, p. 214.

35 Horst Liewald, *Das BGW. Zur Betriebsgeschichte von NARVA – Berliner Glühlampenwerk.* Berlin: Deutsches Technikmuseum, 2004, p. 243. See also Jeannette Madarász, 'Die Realität der Wirtschaftsreform in der DDR. Betriebsalltag in den sechziger Jahren', p. 968, in *DeutschlandArchiv* 6/966 (2003) pp. 966–80.

36 See Roesler, 'Die Produktionsbrigaden', p. 154. See also LAB, C Rep. 409–01 Nr. 214, 'Käthe Kollwitz', 3.6.1960, 25.6.1960 und 23–31.7.1961.

37 See Thomas Reichel, 'Die "durchherrschte Arbeitsgesellschaft" – Zu den Herrschaftsstrukturen und Machtverhältnissen in DDR-Betrieben', p. 91, in Hürtgen, Reichel, *Der Schein der Stabilität*, pp. 85–110.

38 Kott, *Le communisme au quotidien*.

39 Leonore Ansorg, '"Ick hab immer von unten Druck gekriegt und von oben". Weibliche Leitungskader und Arbeiterinnen in einem DDR-Textilbetrieb. Eine Studie zum Innenleben der DDR-Industrie', in *Archiv für Sozialgeschichte* 39 (1999) pp. 123–65. Petra Clemens, *Die aus der Tuchbude – Alltag und Lebensgeschichten Forster Textilarbeiterinnen.* Münster: Waxmann, 1998.

40 Francesca Weil, *Herrschaftsanspruch und Wirklichkeit. Zwei Sächsiche Betriebe in der DDR während der Honecker-Ära.* Cologne: Böhlau, 2000.

41 See Ingrid Deich and Wolfhard Kohte, *Betriebliche Sozialeinrichtungen.* Opladen: Leske+Budrich, 1997.

42 These were all comparatively large companies, state-owned and centrally administered, which have been selected because of the good source base. Nevertheless, large differences between them will become apparent.

43 Kott, *Le communisme au quotidien*, p. 177.

44 Deich and Kohte, *Betriebliche Sozialeinrichtungen*, pp. 155ff.

45 For an outstanding description of the developments leading to and resulting from the creation of *Kombinate*, see Annette Wilczek, *Einkommen – Karriere – Versorgung. Das DDR-Kombinat und die Lebenslage seiner Beschäftigten.* Berlin: Metropol, 2004, pp. 19ff.

46 Rita Aldenhoff-Hübinger, 'Die Ausstrahlung der "Halbleiterpflaume". Folgen einer Betriebsgründung in Frankfurt (Oder)', p. 48 in Dokumentationszentrum Alltagskultur der DDR e.V. (ed.), *Fortschritt, Norm & Eigensinn. Erkundungen im Alltag der DDR.* Berlin: Ch.Links, 1995, pp. 39–51.

47 See Hübner, *Konsens, Konflikt und Kompromiss*, p. 208.

48 See Kott, *Le communisme au quotidien*, pp. 79–83.

49 See Chapter 3.

50 Another example of this attempt to counterbalance the deficiencies of the centrally planned economy was the networking between factories intended to accommodate a semi-legal (if not illegal) exchange of materials. See Steiner, *DDR-Wirtschaftsreform*, p. 35.

51 See Kott, *Le communisme au quotidien*, p. 141.

52 Compare Günther Heydemann and Eckehard Jesse (eds), *Diktaturvergleich als Herausforderung – Theorie und Praxis*. Berlin: Duncker & Humblot, 1998, p. 184. See also Ansorg, 'Ick hab immer von unten Druck gekriegt und von oben', p. 148.
53 See, for example, SAPMO DY24/14230, 10.1.1989, Eberhard Aurich, 'Probleme und Schwierigkeiten von 1.Kreissekretären', pp. 11–13.
54 See Hürtgen, *Zwischen Disziplinierung und Partizipation*, pp. 247ff.
55 BAB, DE 1 / VA 56131, SPK, Notizen zum Beratung des Politbüro (PB) 24.3.1972, p. 8.
56 Kaiser, *Machtwechsel*, chapter 3.
57 Deich and Kohte, *Betriebliche Sozialeinrichtungen*, p. 168. See also LAB C Rep. 411, Nr. 1306, Vol. 5, Stellungnahme und Beschluss der Parteileitung in der Leitungssitzung 28.9.1978. In addition, see interview with K., 30 May 2005 (transcript in possession of author).
58 Kott, *Le communisme au quotidien*, p. 169.
59 Ibid., p. 123.
60 Steiner, *DDR-Wirtschaftsreform*, p. 38.
61 See Günter Mensching, *Ingenieur M. ppm. Einer unter Millionen. Lebenserinnerungen und Ansichten*. Berlin: Nora, 2005, pp. 189ff. See also Dagmar Semmelmann, *Gespräch mit vier Kollegen aus der Tischlerei des O-Betriebes*. (6.9.1978) unpublished, pp. 1–2.
62 See Dagmar Semmelmann, *Gedanken zum sozialistischen Wettbewerb*. (1978–9), unpublished, p. 3.
63 See Harry Müller, *Jugend im Wandel ihrer Werte*. Leipzig: ZIJ, 1985, p. 13.

2 *Transformatorenwerk Berlin*: Success and Failure

1 LAB, C Rep. 411 Nr. 1, Entwicklung Transformatorenwerk 'Karl Liebknecht' (1961).
2 LAB, C Rep. 411 Nr. 1, Entwicklung des TRO nach 1945 (1949–74).
3 For a comprehensive analysis of economic development in the 1960s, see Steiner, *DDR-Wirtschaftsreform*. See also Kopstein, *Politics of Economic Decline*.
4 Kurt Hager, *Erinnerungen*. Leipzig: Faber & Faber, 1996, p. 274.
5 Heike Förster, *Entwicklung von Handlungsstrategien bei Führungskräften in der DDR-Wirtschaft. Eine empirische Untersuchung von Lebens- und Karriereverläufen ehemaliger Betriebs- und Kombinatsdirektoren*. Frankfurt/Main: Peter Lang, 1995, p. 53.
6 LAB C Rep. 411, Nr. 105, Konzeption zur weiteren Verbesserung der Organisation der Leitung im VEB TRO, 4.4.1964.
7 Wilczek, *Einkommen*, p. 38.
8 LAB C Rep. 411 Nr. 237, Arbeit mit dem BKV, dem Frauen- und Jugendförderungsplan im 1.HJ 1963, 12.7.1963.
9 LAB C Rep. 411, Nr. 286, Brief von Skopp, 31.7.1964.
10 LAB C Rep. 411, Nr. 1306, Vol. 3, TRO APO 9 an Gerlatzek, BPO, 6.11.1964.
11 See *Trafo*, July 1964 to January 1965.
12 LAB C Rep. 411, Nr. 159, Protokoll 24.11.1964; C Rep. 411, Nr. 1303, Vol. 1, Protokoll 21.1.1965.

13 Interviews with K., 14 April 2005 and 30 May 2005.

14 Correspondence and interview with D. Meinke in author's possession.

15 Claus Krömke, *Das 'Neue Ökonomische System der Planung und Leitung der Volkswirtschaft' und die Wandlungen des Günter Mittag*. Berlin: Gesellschafts-wissenchaftliches Forum, 1996, pp. 14–15.

16 Ibid., p. 32.

17 For example, throughout 1966 the Minister for Finances, Willi Rumpf, sustained his resistance to the price reforms. Kopstein, *The Politics of Economic Decline*, p. 64.

18 For details see André Steiner, 'Von "Hauptaufgabe" zu "Hauptaufgabe". Zur Wirtschaftsentwicklung der langen 60er Jahre in der DDR', p. 231 in Axel Schildt *et al.*, *Dynamische Zeiten. Die 60er Jahre in den beiden deutschen Gesellschaften*. Hamburg: Christians, 2000, pp. 218–47.

19 Steiner, *DDR-Wirtschaftsreform*, p. 125.

20 See Krömke, *Das 'Neue Ökonomische System'*, p. 19.

21 LAB C Rep. 411, Nr. 105, Vorlage für das Produktionskomitee des VEB TRO, 12.5.1967, p. 5.

22 LAB C Rep. 411, Nr. 24, SED BL Gross-Berlin, Beschluss Nr. 12/62-1, 20.9.1962, pp. 3–4.

23 LAB C Rep. 411, Nr. 105, Vorlage für das Produktionskomitee des VEB TRO, 12.5.1967, p. 1.

24 LAB C Rep. 411, Nr. 1306, Vol. 3, Zillgitt an BPO, Gerlatzek, 20.12.1963.

25 LAB C Rep. 411, Nr. 1306, Vol. 3, Protokoll Nr.1/64, BPO 6.1.1964.

26 LAB C Rep. 411, Nr. 1306, Vol. 3, Untersuchung der Leitungstätigkeit im Betrieb Rummelsburg, 13–18.7.1964.

27 LAB C Rep. 904-023, Nr. 33, Wochenbericht 12.12.1964.

28 LAB C Rep. 411, Nr. 1306, Vol. 3, Protokoll Nr. 24/64, BPO 7.9.1964.

29 LAB C Rep. 411, Nr. 175, Protokoll 22.9.1966 and Nr. 181, Protokoll 21.3.1967.

30 See for example LAB C Rep. 904-023, Nr. 20. See also Krömke, *Das 'Neue Ökonomische System'*, p. 15.

31 LAB C Rep. 411, Nr. 175, Protokoll 24.1.1966.

32 LAB C Rep. 602, Film-Nr. A179/76-182/76, Protokoll, 10.5.1966.

33 Ibid., p. 4.

34 Ibid.

35 The situation was particularly bad, as the TRO was unable to keep to delivery schedules agreed with the Soviet Union. LAB, C Rep. 411 Nr. 175, Sondersitzung 22.9.1966, p. 2.

36 LAB C Rep. 411, Nr. 105, Vorlage für das Produktionskomitee des VEB TRO, 12.5.1967, pp. 1–2.

37 LAB C Rep. 411, Nr. 1333, Vertrauensleute Vollversammlung (VVV), 27.6.67, p. 5.

38 Helmut Müller-Enbergs *et al.*, (eds), *Wer war Wer in der DDR?* Berlin: Ch. Links, 2001, p. 941. See also Günther Buch, *Namen und Daten wichtiger Personen der DDR*. Bonn: Dietz, 1979, p. 363.

39 LAB C Rep. 411, Nr. 1333, VVV, 21.9.1967, p. 2.

40 Ibid., p. 9.

41 BA-SAPMO, DY46/1297, Protokoll, 4.12.1967.

42 LAB C Rep. 411, Nr. 73, Zielsetzung in der Transformatorenentwicklung, 1968–80, 19.11.1968, p. 16.

43 Already in December 1962, a decision was made to enforce this exchange of functionaries. See Steiner, *DDR-Wirtschaftsreform*, p. 75.

44 LAB C Rep. 602, Nr. 1064, Film Nr. A22/76, Kaderprogramm der VVB Hochspannungsgeräte und Kabel, 31.3.1964.

45 Of the 27 works directors listed in *Wer war wer in der DDR?* for the relevant period, only six did not fit this pattern. Those working in the cultural sector tended to stay in their positions throughout the 1960s and into the 1970s. Another reason for not entirely fitting into this pattern were periods of study in Moscow. The personnel files of the Chemical Ministry show matching turnover patterns. See BAB DG 11/2483–5, 6133.

46 Steiner, *DDR-Wirtschaftsreform*, pp. 74–5, pp. 154–5.

47 LAB C Rep. 602, Nr. 1064, Film Nr. A21/76, Programm der Kaderentwicklung, 1.7.1967, pp. 16 and 23.

48 See Caldwell, *Dictatorship*, chapter 4.

49 Wilczek, *Einkommen*, p. 238.

50 Ibid., p. 261.

51 See also Kott, who pinpointed changes in dress code that support this thesis. Kott, *Le communisme au quotidien*, p. 167.

52 LAB C Rep. 411, Nr. 1333, VVV 27.6.1967, p. 5. Various work directors, besides Wunderlich, such as Rudi Rubbel at the BGW and Hermann Danz at the CFW, fit into this category of 'new management'.

53 LAB C Rep. 602 Film Nr. A22/76 (Kt. 2), Kaderprogramm der VVB HuK, 31.3.1964, pp. 16–18. See also Jeannette Madarász, 'Normalization in East German enterprises, 1961 to 1979. The improvement of working and living conditions under Walter Ulbricht and Erich Honecker', in *Debatte* 13/1 (2005) pp. 45–63.

54 BA-SAPMO, DY46/1297, VVB Hochspannungsgeräte SED Grundorganisation, 19.7.67, p. 71.

55 See Caldwell, *Dictatorship*, p. 185. Kott puts this development two years earlier, to 1965. See Kott, *Le communisme au quotidien*, p. 61.

56 LAB C Rep. 411, Nr. 51, Protokoll der Parteiaktivtagung des Industriezweiges Hochspannungsgeräte am 19.7.1967.

57 LAB C Rep. 411 Nr. 1306, Vol. 4, Sonderrapport zur Stufenschalterfertigung in Rummelsburg, 21.1.1970. See also Bericht zur Sekretariatssitzung der KL-SED, 13.3.1970.

58 LAB C Rep. 411, Nr. 1081, Vorlage 19.12.1967.

59 See interview with K., 30 May 2005. He pointed out that throughout the 1970s, the same amount of transformers were constructed annually whilst the financial accounts indicated an increase of productivity.

60 LAB C Rep. 411, Nr. 105, Protokoll über die Beratung der Kombinats- und Werkdirektoren der künftigen VVB AEA am 27.11.1969, p. 3.

61 LAB C Rep. 411, Nr. 1306, Vol. 4, Bericht 'Bisherige Planerfüllung', about August 1970, p. 5.

62 LAB C Rep. 411, Nr. 1306, Vol. 4, Konsultation mit der SED-KL Köpenick, 1.12.1970, p. 6.

63 LAB C Rep. 411, Nr. 178, Protokoll Nr. 26/75, Werkleitungssitzung 21.7.1975.

64 LAB C Rep. 411, Nr. 1306, Vol. 5, Stellungnahme und Beschluss der Parteileitung in der Leitungssitzung 28.9.1978.

65 See interview with K., 30 May 2005.
66 LAB C Rep. 411, Nr. 175, Protokoll 3.5.1966.
67 BA-SAPMO C Rep. 902/2641, BL SED, 15.7.1968.
68 LAB C rep. 411, Nr. 193, Vorlage 28.11.1968.
69 LAB C Rep. 411, Nr. 1287, Vol. 2, Kurzinformation Fluktuationssituation, 7.9.1970.
70 LAB C Rep. 411, Nr. 1031, Vorlage, 14.12.1973.
71 LAB C Rep. 411, Nr. 1287, Vol. 2, Vorlage, 22.10.1970.
72 LAB C Rep. 411, Nr. 1287, Vol. 2, Vorlage, 25.2.1977.
73 Uta Bruhm-Schlegel, *Arbeiterjugend und sozialistischer Betrieb*. Leipzig: ZIJ, 1977, p. 15.
74 In 1989 most East Germans proudly looked back at long years (up to 30 years and more) of working for the same employer.
75 LAB C Rep. 411, Nr. 1511, Fluktuationsanalyse, 18.7.1979.
76 Ibid.
77 Statistical trends taken from Gunnar Winkler (ed.), *Geschichte der Sozialpolitik der DDR, 1945–85*. Berlin: Akademie, 1989, p. 394.
78 LAB C Rep. 411, Nr. 1504, Untersuchung zu den Ursachen des hohen Krankenstandes, 27.11.1973 and Analyse des Krankenstandes 1978, 30.3.1979. In comparison, average sickness rates in the FRG in the 1970s were just above 5 per cent and in 2003 were about 3.61 per cent. (Statistics according to BMGS, 29.12.2003.) These rates were also high in comparison to other comparable East German enterprises, see LAB C Rep. 411, Nr. 1289 Bd. 2, Vorlage 8.9.1976, p. 1.
79 Rainer Deppe and Dietrich Hoβ, *Sozialistische Rationalisierung*. Frankfurt/ Main: Campus, 1980, pp. 40–54.
80 LAB C Rep. 411, Nr. 185, Protokoll 27/78, p. 3.
81 In particular a lack of building capacity, of which the greatest part was used for the building of accommodation blocs, hindered individual enterprises from improving working and living conditions for their workforce. See for example LAB C Rep. 411, Nr. 1306, Bd. 5, Brief 25.3.1977. For a more detailed account of these developments, see Chapter 3.
82 LAB C Rep. 904–023, Nr. 66, Bericht 11.6.1979, p. 2.
83 Ibid.
84 Ibid., p. 3.
85 For a detailed analysis of these issues, see Thomas Lindenberger, '"Asoziale Lebensweise": Herrschaftslegitimation, Sozialdisziplinierung und die Konstruktion eine "negativen Milieus" in der SED-Diktatur', in *Geschichte und Gesellschaft* 31/2 (2005) pp. 227–54.
86 Müller, *Jugend*, p. 13.
87 LAB C Rep. 904-023, Nr. 65, SED Bericht Mai 1978, p. 3.
88 Semmelmann was probably the first to experiment with oral history in the GDR and belonged to the group of GDR historians looking after Lutz Niethammer and his team during their research for *Die volkseigene Erfahrung* in 1987.
89 Semmelmann, *Gedanken*, p. 1.
90 Semmelmann, *Gespräch*, p. 9.

3 *Berliner Glühlampenwerk*: Working and Living Conditions

1 For an extensive overview of the history of the BGW, see Liewald, *BGW*.
2 See, for example, LAB, C Rep. 902/848, Bericht über die Entwicklung der sozialistischen Brigaden im VEB BGW, 16.6.60, p. 9.
3 LAB, C Rep. 409–01, Nr. 17, Protokolle Januar bis August 1964.
4 See also SAPMO, DY46/2928, Januar 1965, Programm zur Verbesserung der Arbeits- und Lebensbedingungen (ALB) der Werktätigen im BGW (2.Entwurf), R.Rubbel, p. 1.
5 See LAB, C Rep. 409–01 Nr. 214. See also Madarász, 'Die Realität der Wirtschaftsreform', pp. 966–80.
6 LAB, C Rep. 409–01, Nr. 17, Dienstbesprechung 7.5.1963, p. 6.
7 LAB, C Rep. 409–01, Nr. 17, Dienstbesprechung 7.7.1964, p. 3.
8 LAB, C Rep. 409–01, Nr. 17, Dienstbesprechung 28.4.1964, p. 7.
9 See Liewald, *BGW*, p. 97f.
10 According to one economic functionary working at the BGW at the time, Rubbel had accepted the BGW assignment only under the condition that he would be allowed to do as he thought fit to rehabilitate the enterprise. See questionnaire in author's possession.
11 Liewald, *BGW*, pp. 97–8.
12 LAB, C Rep. 409-01 Nr. 17, Dienstbesprechung, 3.8.1964; Direktionssitzung und -beratung, 21.8.1964.
13 LAB, C Rep. 409-01 Nr. 215, *Lichtquelle* 14.8.1964.
14 See, for example, LAB, C Rep. 409-01 Nr. 215, 'Lunik III', 27.8.1964.
15 LAB, C Rep. 409-01 Nr. 214, Brigadetagebuch der Brigade 'Käthe Kollwitz', 30.9.1964.
16 LAB, C Rep. 409-01 Nr. 216, Brigadetagebuch der Brigade 'Käthe Kollwitz', 'Lunik III', see 25–30.10.1965, 1–6.11.1965, 22–27.11.1965.
17 See B. R., questionnaire 6.3.2005.
18 LAB, C Rep. 409-01 Nr. 54, Protokoll der erweiterten Parteileitungssitzung 18.1.1965, p. 6f; LAB, C Rep. 409-01 Nr. 17, Dienstbesprechung 14.9.1964, p. 4.
19 LAB, C Rep. 409-01 Nr. 54, Protokoll der erweiterten Parteileitungssitzung, 18.1.1965, p. 13.
20 LAB, C Rep. 409-01 Nr. 17, Dienstbesprechung 21.8.1964, p. 2.
21 A similar strategy was followed by Christa Bertag, when she became works director of the VEB Kosmetik-Kombinats Berlin in 1986. Christa Bertag 'Wir dachten, wir finden schon eine Lösung', p. 245 in Theo Pirker *et al.*, *Der Plan als Befehl und Fiktion–Wirtschaftsführung in der DDR*. Opladen: Westdeutscher, 1995, pp. 237–54.
22 LAB, C Rep. 409-01 Nr. 17, Dienstberatung 30.9.1964, p. 4.
23 Liewald, *BGW*, pp. 99–100.
24 See BAB DY46 / 3875, Industriekommission des FDGB ZV to Hella Wedel, BGW, 10.11.1964; SAPMO DY46 / 2928, Januar 1965, Programm zur Verbesserung der ALB, Rubbel.
25 Liewald, *BGW*, p. 243. See also by the same author, *BGW – Nachlese* (2005), p. 16.

26 SAPMO, DY46 / 2928, Januar 1965, Programm zur Verbesserung der ALB, Rubbel, pp. 7, 11.
27 See, for example, LAB, C Rep. 411 Nr. 1081, Vorlage: Konzeption der Preisarbeit, Rahmel, 19.12.1967.
28 Walter Ulbricht speaking at the fifth plenary session of the ZK SED, cited by the SPK, HA Perspektivplanung, 8.2.1965, Information über den gegenwärtigen Stand der Ausarbeitung von Konzeptionen zur perspektivischen Entwicklung der ALB der Werktätigen in den Betrieben, p. 1, in BAB, DE 1, VA 43570.
29 BAB, DE 1, VA 48523, PB Beratung des 'Berichtes über die Verbesserung der ALB der Werktätigen', 29.9.1964.
30 BAB, DE 1, VA 43570, Ministerrat DDR, SPK, HA Perspektivplanung, 3.6.1965.
31 SAPMO, DY46 / 3875, Industriekommission an Hella Wedel, 10.11.1964.
32 SAPMO, DY46 / 2928, Januar 1965, Programm zur Verbesserung der ALB, Rubbel.
33 BAB, DE 1/ VA 43570, SPK, HA Perspektivplanung, 8.2.1965, Information über den gegenwärtigen Stand der Ausarbeitung von Konzeptionen zur perspektivischen Entwicklung der ALB.
34 Ministerratesbeschluss über die Verbesserung der ALB, 9.5.1965.
35 Archival material supporting such conjecture has so far not been found. The FDGB's naming (and thereby shaming) to the SPK of other enterprises that had developed similar programmes for the improvement of working and living conditions undermines this theory.
36 Biermann, *Demokratisierung?*, p. 73.
37 See Chapter 6.
38 Staatsratsbeschluss zur Weiterentwicklung der Haushalts- und Finanzwirtschaft der Städte und Gemeinden, 15.9.1967.
39 Verordnung des Ministerrates, 17.7.1968, Gestaltung der Vertragsbeziehungen zwischen den Räten der Stadt und Gemeinden und den Betrieben zur weiteren Verbesserung der ALB der Werktätigen.
40 BLHA, 730/SG 106, Spigath cited in Werner Kalz, Schlussfolgerungen aus der territorialen Koordinierung des Perspektivplanes für die Gestaltung der Zusammenarbeit zwischen VVB und Bezirksorganen. Januar 1968, p. 21.
41 Deich and Kohte, *Betriebliche Sozialeinrichtungen*, p. 28.
42 BLHA Rep. 704 HFO 447.
43 LAB C Rep. 411, Nr. 1306, Vol. 5, Brief Friedrich an Otto Seidel, 1.Sekretär SED-KL, 25.3.1977.
44 LAB C Rep. 411, Nr. 1319, BGL-Sitzung, 20.11.1974, 27.8.1975.
45 See Chapter 2.
46 See Chapter 5.
47 See interviews with former employees of TRO, conducted by the author in 2005.
48 See for example the activities of Werner Frohn at the EVW described by Knortz, *Innovationsmanagement*, p. 96. See also Pirker *et al.*, *Der Plan als Befehl und Fiktion*, specifically the interview with Wolfgang Biermann.
49 Knortz, *Innovationsmanagement*, pp. 236–7. See also Deich and Kohte, *Betriebliche Sozialeinrichtungen*, p. 196.

4 *Erdölverarbeitungswerk Schwedt*: Privileged Within a Shortage Economy

1 See interview with Werner Hager, 1 July 2005, and other former employees of the EVW (transcripts in possession of the author). See also the novel describing the early stages of construction in Schwedt, K.-H. Jakobs, *Beschreibung eines Sommers*. Berlin: Verlag Neues Leben, 1961.

2 Erich Dannehl *et al.*, *Ein Werk des Sozialismus, der Freundschaft und der Jugend. Geschichte des VEB PCK Schwedt, Stammbetrieb von 1959–1981*. Berlin: Tribüne, 1985, p. 71.

3 Ibid., p. 53.

4 Ibid., p. 58.

5 See BLHA Rep. 703 EVW 258 and 274, Analyse der Arbeitskräfte, des Lohnfonds und der Arbeitszeit, 30.10.1967, p. 1.

6 Dannehl *et al.*, *Ein Werk des Sozialismus*, p. 61.

7 BLHA Rep. 703 EVW 258, Bericht zur Werkleitersitzung: Werbung von Arbeitskräften, 20.1.1964. See also Jahresanalyse über die AK Zuführung und die Fluktuation in 1965 (Version 1).

8 BLHA Rep. 703 EVW 263, Wirkungsweise ökonomischer Hebel in der Sphäre der materiellen Interessiertheit, 27.8.1965, pp. 30–1.

9 BLHA Rep. 703 EVW 421, Entwurf einer überarbeiteten Werksvereinbarung des EVW zwischen EVW und BGL.

10 BLHA, Rep. 703 EVW 264, Vorlage, 21.9.1965, p. 6 and Vorlage, 14.9.1965, p. 2.

11 BLHA Rep. 703 EVW 306, Realisierungsstand per 31.12.1965 des Wettbewerbs zur Realisierung von Massnahmen zum Gesundungsprogramm der BMSR Technik im EVW Schwedt, p. 1.

12 BLHA Rep. 703 EVW 260, Protokoll Werkleitungssitzung, 29.10.1965.

13 Compare with Renate Hürtgen's study of trade union functionaries, the *Vertrauensleute*. Hürtgen asserts that basic working class and trade union traditions died away in the 1960s. See Hürtgen, *Zwischen Disziplinierung und Partizipation*, p. 324.

14 BLHA Rep. 703 EVW 365, Staatliche Aufgaben 1967, VEB EVW Schwedt, 1.8.1966, p. 30.

15 These individual agreements should not be confused with the community contracts required officially from 1968 onwards.

16 BLHA Rep. 703 EVW 411, Brief Hager an Oberbürgermeister Mattscherodt, 5.6.1967.

17 BLHA Rep. 703 EVW 302, Vorlage für die BPO, Abt. TMM, 21.11.1967, Abt. TMB, 21.11.1967.

18 BLHA Rep. 703 EVW 374, Kommunalvertrag 1969/70 EVW – Rat der Stadt Schwedt, 13.9.1969.

19 See Aldenhoff-Hübinger, 'Die Ausstrahlung der "Halbleiterpflaume"', p. 48. See also http://de.wikipedia.org/wiki/Schwedt/Oder#Einwohnerentwicklung. (18.08.2005).

20 Knortz, *Innovationsmanagement*, p. 239.

21 Biermann, *Demokratisierung?*, p. 58.

22 BLHA Rep. 703 EVW 272, Protokoll, 23.5.1966, p. 3.

23 See interview with Werner Hager, 1 July 2005.

24　Dannehl *et al.*, *Ein Werk des Sozialismus*, pp. 114–5.
25　BLHA Rep. 703 EVW 302, Ursachen der Fluktuation – Massnahmen zur Festigung der Stammbelegschaft, 20.11.1967.
26　Dannehl *et al.*, *Ein Werk des Sozialismus*, p. 115.
27　Ibid., p. 116.
28　See interview with Werner Hager, 1 July 2005.
29　BLHA Rep. 703 EVW 416, various economic functionaries were replaced between September and December 1968. See also Rep. 703 EVW 368, Protokoll über die Plananlaufbesprechung Plan 1969 am 2.1.1969, p. 4.
30　BLHA Rep. 703 EVW 393, Vorschläge für die politisch-ideologische Vorbereitung und Realisierung der Kombinatsbildung im EVW Schwedt, 10.8.1969, p. 1.
31　Dannehl *et al.*, *Ein Werk des Sozialismus*, pp. 116–20.
32　Highlighting the farcical nature of East German economic planning is not intended to deny the initial fascination central state planning carried world-wide after the Second World War. See Caldwell, *Dictatorship*, p. 3.
33　See Steiner, *DDR-Wirtschaftsreform*, pp. 30–4.
34　BLHA Rep. 703 EVW 67, Schlussfolgerungen über die ökonomische Arbeit des Jahres 1962, 20.2.1963.
35　BLHA Rep. 703 EVW 74, Analyse 31.5.1963, p. 6.
36　BLHA Rep. 703 EVW 74, Analyse 30.4.1963.
37　BLHA Rep. 703 EVW 74, Analyse 31.7.1963.
38　BAB, DE 1, VA 51535, Wyschofsky an Apel, 12.6.1965.
39　Protokoll des VII. Parteitages der SED, Berlin 1967, Bd.III, p. 509 Cited in Biermann, *Demokratisierung?* p. 66.
40　BAB, DE 1, VA 56120, SED-KL, SPK, 2.12.1970.
41　Ibid.
42　BAB, DE 1, VA 56120, Oelschlägel an Mittag, 27.11.1970, p. 2.
43　Ibid., pp. 3–4.
44　BAB, DE 1, VA 56121, Notizen über die Beratung des Volkswirtschaftsplanes 1972 am 9.11.1971 im PB, pp. 12–14.
45　SAPMO, DY 30 / 2703, Probleme der weiteren Vervollkommnung der Leitung und Planung, 24.1.1972.
46　BAB, DE 1, VA 56114, Berthold an Schürer, 16.11.1972.
47　SAPMO, DG 11 / 1138, Abteilung Rationalisierung und Investitionen, 18.6.1973.
48　Knortz, *Innovationsmanagement*, p. 237.
49　See Deich and Kohte, *Betriebliche Sozialeinrichtungen*.
50　Ibid., pp. 155ff.
51　Knortz, *Innovationsmanagement*, p. 237.
52　Ibid., p. 236.
53　For similar assessments see Wolfgang Biermann, 'Man musste ein König der Improvisation sein', p. 220, in Pirker, *Der Plan als Befehl und Fiktion*, pp. 213–35.
54　Hager was remembered by others, and describes himself, as somebody who was supportive of the East German political system. Not atypically for leading economic functionaries of his generation (born 1925), he became a member of the SED early on. He took this step at least partly in reaction to his war time experiences. See interview with Werner Hager, 1 July 2005.
55　Biermann, *Demokratisierung?* p. 77.

56 Biermann, 'König der Improvisation', pp. 198ff.
57 Knortz, *Innovationsmanagement*, p. 210.
58 Ibid., pp. 165–6.
59 Ibid., p. 186.
60 See Kopstein, *Politics of Economic Decline*, p. 2. See also Steiner, *DDR-Wirtschaftsreform*, p. 556.
61 Knortz, *Innovationsmanagement*, p. 186.
62 Ibid., p. 236; Compare with BLHA 730 / SG 152, Dissertation Werner Frohn, 17.10.1980, Autorenreferat, p. 1.
63 BLHA 730/SG 152, Dissertation Werner Frohn, p. 3.
64 Ibid., p. 15.
65 Knortz, *Innovationsmanagement*, p. 165.
66 Dannehl *et al.*, *Ein Werk des Sozialismus*, pp. 158ff.
67 SAPMO DY46/3332, FDGB ZV IG Metall, Abt. E/E, 30.11.1966.

5   Halbleiterwerk Frankfurt/Oder: Falling Behind the Times

1 Deich and Kohte, *Betriebliche Sozialeinrichtungen*, pp. 192–4.
2 An earlier abbreviation (HWF) was later changed to HFO, which will be used throughout this study to avoid confusion.
3 For a useful chronicle of the HFO's history and many of the events described in this chapter, see BPO des HFO, *Menschen – Maschinen – Mikroelektronik. Zur Geschichte des VEB Halbleiterwerk Frankfurt/Oder.* Neubrandenburg: HFO, 1979.
4 BLHA Rep. 704 HFO 1185, Rechenschaftsbericht Konfliktkommission, 1963, p. 9.
5 See BLHA Rep. 704 HFO 9, Analyse der Produktion 1959 and Jahres-Komplex-Analyse 1960, April 1961.
6 BLHA Rep. 704 HFO 9, Rentabilitätsberatung, 2.7.1962, p. 4.
7 BLHA Rep. 704 HFO 9, Rechenschaftslegung der Investitionstätigkeit des HFO vor dem Leiter der Elektronischen Industrie im VWR, 11.6.1963, p. 7.
8 BLHA Rep. 704 HFO 9, Rentabilitätsberatung, 2.7.1962, p. 4.
9 See, for example, BLHA Rep. 704 HFO 9, Leitungssitzungen 1959–63.
10 BLHA Rep. 704 HFO 9, Leitungssitzung, 9.10.1963, p. 3.
11 Ibid., p. 5.
12 BLHA Rep. 704 HFO 78, Leitungssitzung HFO, 6.12.1961, p. 13. See also BAB, DE 1 / VA 51754, SPK, Abt. Elektrotechnik, Massnahmen zur Sicherung der einheitlichen Leitung des VEB Halbleiterwerk F/O und des Instituts für Halbleitertechnik, 28.1.1964.
13 Steiner, *DDR-Wirtschaftsreform*, p. 135.
14 Rita Röhr, *Hoffnung. Hilfe. Heuchelei. Geschichte des Einsatzes polnischer Arbeitskräfte in Betrieben des DDR-Grenzbezirks Frankfurt/Oder 1966–1991.* Berlin: Berliner Debatte, 2001, pp. 71–3.
15 For more information on the subject, see Klaus J. Bode and J. Oltmer, *Migration, Normalfall Migration.* Bonn: BPB, 2004, pp. 90–6. See also Marianne Krüger-Potratz, *Anderssein gab es nicht. Ausländer und Minderheiten in der DDR.* Münster: Waxmann, 1991.
16 BLHA Rep. 704 HFO 261, Entwicklung und Einschätzung der Wirkungsweise der Betriebszeitung und des Einflusses der Parteileitung auf die inhaltliche Gestaltung, 3.9.1968, p. 8.

17 BLHA Rep. 704 HFO 193, Information zu den polnischen Bürgern, die im HFO tätig sind, 22.6.1972. For more details on the employment of Polish workers in East German factories in and around Frankfurt/Oder, see Röhr, *Hoffnung*.

18 A collection of diverse memory reports, written in 1995–6, were published by the Seniorenbeirat der Stadt Frankfurt/Oder in a small booklet, *Zeitzeugen berichten. Erinnerungen, Erlebnisse, Begebenheiten aus Frankfurt/Oder und Słubice*. Frankfurt/Oder: Land Brandenburg, 2005.

19 See for example SAPMO, DY 30 / 2146, Beratung des Sekretariats des ZK mit den 1. Sekretären der BL, 15.11.1972, p. 9. See also SAPMO, DY 30 IV B 2/5/656, Fernschreiben BL SED F/O an ZK SED, Parteiinformation, 31.7.1979.

20 B.B., cited from *Zeitzeugen berichten*, pp. 70–1.

21 Röhr, *Hoffnung*, pp. 79, 82.

22 H.R., cited from *Zeitzeugen berichten*, p. 76.

23 Ibid., B.B., p. 71.

24 Ibid., p. 69.

25 Ibid., p. 70. See also C.M., cited from *Zeitzeugen berichten*, p. 76.

26 See Madarász, 'Normalisation in East German enterprises', pp. 45–63.

27 Aldenhoff-Hübinger, 'Die Ausstrahlung der "Halbleiterpflaume"', p. 48. See also http://de.wikipedia.org/wiki/Frankfurt_%28Oder%29#Einwohnerentwicklung. (18.08.2005).

28 BLHA Rep. 704 HFO 105, Plan zur Verbesserung der ALB 1968, 9.2.1968.

29 See Chapter 4.

30 Olaf Klenke, 'Globalisierung, Mikroelektronik und das Scheitern der DDR-Wirtschaft', p. 423, in *DeutschlandArchiv* 3 (2002) pp. 421–8.

31 André Steiner, 'Zwischen Konsumversprechen und Innovationszwang – Zum wirtschaftlichen Niedergang der DDR', p. 160, in Konrad Jarausch and Martin Sabrow (eds), *Weg in den Untergang – Der innere Zerfall der DDR*. Göttingen: Vandenhoeck & Ruprecht, 1999, pp. 153–92.

32 SAPMO DY 30/2937, Abt. Bauwesen, Information über Auswirkungen zentraler Festlegungen auf die Erhöhung des Verwaltungsaufwandes, 3.1.1972; see also Abt. Maschinenbau und Metallurgie an Mittag, 4.1.1972.

33 SAPMO, DY 30 / 2703, Abt. Sozialistische Wirtschaftsführung, Vermerk über Aussprachen in Mühlhausen und Dresden, 18.5.1972, p. 3.

34 Ibid., p. 5.

35 Ibid., p. 3.

36 SAPMO DY 30/2704, Abt. Parteiorgane des ZK, 9.3.1973.

37 For a more detailed analysis of the subject, see Jörg Roesler, 'Kombinate in der Geschichte der DDR. Von den ersten VVB bis zur durchgängigen Kombinatsbildung', in *Jahrbuch für Geschichte* 31 (1984) pp. 221–71.

38 Steiner, 'Zwischen Konsumversprechen und Innovationszwang', p. 160.

39 Cited from Kott, *Le communisme au quotidien*, p. 193.

40 Steiner, 'Zwischen Konsumversprechen und Innovationszwang', p. 160.

41 SAPMO DY 30/2704, Abt. Sozialistische Wirtschaftsführung: Problemberatungen mit Berliner Kombinatsdirektoren am 27.7.1973, p. 2.

42 SAPMO, DY 30/vorl.SED 27972/I, Information zu Fragen der Arbeitskonflikte und Austritte bzw. Austrittsandrohungen aus dem FDGB, p. 3.

43 BLHA Rep. 704 HFO 105, Erläuterungen zum Planteil ALB zum Planentwurf 1971–5 für den Stammbetrieb HFO, 21.8.1970, p. 1.

44 BLHA Rep. 704 HFO 105, Einschätzung über Stand und Entwicklung nach einem Jahr Kombinatsbildung, 4.12.1970, p. 1.
45 Ibid., p. 2.
46 BLHA Rep. 704 HFO 261, BPO HFO an SED-KL, Einschätzung des Bewusstseinsstandes im HFO, 22.1.1968.
47 BLHA Rep. 704 HFO 261, Parteileitungssitzung 6.8.1968, p. 8.
48 BLHA Rep. 704 HFO 261, Beschluss der Leitung der BPO zum Stand der Planerfüllung 1968, 15.10.1968.
49 BLHA Rep. 704 HFO 261, Entwicklung und Einschätzung der Wirkungsweise der Betriebszeitung und des Einflusses der Parteileitung auf die inhaltliche Gestaltung, 3.9.1968, pp. 7–8.
50 Ibid., p. 4.
51 BLHA Rep. 704 HFO 105, Bericht des Direktors für Sozialökonomie, 27.12.1972, pp. 3, 10.
52 Ibid., p. 9.
53 BLHA Rep. 704 HFO 366, Brief Sommer an General Direktor (GD) des VVB, 17.10.1972.
54 BLHA Rep. 704 HFO 361, Die politisch-ideologische Arbeit bei der Durchsetzung der Partei- und Staatsdisziplin, 2.6.1972; See also HFO 1101, Protokoll, 4.7.1973.
55 BLHA Rep. 704 HFO, Überarbeitung der Zuarbeit entsprechend dem Protokoll zur Abstimmung der Arbeitskräfteentwicklung, 29.10.1975, pp. 3–4.
56 Deich and Kohte, *Betriebliche Sozialeinrichtungen*, p. 28.
57 BLHA Rep. 704 HFO 1135, Protokoll 3/77, 5.1.1977, p. 2.
58 BLHA Rep. 704 HFO 415.
59 BLHA Rep. 704 HFO 429.
60 BLHA Rep. 704 HFO 500.
61 BLHA Rep. 704 HFO 668.
62 Ibid.
63 BLHA Rep. 704 HFO 15; HFO 36 Erfüllung der geplanten Arbeitsproduktivität, 21.10.1966, p. 2; HFO 1107 Vorlage 6/75, 14.5.1975, p. 2; HFO 1134 Vorlage 3/78, 26.1.1978, p. 2; HFO 1143 BGL-Sitzung 5.12.1979, p. 4.
64 BLHA Rep. 704 HFO 361, Die politisch-ideologische Arbeit und Führungstätigkeit zur Durchsetzung der Beschlüsse des VIII.Parteitages, 5.10.1971.
65 BLHA Rep. 704 HFO 671, Protokolle 7/77, 8/77.
66 The firm was founded in 1862, survived the GDR as a state-owned factory and is now in private ownership again.
67 Müller-Enbergs, *Wer war Wer in der DDR?*, p. 894.
68 The BGW, for example, underwent a similar development of being made part of a *Kombinat* twice, once in 1969 and then again in 1978, just as the HFO. However, in both instances the BGW remained the parent unit within NARVA and proved reasonably successful as an individual factory.
69 Steiner, 'Zwischen Konsumversprechen und Innovationszwang', p. 170.
70 Andre Beyermann, *Staatsauftrag: 'Höchstintegration'. Thüringen und das Mikroelektronikprogramm der DDR*. Bonn: BPB, 2005, see http://www.thueringen.de/de/lzt/thueringen/blaetter/micro/print.html (18.08.2005).
71 Ibid.
72 Compare, for example, protocols of works directors' meetings as recorded in BLHA Rep. 704 HFO 735 (1979) and HFO 671 (1977).

73   Aldenhoff-Hübinger, 'Die Ausstrahlung der "Halbleiterpflaume"', p. 48.
74   BLHA Rep. 704 HFO 736, Politische Führungskonzeption ... zur Realisierung und gezielten Überbietung des Politbürobeschlusses vom 26.6.1979, 13.11.1979.
75   Beyermann, *Staatsauftrag: 'Höchstintegration'*.
76   For further information on the history of the *VEB Kombinat Robotron*, see http://rechentechnik.foerderverein-tsd.de/robotron/ (18.8.2005).
77   All excerpts taken from *Zeitzeugen berichten*.

6   *Chemiefaserwerk Premnitz*: Creating a Home for Thousands

1   In this text, the *Chemiefaserwerk Premnitz* will be referred to as 'CFW' throughout to avoid confusion, although at some stage it was also abbreviated 'CFP'.
2   All the figures given are rounded down. Cited from Jutta Bartz, *Die Entwicklung der Stadt Premnitz, 1949–1979. Vom Dorf zur Chemiearbeiterstadt.* Premnitz: 1979, pp. 4–5.
3   See interview with Hermann Danz, February 2005 (transcript in author's possession).
4   BLHA Rep. 503 CFW 633, Betriebscharakteristik des CFW, 31.12.1960.
5   BLHA Rep. 503 CFW 938, Vorlage, 27.1.1961.
6   BLHA Rep. 503 CFW 938, Vorlage, 28.3.1961.
7   BLHA Rep. 503 CFW 938, Vorlage, 4.5.1961.
8   BLHA Rep. 503 CFW 629, Die verbesserte Anwendung des Prinzips der materiellen Interessiertheit, 31.5.1963.
9   BLHA Rep. 503 CFW 650, Direktionssitzung 4.5.1964.
10   BLHA Rep. 503 CFW 4343, Aussprache mit der Intelligenz, 11.10.1965.
11   BLHA Rep. 503 CFW 6645, Thesen für Rechenschaftsbericht des Werkdirektors für VVV 23.2.1966, p. 4.
12   BLHA Rep. 503 CFW 5236, 15.3.1970, Grundkonzeption zur Verbesserung der ALB für den Zeitraum 1970–5, p. 39.
13   See interview with Hermann Danz.
14   BLHA Rep. 503 CFW 4343, Rechenschaftsbericht der APO 6, 24.3.1965, p. 5.
15   BLHA Rep. 503 CFW 6635, Bericht des Werkdirektors vor dem Sekretariat der BL SED Potsdam, 25.8.1967, p. 5.
16   Ibid.
17   BLHA Rep. 503 CFW 6743, Danz: Gedanken, Vorstellungen, Thesen, Antwort auf Fragen, 17.12.1967.
18   BLHA Rep. 503 CFW 6635, Vorlage für das Sekretariat der SED-BL, 21.8.1967, p. 2.
19   BLHA Rep. 503 CFW 6743, Danz: Gedanken, Vorstellungen, Thesen, Antwort auf Fragen, 17.12.1967, p. 33.
20   Ibid., p. 55.
21   According to Danz, he was able to build up a working relation with Dorn after some time. This view, however, is opposed by accounts from other economic functionaries, who felt that Danz was dominated by Dorn throughout his time at the CFW. See interview.

22 BLHA Rep. 503 CFW 4003, Situationsbericht zum Stand der Investitionsvorhaben CFW Premnitz per 30.6.1969.

23 BLHA Rep. 503 CFW 5223, Thesen zum Bericht für die VVV, 30.3.1971, p. 3.

24 BLHA Rep. 503 CFW 3901, Festlegungen der Dienstbesprechung des GD des Chemiefaserkombinates vom 8.2.1971, p. 1.

25 BLHA Rep. 503 CFW 3901, Danz: Mitteilung an Leitung der BPO, 29.1.1973 zu VD 9.1–1/73, 11.1.1973, Überprüfung der Leitungstätigkeit des Betriebsdirektors, p. 4.

26 Ibid., p. 8.

27 Ibid., p. 19.

28 Ibid., p. 1.

29 BLHA Rep. 503 CFW 6635, Niederschrift über die Aussprache mit dem Genossen Baum, BL SED Potsdam 18.11.1969, p. 3.

30 Ibid., p. 6.

31 BLHA Rep. 503 CFW 6635, Danz an Baum, 16.12.1969, p. 1.

32 BLHA Rep. 503 CFW 5236, 15.3.1970, Grundkonzeption zur Verbesserung der ALB für den Zeitraum 1970–5, p. 13.

33 BLHA Rep. 503 CFW 5654, Bericht über den Stand der Erfüllung der Massnahmen aus den abgeschlossenen Kommunalverträgen des CFW, 15.10.1971. The following two legal rulings were most often employed to support the extensive co-operation between the CFW, the town of Premnitz and other municipalities and villages: State council, 16.4.1970, Die weitere Gestaltung des Systems der Planung und Leitung der wirtschaftlichen und gesellschaftlichen Entwicklung, der Versorgung und Betreuung der Bevölkerung in den Bezirken, Kreisen, Städten und Gemeinden – zur Entwicklung sozialistischer Kommunalpolitik (GBl. Teil I, Nr.10 vom 12.5.1970); and Council of Ministers, 8.7.1970, Richtlinie für die Planung und Finanzierung gemeinsamer Massnahmen zwischen den Räten der Städte und Gemeinden und den Betrieben und Kombinaten für die Entwicklung sozialistischer ALB im Territorium. Both rulings were crucial to the further co-operation between local administrations and state-owned concerns with regard to the improvement of working and living conditions.

34 BLHA Rep. 503 CFW 5654, Bericht über den Stand der Erfüllung der Massnahmen aus den abgeschlossenen Kommunalverträgen des CFW, 15.10.1971.

35 Deich and Kohte, *Betriebliche Sozialeinrichtungen*, p. 143.

36 Although the main focus of this study is on state-owned concerns, it should be at least mentioned that Honecker's accession to power put an end to most private firms that had endured in spite of the many drawbacks that had been implemented over the years to make their survival less likely. In 1972, the remaining private companies with state participation, which were mostly small but had supplied crucial consumer goods, were taken into state ownership. This step was taken without proper consideration for its impact on the East German economy. Particularly the provision of consumer goods, which had been a problem anyway, was undermined both in terms of variety and the sheer mass of goods available to the population. Suddenly, small but crucial implements were not produced any more, or there was a noticeable reduction in the shapes, sizes and colours of jumpers. Central decision makers were forced to order state-owned concerns to start

producing consumer goods such as furniture and lawn mowers in addition to their normal product line. The CFW started to produce cassette tapes for tape recorders in 1975.

37 BLHA Rep. 503 CFW 5009, Beratung mit Genossen Wambutt, Abt. Grundstoffindustrie, ZK SED, 21.7.1972, p. 2.
38 BLHA Rep. 704 HFO 1100, Festlegungen aus der Sitzung der BGL, 17.5.1972, p. 5.
39 BLHA Rep. 704 HFO 447.
40 BLHA Rep. 503 CFW 4252, Übersicht zur Entwicklung des CFW, 26.7.76, p. 4.
41 BLHA Rep. 503 CFW 3901, Übersicht zur Entwicklung des CFW, 20.12.1972.
42 BLHA Rep. 503 CFW 4203, Protokoll Leitungssitzung APO und AGL, 21.5.1974, pp. 1–3.
43 BLHA Rep. 503 CFW 4692, Thesen zum Referat der BGL für die VVV, 17.4.1975.
44 BLHA Rep. 503 CFW 5657, Dienstbesprechung 43/75, 27.10.1975.
45 BLHA Rep. 503 CFW 5657, 179/76, 15.3.1976, p. 4.
46 BLHA Rep. 503 CFW 5482, Vorbereitung der Aussprache des Bürgermeisters mit dem Betriebsdirektor, 15.12.1978 und beim Rat der Stadt, 13.12.1978.
47 BLHA Rep. 704 HFO 1095, BGL-Sitzung 22.5.1962.
48 BLHA Rep. 704 HFO 1099, BGL-Sitzung 15.12.1971, p. 3.
49 BLHA Rep. 704 HFO 594, Direktionssitzung 15.12.1971, p. 7.
50 BLHA Rep. 704 HFO 512, Überarbeitung der Zuarbeit entsprechend dem Protokoll zur Abstimmung der Arbeitskräfteentwicklung, 29.10.1975, p. 3.
51 BLHA Rep. 704 HFO 1135, Protokoll 3/77, 5.1.1977, p. 2.
52 BLHA Rep. 704 HFO 1138, 15.5.1978, 25.7.1978.
53 BLHA Rep. 503 CFW 750, Statistisches Material, 20.4.1969, p. 27.
54 BLHA Rep. 503 CFW 4003, Brief an Ministerium für Chemische Industrie, 28.2.1969, p. 2.
55 BLHA Rep. 503 CFW 4985, Analyse, 23.8.1974, pp. 2, 6.
56 BLHA Rep. 503 CFW 5189, Analyse, 26.8.1980, p. 1.
57 BLHA Rep. 503 CFW 4276, Dienstbesprechung 27.12.1979.
58 See, for example, André Steiner, *Von Plan zu Plan. Eine Wirtschaftsgeschichte der DDR*. Munich: DVA, 2004, p. 188.

7 Conflicts and Solutions

1 Helke Stadtland, 'Konfliktlagen und Konfliktformen. Arbeiter in der DDR zwischen Integration, Disziplinierung und Verweigerung', p. 367, in Hübner *et al.* (eds), *Arbeiter im Staatssozialismus*, pp. 357–81.
2 Renate Hürtgen, *Zwischen Disziplinierung und Partizipation*, pp. 247ff.
3 Renate Hürtgen, 'Konfliktverhalten der DDR-Arbeiterschaft und Staatsrepression im Wandel', p. 393, in Hübner *et al.* (eds), *Arbeiter im Staatssozialismus*, pp. 383–403.
4 Ibid., p. 384.
5 Originally, the term was devised for a study of workers in Imperial, Weimar and Nazi Germany. See Alf Lüdtke, *Eigen-Sinn, Fabrikalltag, Arbeitererfahrungen und Politik vom Kaiserreich bis in den Faschismus*. Hamburg:

Ergebnisse, 1993. Translated directly into English, the term *Eigensinn* means 'obstinacy' or 'stubbornness'. However, the hyphen between 'Eigen' (individual) and 'Sinn' (sense) highlights the wider meaning of the term within Lüdtke's concept of 'Eigen-Sinn'.

6 Lüdtke, *Eigen-Sinn*, p. 172. See also Thomas Lindenberger (ed.), *Herrschaft und Eigen-Sinn in der Diktatur – Studien zur Gesellschaftsgeschichte der DDR*. Cologne: Böhlau, 1999.

7 See Lindenberger, *Herrschaft und Eigen-Sinn*.

8 In the introduction to *Herrschaft und Eigen-Sinn*, Lindenberger describes functionaries as border guards (*Grenzwächter*) of the various sections of everyday-life (*Lebenswelten*). See Lindenberger, 'Die Diktatur der Grenzen. Zur Einleitung', p. 34 in Lindenberger, *Herrschaft*.

9 See, for example, LAB, C Rep. 409–01 Nr. 216. See also, Madarász, Die Realität der Wirtschaftsreform, pp. 968ff.

10 LAB, C Rep. 409-01 Nr. 216, p. 1.

11 Thomas Reichel, '"Jugoslawische Verhältnisse"? – Die "Brigaden der sozialistischen Arbeit" und die "Syndikalismus" Affäre (1959–62)', p. 72 in Lindenberger, *Herrschaft*. For an example describing the disillusionment of the brigade 'Erich Mühsam' at the BGW in 1964, see also Kott, *Le communisme au quotidien*, p. 140.

12 SAPMO, DY46/2939, ZV IG Metall, 19.1.62, pp. 8–9.

13 Ibid., p. 7.

14 Ibid., p. 13.

15 Ibid., pp. 16f.

16 Wilczek, *Einkommen*, pp. 240ff.

17 See examples from the conflict commission of the TRO: LAB, C Rep. 411/1358 (for example, Beschluss, 15.6.1970).

18 LAB C Rep. 411 Nr. 1358, Justitiar der Berliner Betriebe, 24.9.1953.

19 For a more detailed analysis of the conflict commissions, see Wolfgang Kohte, 'Konfliktkommissionen zwischen paternalistischer Interessenwahrnehmung und ordnender Erziehung', in Hürtgen and Reichel (eds), *Schein der Stabilität*, pp. 249–62. See also Kott, *Le communisme au quotidien*, pp. 96ff.

20 Kott, *Le communisme au quotidien*, p. 97.

21 LAB, C Rep. 411/1358, Technische Direktion an Genosse Dietzsch, 11.3.1965.

22 See Kott, *Le communisme au quotidien*, p. 147.

23 Lüdtke, *Eigen-Sinn*, p. 143.

24 Weil, *Herrschaftsanspruch und Wirklichkeit*, pp. 72ff.

25 LAB, C Rep. 409–01 Nr. 214, Kollwitz, 10.1.1961.

26 SAPMO, DY46/2934, FDGB ZV IG Metall, 15.6.1965.

27 LAB, C Rep. 411 Nr. 1357.

28 For a specific example of this politicization process and its implications for productivity, see Madarász, 'Die Realität der Wirtschaftsreform', p. 969.

29 In a survey by the author among former employees of the five state-owned factories under discussion, which was based on a combination of questionnaires and selective interviews, the vast majority of those questioned were members of one or more mass organizations. Most described this as a 'normal' part of East German life, which did not need to be explained further. (Questionnaires and transcripts in author's possession.)

30   Many East Germans still react positively to catchwords such as solidarity
      and social equality, many still view history according to the Marxist inter-
      pretation, and most still maintain a world view in which the state is
      expected to provide social security and fairness, become more involved in
      economic processes, and be more controlling with regard to public beha-
      viour, education of the young and punishment of those that do not comply
      with the 'rules'. In 2005, the election campaign of the then-new *Links-*
      Partei, which incorporated the *Partei des Demokratischen Sozialismus* (PDS),
      which succeeded the East German SED, targeted East German voters with a
      whole set of promises and slogans based on this world view. In the election,
      the *Links-Partei* was extremely successful, especially in the East German
      electoral districts. For further information on the *Links-Partei*, see
      http://sozialisten.de (6.9.2005).
31   See Kott, *Le communisme au quotidien*, p. 62.
32   Ibid., p. 59.
33   See Madarász, *Conflict and Compromise*, pp. 65, 74.
34   Answers to the questionnaire suggest that SED members tended to
      approach the party secretary or use other contacts rather than using trade
      union functionaries when trying to solve conflicts. On conflicts within the
      SED, see Thomas Klein, Wilfriede Otto and Peter Grieder, *Visionen:*
      Repression und Opposition in der SED (1949–1989). Frankfurt/Oder: Editionen,
      1996.
35   See, for example, BStU, MfS SED-KL1776 for party proceedings in the Berlin
      section of the MfS in 1976. In that year about 40 per cent of all cases were
      linked to abuse of alcohol.
36   SAPMO, DY 30/vorl.SED 27972/I, 11.3.1981.
37   See, for example, SAPMO, DY 30 IV B 2/5/1330, Parteiverfahren 1975, p. 4.
38   SAPMO, DY 30 IV B 2/5/1348, Parteiverfahren 1977, p. 1.
39   For a detailed analysis of the first and second brigade movement, see Jörg
      Roesler, 'Die Produktionsbrigaden'. See also Hübner, *Konsens, Konflikt und*
      Kompromiss, and Kott, *Le communisme au quotidien*, pp. 127ff.
40   See Jörg Roesler, 'Probleme des Brigadealltags. Arbeitsverhältnisse und
      Arbeitsklima in volkseigenen Betrieben 1950–89', in *Aus Politik und*
      Zeitgeschichte B38 (1997) pp. 3–17.
41   See Steiner, *DDR-Wirtschaftsreform*. See also Caldwell, *Dictatorship*, chapter
      1.
42   See Roesler, *'Das Brigadetagebuch'*, p. 158. See also Madarász, 'Die Realität
      der Wirtschaftsreform', p. 970.
43   LAB, C Rep. 411 Nr. 682, Der Einfluss der sozialistischen Gemeinschaft-
      sarbeit auf die Weiterentwicklung sozialistischer Gemeinschaftsbeziehungen
      ..., 20.10.1969.
44   Semmelmann, *Gedanken*.
45   Semmelmann, *Gespräch*, pp. 1–2.
46   For a detailed discussion of the role of the Stasi in East German factories,
      see Hertle and Gilles, 'Stasi in der Produktion'. See also Hürtgen,
      'Konfliktverhalten', pp. 388ff.
47   All information on this IM and his reports has been taken from MfS BV
      Berlin AIM 3206/89, vols 1–3.
48   See Chapter 2.

49 Ibid.
50 MfS, BVfS Frankfurt / O AKG 448, p. 36.

Conclusion: Normality in the GDR

1   For further details on the impact of the Helsinki agreement on the GDR, see for example Bernd Eisenfeld, 'Reaktionen der DDR-Staatssicherheit auf Korb III des KSZE-Prozesses', in *DeutschlandArchiv* 6 (2005) pp. 1000–8.
2   See for example Felix Mühlberg, 'Eingaben als Instrument informeller Konfliktbewältigung', in Badstübner, *Befremdlich Anders*, pp. 233–70.
3   Norbert Haase, Lothar Reese and Peter Wensierski (eds), *VEB – Nachwuchs – Jugend in der DDR*. Reinbeck: Rowohlt, 1983, pp. 42–3.
4   Questionnaire, K.S. (1997).
5   Ralf Schwarzer and Matthias Jerusalem, *Gesellschaftlicher Umbruch als kritisches Lebensereignis – Psychosoziale Krisenbewältigung von Übersiedlern und Ostdeutschen*. Munich: Juventa, 1994, p. 35.
6   Gabriele Eckart, *So sehe ick die Sache': Protokolle aus der DDR – Leben im havelländischen Obstanbaugebiet*. Cologne: Kiepenheuer & Witsch, 1984, p. 66.
7   Günter de Bruyn, *Vierzig Jahre. Ein Lebensbericht*. Frankfurt/Main: Fischer, 1998, p. 110.
8   Walter Friedrich, 'Zur Theorie und Terminologie der marxistischen Jugendforschung I', p. 16 in *Jugendforschung* 7 (1968).
9   Ibid.
10 Müller, *Jugend*, pp. 13–14. See also Dieter Geulen, *Politische Sozialisation in der DDR. Autobiographische Gruppengespräche mit Angehörigen der Intelligenz*. Opladen: Leske+Budrich, 1998, p. 103. See also Ina Merkel, *Utopie und Bedürfnis. Die Geschichte der Konsumkultur in der DDR*. Cologne: Böhlau, 1999, p. 160. See also Mühlberg, *Bürger, Bitten und Eingaben*, p. 27.
11 A similar development can be traced in brigade diaries when those from the early 1960s are compared with brigade diaries written in the late 1970s or 1980s. See Roesler, 'Das Brigadetagebuch', p. 158.
12 Cited by Semmelmann, *Gespräch*, p. 4.

Bibliography

Adorno, Theodor W., Horkheimer Max, 'Individium' and 'Gesellschaft', in Soziologische Exkurse. Vol.4 Frankfurt and Main: Europäische Verlagsansthalt, 1956, pp. 40–54.

Aldenhoff-Hübinger, Rita, 'Die Ausstrahlung der "Halbleiterpflaume". Folgen einer Betriebsgründung in Frankfurt (Oder)', in Dokumentationszentrum Alltagskultur der DDR e.V. (ed.), *Fortschritt, Norm & Eigensinn. Erkundungen im Alltag der DDR*. Berlin: Ch.Links, 1995, pp. 39–51.

Alheit, Peter and Hanna Haack, *Die vergessene 'Autonomie' der Arbeiter. Eine Studie zum frühen Scheitern der DDR am Beispiel der Neptunwerft*. Berlin: Dietz, 2004.

Ansorg, Leonore, '"Ick hab immer von unten Druck gekriegt und von oben". Weibliche Leitungskader und Arbeiterinnen in einem DDR-Textilbetrieb. Eine Studie zum Innenleben der DDR-Industrie', in *Archiv für Sozialgeschichte* 39 (1999) pp. 123–65.

Badstübner, Evemarie, *Befremdlich Anders: Leben in der DDR*. Berlin: Dietz, 2000.

Bartz, Jutta, *Die Entwicklung der Stadt Premnitz, 1949–1979. Vom Dorf zur Chemiearbeiterstadt*. Premnitz: 1979.

Bertag, Christa, 'Wir dachten, wir finden schon eine Lösung', in Pirker, *Der Plan als Befehl und Fiktion*, pp. 237–54.

Beyermann, Andre, *Staatsauftrag: 'Höchstintegration'. Thüringen und das Mikroelektronikprogramm der DDR*. Bonn: BPB, 2005, see http://www.thueringen.de/de/lzt/thueringen/blaetter/micro/print.html. (18.08.2005).

Biermann, Wolfgang, *Demokratisierung in der DDR? Ökonomische Notwendigkeiten, Herrschaftsstrukturen, Rolle der Gewerkschaften 1961–1977*. Cologne: Wissenschaft und Politik, 1978.

Biermann, Wolfgang, 'Man musste ein König der Improvisation sein', in Pirker, *Der Plan als Befehl und Fiktion*, pp. 213–35.

Bode, Klaus J. and J. Oltmer, *Migration, Normalfall Migration*. Bonn: BPB, 2004.

Bourdieu, Pierre, 'Sur le puvoir symbolique' in *Annales*, 32/3, May–June 1977, pp. 405–11.

BPO des HFO (ed.), *Menschen – Maschinen – Mikroelektronik. Zur Geschichte des VEB Halbleiterwerk Frankfurt/Oder*. Neubrandenburg, 1979.

Bruhm-Schlegel, Uta, *Arbeiterjugend und sozialistischer Betrieb*. Leipzig: ZIJ, 1977.

Buch, Günther, *Namen und Daten wichtiger Personen der DDR*. Bonn: Dietz, 1979.

Caldwell, Peter C., *Dictatorship, State Planning, and Social Theory in the GDR*. Cambridge: Cambridge University Press, 2003.

Clemens, Petra, *Die aus der Tuchbude – Alltag und Lebensgeschichten Forster Textilarbeiterinnen*. Münster: Waxmann, 1998.

Cosentino, Christina and Wolfgang Müller (eds), '*im widerstand/im missverstand?' Zur Literatur und Kunst des Prenzlauer Bergs*. DDR Studien, Vol. 8. New York: Peter Lang, 1995.

Dale, Gareth, *Between State Capitalism and Globalisation. The Collapse of the East German Economy*. Bern: Peter Lang, 2004.

Dannehl, Erich *et al.*, *Ein Werk des Sozialismus, der Freundschaft und der Jugend. Geschichte des VEB PCK Schwedt, Stammbetrieb von 1959–1981*. Berlin: Tribüne, 1985.

de Bruyn, Günter, *Vierzig Jahre. Ein Lebensbericht*. Frankfurt/Main: Fischer, 1998.

Deich, Ingrid and Wolfhard Kohte, *Betriebliche Sozialeinrichtungen*. Opladen: Leske+Budrich, 1997.

Deppe, Rainer and Dietrich Hoß, *Sozialistische Rationalisierung*. Frankfurt/M: Campus, 1980.

Eckart, Gabriele, *'So sehe ick die Sache': Protokolle aus der DDR – Leben im havelländischen Obstanbaugebiet*. Cologne: Kiepenheuer & Witsch, 1984.

Eisenfeld, Bernd, 'Reaktionen der DDR-Staatssicherheit auf Korb III des KSZE-Prozesses', in *DeutschlandArchiv* 6 (2005) pp. 1000–8.

Emmerich, Wolfgang, *Kleine Literaturgeschichte der DDR*. Leipzig: Kiepenheuer, 1997.

Förster, Heike, *Entwicklung von Handlungsstrategien bei Führungskräften in der DDR-Wirtschaft. Eine empirische Untersuchung von Lebens- und Karriereverläufen ehemaliger Betriebs- und Kombinatsdirektoren*. Frankfurt/M: Peter Lang, 1995.

Friedrich, Walter, 'Jugend und Jugendforschung in der ehemaligen DDR-Forschung', in W. Melzer *et al.* (eds), *Osteuropäische Jugend im Wandel – Ergebnisse vergleichender Jugendforschung in der Sowjetunion, Polen, Ungarn und der ehemaligen DDR*. Munich: Juventa, 1991, pp. 172–83.

Friedrich, Walter, 'Zur Theorie und Terminologie der marxistischen Jugendforschung I', in *Jugendforschung* 7 (1968).

Fulbrook, Mary, 'Arbeiter in sozialen und politischen Konfliktkonstellationen', in Hübner *et al.*, *Arbeiter im Staatssozialismus*, pp. 347–56.

Fulbrook, Mary, *The People's State. East German Society from Hitler to Honecker*. Yale: Yale University Press, 2005.

Geulen, Dieter, *Politische Sozialisation in der DDR. Autobiographische Gruppengespräche mit Angehörigen der Intelligenz*. Opladen: Leske+Budrich, 1998.

Giddens, Anthony, *The Constitution of Society: Outline of the Theory of Structuration*. Berkeley: University of California Press, 1984.

Gieseke, Jens, *Die DDR-Staatssicherheit: Schild und Schwert der Partei*. Bonn: BPB, 2000.

Haase, Norbert, Lothar Reese and Peter Wensierski (eds), *VEB – Nachwuchs – Jugend in der DDR*. Reinbeck: Rowohlt, 1983.

Hager, Kurt, *Erinnerungen*. Leipzig: Faber & Faber, 1996.

Heldmann, Philipp, *Herrschaft, Wirtschaft, Anoraks. Konsumpolitik in der DDR der Sechzigerjahre*. Göttingen: Vandenhoeck & Ruprecht, 2004.

Hertle, Hans-Hermann and Franz-Otto Gilles, 'Stasi in der Produktion – Die "Sicherung der Volkswirtschaft" am Beispiel der Struktur und Arbeitsweise der Objektdienststellen des MfS in den Chemiekombinaten', in Henke, Klaus-Dietmar and Roger Engelmann (eds), *Aktenlage – Die Bedeutung der Unterlagen des Staatssicherheitsdienstes für die Zeitgeschichtsforschung*. Berlin: Ch. Links, 1995, pp. 118–37.

Heydemann, Günther and Eckehard Jesse (eds), *Diktaturvergleich als Herausforderung – Theorie und Praxis*. Berlin: Duncker & Humblot, 1998.

Hornbostel, Stefan, 'Spätsozialismus, Legitimierung und Stabilität', in Hannah-Arendt-Institut (ed.), *Repression und Wohlstandsversprechen – Zur Stabilisierung von Parteiherrschaft in der DDR und der CSSR*. Dresden: Hannah-Arendt-Institut, 1999, pp. 13–25.

Hübner, Peter, 'Betriebe als Träger der Sozialpolitik, betriebliche Sozialpolitik', in Bundesministerium für Gesundheit und Soziale Sicherung und Bundesarchiv (ed.), *Geschichte der Sozialpolitik in Deutschland seit 1945*. Vol. 8: Hoffmann, Dierk; Schwartz, Michael (eds), *DDR 1949–61, Im Zeichen des Aufbaus des Sozialismus*. Baden-Baden: Nomos, 2004, pp. 727–73.

Hübner, Peter, 'Der Betrieb als Ort der Sozialpolitik in der DDR', in Boyer, Christoph and Peter Skyba (eds), *Repression und Wohlstandsversprechen – Zur Stabilisierung von Parteiherrschaft in der DDR und der CSSR*. Dresden: Hanna-Arendt-Institut, 1999, pp. 63–74.

Hübner, Peter, *Konsens, Konflikt und Kompromiss – Soziale Arbeiterinteressen und Sozialpolitik in der SBZ/DDR 1945–70*. Berlin: Akademie, 1995.

Hübner, Peter, 'Norm, Normalität, Normalisierung: Quellen und Ziele eines gesellschaftspolitischen Paradigmawechsels im sowjetischen Block um 1970', in *Potsdamer Bulletin für Zeithistorische Studien* 28/29 (2003) pp. 24–40.

Hübner, Peter and Jürgen Danyel, 'Soziale Argumente im politischen Machtkampf: Prag, Warschau, Berlin 1968–1971', in *ZfG* 9 (2002) pp. 804–32.

Hübner, Peter, Christoph Klessmann and Klaus Tenfelde (eds), *Arbeiter im Staatssozialismus. Ideologischer Anspruch und soziale Wirklichkeit*. Cologne: Böhlau, 2005.

Huinink, Johannes, Karl Ulrich Mayer *et al.*, *Kollektiv und Eigensinn – Lebensverläufe in der DDR und danach*. Berlin: Akademie,1995.

Hürtgen, Renate, 'Konfliktverhalten der DDR-Arbeiterschaft und Staatsrepression im Wandel', in Hübner *et al.*, *Arbeiter im Staatssozialismus*, pp. 383–403.

Hürtgen, Renate, *Zwischen Disziplinierung und Partizipation. Vertrauensleute des FDGB im DDR-Betrieb*. Cologne: Böhlau, 2005.

Hürtgen, Renate and Thomas Reichel (eds), *Der Schein der Stabilität – DDR-Betriebsalltag in der Ära Honecker*. Berlin: Metropol, 2001.

Kaelble, Hartmut, Jürgen Kocka and Hartmut Zwahr (eds), *Sozialgeschichte der DDR*. Stuttgart: Klett-Cotta, 1994.

Kaiser, Monika, *Machtwechsel von Ulbricht zu Honecker. Funktionsmechanismen der SED-Diktatur in Konfliktsituationen 1962–1972*. Berlin: Akademie, 1997.

Kaufmann, Werner, *Einfluss und Auswirkungen der neuen Technik auf die Entwicklung des Arbeitsvermögens der Werktätigen des Betriebsteils Leuchtstofflampe im VEB BGW*. Unpublished, University of Rostock (1966).

Keiser, Sarina, *Ostdeutsche Frauen zwischen Individualisierung und Re-Traditionalisierung – Ein Generationenvergleich*. Hamburg: Dr.Kovac, 1997.

Klein, Thomas, Otto Wilfriede and Peter Grieder *Visionen: Repression und Opposition in der SED (1949–1989)*. Frankfurt/O: Editionen, 1996.

Klenke, Olaf, 'Globalisierung, Mikroelektronik und das Scheitern der DDR-Wirtschaft', in *DeutschlandArchiv* 3 (2002) pp. 421–8.

Knortz, Heike, *Innovationsmanagement in der DDR 1973/79–1989. Der sozialistische Manager zwischen ökonomischen Herausforderungen und Systemblockaden*. Berlin: Duncker & Humblot, 2004.

Kohli, Martin, 'Die DDR als Arbeitsgesellschaft? Arbeit, Lebenslauf und soziale Differenzierung', in Kaelble *et al.*, *Sozialgeschichte*, pp. 31–61.

Kohte, Wolfgang, 'Konfliktkommissionen zwischen paternalistischer Interessenwahrnehmung und ordnender Erziehung', in Hürtgen and Reichel (eds), *Der Schein der Stabilität*, pp. 249–62.

Kopstein, Jeffrey, *The Politics of Economic Decline in East Germany, 1945–1989*. Chapel Hill: University of North Carolina, 1997.

Kott, Sandrine, *Le communisme au quotidien. Les Enterprises d'Etat dans la société est-allemande*. Paris: Edition Belin, 2001.

Kott, Sandrine, 'Pour une histoire sociale du pouvoir en Europe communiste', in *Revue d'histoire moderne et contemporaire* 49 (2002) pp. 5–23.

Krömke, Claus, *Das 'Neue Ökonomische System der Planung und Leitung der Volkswirtschaft' und die Wandlungen des Günter Mittag*. Berlin: Gesellschafts-wissenchaftliches Forum, 1996.

Krüger-Potratz, Marianne, *Anderssein gab es nicht. Ausländer und Minderheiten in der DDR*. Münster: Waxmann, 1991.

Liewald, Horst, *Das BGW. Zur Betriebsgeschichte von NARVA – Berliner Glühlampenwerk*. Berlin: Deutsches Technikmuseum, 2004.

Liewald, Horst, *Das BGW. Nachlese*. Berlin: Deutsches Technikmuseum, 2005.

Lindenberger, Thomas, (ed.), *Herrschaft und Eigen-Sinn in der Diktatur–Studien zur Gesellschaftsgeschichte der DDR*. Cologne: Böhlau, 1999.

Lindenberger, Thomas, '"Asoziale Lebensweise": Herrschaftslegitimation, Sozialdisziplinierung und die Konstruktion eine "negativen Milieus" in der SED-Diktatur', in *Geschichte u. Gesellschaft* 31(2005) pp. 2, 227–54.

Lüdtke, Alf, *Eigen-Sinn. Fabrikalltag, Arbeitererfahrungen und Politik vom Kaiserreich bis in den Faschismus*. Hamburg: Ergebnisse, 1993.

Lüdtke, Alf, 'Meister der Landtechnik oder: Grenzen der Feldforschung? Annäherungen an einen "Qualitätsarbeiter" auf dem Lande im Bezirk Erfurt', in Münkel, Daniela and Jutta Schwarzkopf (eds), *Geschichte als Experiment. Studien zu Politik, Kultur und Alltag im 19. und 20. Jahrhundert*. Frankfurt/Main: Campus, 2004.

Madarász, Jeannette, *Conflict and Compromise in East Germany, 1971–89. A Precarious Stability*. Basingstoke: Palgrave, 2003.

Madarász, Jeannette, 'Die Realität der Wirtschaftsreform in der DDR. Betriebsalltag in den sechziger Jahren', in *DeutschlandArchiv* 6 (2003) pp. 966–80.

Madarász, Jeannette, 'Normalisation in East German enterprises, 1961 to 1979. The improvement of working and living conditions under Walter Ulbricht and Erich Honecker', in *Debatte*, 13/1 (2005) pp. 45–63.

Madarász, Jeannette, 'Normalisierung in der Diktatur? Potentiale und Limitationen eines Konzepts im Kontext der DDR-Geschichte, 1961–79', in Wagner, Helmut (ed.), *Europa und Deutschland–Deutschland und Europa*. Münster: LIT, 2005, pp. 335–55.

Mensching, Günter, *Ingenieur M. ppm. Einer unter Millionen. Lebenserinnerungen und Ansichten*. Berlin: Nora, 2005.

Merkel, Ina, *Utopie und Bedürfnis. Die Geschichte der Konsumkultur in der DDR*. Cologne: Böhlau, 1999.

Michaelis, Rolf, 'Frauen–Führungskader in der VVB', in Grandke, Anita: *Frau und Wissenschaft*. Berlin: DadW, 1968, pp. 48–50.

Mühlberg, Felix, *Bürger, Bitten und Behörden: Geschichte der Eingabe in der DDR*. Berlin: Dietz, 2004.

Mühlberg, Felix, 'Eingaben als Instrument informeller Konfliktbewältigung', in Badstübner: *Befremdlich Anders*, pp. 233–70.

Müller, Harry, *Jugend im Wandel ihrer Werte.* Leipzig: ZIJ, 1985.

Müller-Enbergs, Helmut, Jan Wielgohs and Dieter Hoffmann (eds), *Wer war Wer in der DDR?* Berlin: Ch. Links, 2001.

Pirker, Theo, M. Rainer Lepsius, Rainer Weinert and Hans-Hermann Hertle, *Der Plan als Befehl und Fiktion – Wirtschaftsführung in der DDR.* Opladen: Westdeutscher, 1995.

Pollack, Detlef, 'Die konstitutive Widersprüchlichkeit der DDR. Oder: War die DDR-Gesellschaft homogen?', in *Geschichte und Gesellschaft* 24 (1998) pp. 100–31.

Reichel, Thomas, '"Jugoslawische Verhältnisse"? – Die "Brigaden der sozialistischen Arbeit" und die "Syndikalismus" Affäre (1959–62)', in Lindenberger, *Herrschaft,* pp. 45–73.

Reichel, Thomas, 'Die "durchherrschte Arbeitsgesellschaft" – Zu den Herrschaftsstrukturen und Machtverhältnissen in DDR-Betrieben', in Reichel Hürtgen, *Der Schein der Stabilität,* pp. 85–110.

Ritzer, George, *Modern sociological theory.* London: Sage, 2001.

Röbenack, Silke, '*Aber meistens einfach nur ein Kollege' Über die ersten Betriebsräte in Ostdeutschland.* Munich: Rainer Hampp, 2005.

Roesler, Jörg, '*Das Brigadetagebuch – betriebliches Rapportbuch, Chronik des Brigadelebens oder Erziehungsfibel?'* in Badstübner: *Befremdlich Anders,* pp. 151–66.

Roesler, Jörg, 'Die Produktionsbrigaden in der Industrie der DDR. Zentrum der Arbeitswelt?', in Kaelble *et al.,* *Sozialgeschichte,* pp. 144–70.

Roesler, Jörg, 'Jugendbrigaden im Fabrikalltag der DDR 1948–1989', in *Aus Politik und Zeitgeschichte.* B28 (1999) pp. 21–31.

Roesler, Jörg, 'Kombinate in der Geschichte der DDR. Von den ersten VVB bis zur durchgängigen Kombinatsbildung', in *Jahrbuch für Geschichte* 31 (1984) pp. 221–71.

Roesler, Jörg, 'Probleme des Brigadealltags. Arbeitsverhältnisse und Arbeitsklima in volkseigenen Betrieben 1950–89', in *Aus Politik und Zeitgeschichte* B38 (1997) pp. 3–17.

Röhr, Rita, *Hoffnung. Hilfe. Heuchelei. Geschichte des Einsatzes polnischer Arbeitskräfte in Betrieben des DDR-Grenzbezirks Frankfurt/Oder 1966-1991.* Berlin: Berliner Debatte, 2001.

Rousseau, Jean Jacques, *Du contrat social ou principes ou droit politique.* Amsterdam: Rey, 1762.

Schnelle, Gertraude, 'Technische Revolution und Gleichberechtigung', in Grandke, *Frau und Wissenschaft,* pp. 93–5.

Schroeder, Klaus and Steffen Alisch, *Der SED–Staat – Geschichte und Strukturen der DDR.* Munich: Ernst Vögel, 1998.

Schüle, Annegret, *Die Spinne – Die Erfahrungsgeschichte weiblicher Industriearbeit im VEB Baumwollspinnerei.* Leipzig: Universitätsverlag, 2001.

Schwarzer, Ralf and Matthias Jerusalem, *Gesellschaftlicher Umbruch als kritisches Lebensereignis – Psychosoziale Krisenbewältigung von Übersiedlern und Ostdeutschen.* Munich: Juventa, 1994.

Semmelmann, Dagmar, *Gedanken zum sozialistischen Wettbewerb.* (1978–9), unpublished notes.

Semmelmann, Dagmar, *Gespräch mit vier Kollegen aus der Tischlerei des O-Betriebes.* (6.9.1978), unpublished notes.

Seniorenbeirat der Stadt Frankfurt/O, (ed.), *'Zeitzeugen berichten'. Erinnerungen, Erlebnisse, Begebenheiten aus Frankfurt/Oder und Słubice.* Frankfurt/Oder: Land Brandenburg, 2005.

Soares do Bem, Arim, *Das Spiel der Identitäten in der Konstitution von 'Wir'-Gruppen. Ost- und Westdeutsche Jugendliche und in Berlin geborene Jugendliche ausländischer Herkunft im gesellschaftlichen Umbruch.* Frankfurt/M: Peter Lang, 1998.

Solga, Heike, *Auf dem Weg in eine klassenlose Gesellschaft? Klassenlagen und Mobilität zwischen Generationen in der DDR.* Berlin: Akademie, 1995.

Stadtland, Helke, 'Konfliktlagen und Konfliktformen. Arbeiter in der DDR zwischen Integration, Disziplinierung und Verweigerung', in Hübner, *Arbeiter im Staatssozialismus*, pp. 357–81.

Stanley, Liz, *The auto/biographical I.* Manchester: Manchester University Press, 1992.

Steiner, André, *Die DDR-Wirtschaftsreform der sechziger Jahre – Konflikt zwischen Effizienz- und Machtkalkül.* Berlin: Akademie, 1999.

Steiner, André, 'Von "Hauptaufgabe" zu "Hauptaufgabe". Zur Wirtschaftsentwicklung der langen 60er Jahre in der DDR', in Axel Schildt *et al.*, *Dynamische Zeiten. Die 60er Jahre in den beiden deutschen Gesellschaften.* Hamburg: Christians, 2000, pp. 218–47.

Steiner, André, *Von Plan zu Plan. Eine Wirtschaftsgeschichte der DDR.* Munich: DVA, 2004.

Steiner, André, 'Zwischen Konsumversprechen und Innovationszwang–Zum wirtschaftlichen Niedergang der DDR', in Konrad Jarausch and Martin Sabrow (eds), *Weg in den Untergang – Der innere Zerfall der DDR.* Göttingen: Vandenhoeck & Ruprecht, 1999, pp. 153–92.

Vollnhals, Clemens, *Das Ministerium für Staatssicherheit – Ein Instrument totalitärer Herrschaftsausübung.* Berlin: BStU, 1995.

Weil, Francesca, *Herrschaftsanspruch und Wirklichkeit. Zwei Sächsiche Betriebe in der DDR während der Honecker-Ära.* Cologne: Böhlau, 2000.

Wilczek, Annette, *Einkommen – Karriere – Versorgung. Das DDR-Kombinat und die Lebenslage seiner Beschäftigten.* Berlin: Metropol, 2004.

Winkler, Gunnar, *Geschichte der Sozialpolitik der DDR, 1945–85.* Berlin: Akademie, 1989.

Zachmann, Karin, 'Frauen für die technische Revolution – Studentinnen und Absolventinnen Technischer Hochschulen in der SBZ/DDR', in Gunilla-Friederike Budde (ed.), *Frauen arbeiten. Weibliche Erwerbstätigkeit in Ost- und Westdeutschland nach 1945.* Göttingen: Vandenhoeck & Ruprecht, 1997, pp. 121–56.

Index

Apel, Erich   47, 69, 94

Berlin Wall   1, 2, 4, 5, 37, 172
Berliner Glühlampenwerk   32, 66–85
  NARVA   67, 70
  sickness and turnover rates   24, 80
  social efforts   73–80
Betriebskollektivvertrag   36, 40

Chemiefaserwerk Premnitz   33, 123–40
  SED organization, BPO   32, 128,
    129
  sickness and turnover rates   126,
    134–7
  social efforts   125, 134–9
Chemical Programmes   35, 66, 86, 124
Cold War   1, 4
Conflict commissions   148
Cybernetics   52
COMECON   92

Danz, Hermann   124, 125, 127–33
DFD   154
Dorn, Erich   128

Economic reforms   *see* NES
Economy   22, 34
  economic plans   24, 28, 45–51,
    93–100, 150
  prize reform   57
  rationalization   28
  shortage economy   12, 27–8, 109,
    171
Eigen-Sinn   142–4
Energy Programme   35, 44, 66
Erdölverarbeitungswerk Schwedt   33,
    35, 86–104
  PCK   93
  SED organization, BPO   88, 90, 92,
    98
  sickness and turnover rates   75, 88
  social efforts   88
  Weniger produzieren mehr   99–100

Factories, state-owned   30–6
  brigades   29, 59, 60, 101, 146,
    156–7; brigade diaries 68, 70,
    145, 147–8, 157–8
  status   34, 35, 97–102, 136–7
FDGB   70, 76, 77, 153, 155
FDJ   45, 70–1, 87, 154
FRG   1, 8, 23, 52, 170
  unification   6–7, 170
Friedrich, Manfred   55, 56
Frohn, Werner   33, 92, 93, 98
Functionaries   5, 45
  economic 45, 52–3, 68; *see also*
    Works directors
  party   32

Germany, Federal Republic of   1, 8,
    23, 52, 170
Gorbachev, Mikhail   16, 160

Hager, Kurt   44
Hager, Werner   87, 90, 92, 98
Helsinki conference   14
Hermlin, Stephan   13
Halbleiterwerk Frankfurt/Oder   33, 35,
    105–22
  Institut für Halbleitertechnik   107
  Kombinat VEB Mikroelektronik Erfurt
    116
  Polish workers   108–10
  SED organization (BPO)   113–14
  sickness and turnover rates   115
  social efforts   110, 115, 135
  VEB Kombinat Halbleiterwerk   108,
    116
Hertwig, Jochen   99
Honecker, Erich   5–7, 14, 37, 52–3,
    78–9, 96, 99, 113, 168
  Unity of Social and Economic
    Policy   19, 25

Individualization   3, 12–16, 37, 41,
    60, 156, 174

Kombinat 93, 96–8, 101–2, 111–19

Local authorities 75–6, 79, 90, 130–3

Marxism-Leninism 144, 153
Mass organizations 153–4
 see also DFD, FDGB, FDJ, SED
Microelectronics Programmes 73,
 117–18
Ministry for Chemical Industries 93
Ministry for Electronics and Electrical
 Engineering 52, 55, 117
Ministry of Security *see* Stasi
Mittag, Günter 95, 99, 111, 112

NES 1, 5, 14, 24, 44–7, 61, 95, 152
 material interest 25, 145, 152, 159
 see also working and living
 conditions
Neumann, Alfred 88
Normalization 11–12, 167, 172–3,
 175

Oil crisis 117

Petitions 15, 38, 152, 174
Popular upheaval 35
 1953, 17 June 2, 4, 169
 1989 3, 7, 16, 170
Prague Spring 1, 37, 79
Productivity 24, 126, 145
 soft norms 45–7, 100

Rousseau, Jean-Jacques *see* Social
 Contract
Routinization 22, 36–41, 157, 174
 in factories 38–41
Rubbel, Rudi 32, 69–73

SED 1
 functionaries 32
 members 34, 154–5
 party conferences 95, 106, 107, 127
 SED BL Potsdam 155
 SED BL Berlin 48, 51–2, 57, 70
Social Contract 10–11
Social policy 2, 23, 25–6, 81
Socialist personality 3, 13, 60, 145,
 158, 171

Sommer, Elmar 107, 116
Soviet Union 22, 44, 47, 66, 170
SPK 46, 51, 77, 94, 95ff
Stalin, Josef 4
Stasi 5, 27, 147
 IM 160–5
Strike 142, 147

Theft 148–9
Transformatorenwerk Berlin 32, 35,
 43–65
 Rummelsburg 49–50
 SED organization, BPO 48, 49–51,
 54–5
 sickness and turnover rates 56–9
 social efforts 56–63

Ulbricht, Walter 5, 37, 53, 74, 95–6,
 98, 163
Unity of Social and Economic Policy
 see Honecker, Erich

Verner, Paul 32, 55, 69, 72
Vom Ich zum Wir 5, 157
VVB 21, 24, 49, 52
 *VVB Automatisierungs- und
  Elektroanlagenbau* 55
 *VVB Bauelemente und
  Vakuumtechnik* 106–7
 VVB Hochspannungsgeräte 5, 54
 VVB Hochspannungsgeräte und Kabel
  43, 50–1
 VVB Mineralöle 93
 *VVB Mineralöle und organische
  Grundstoffe* 89, 94
VWR 57

Wedler, Heinz 116
WOA 58
Women 6, 32, 67, 68
 working mothers 73–4, 126
Workforce 28–9, 40, 57, 142,
 158
 bonuses 49, 57, 71, 73
 salaries 70, 71
 wages 45, 89, 99, 145; workers
  22–3, 27; *Neuerer* 40; Polish
  see HFO
Working mothers *see* women

Working and living conditions
  26–7, 74, 145
  improvement of   5, 19, 23, 36, 57,
    73–82
  Kultur- und Sozialfond   115, 134
Works directors   7, 24, 32–3, 38–9,
  51–4, 66, 81, 98–9, 149
Wunderlich, Helmut   32–3, 51, 55
Wyschofsky, Günther   32, 94, 99

Young people   6, 59, 169–70

ZIJ   58
  Friedrich, Walter   173
ZK SED   37, 47, 75, 101
  Department for Economic
    Management   96
  Department for Rationalization and
    Investment   57